Chinese Heritage in British Christianity

Chinese Heritage in British Christianity

More than Foreigners

Edited by Alexander Chow

scm press

© The editor and contributors 2025

Published in 2025 by SCM Press
Editorial office
3rd Floor, Invicta House,
110 Golden Lane,
London EC1Y 0TG, UK
www.scmpress.co.uk

SCM Press is an imprint of Hymns Ancient & Modern Ltd
(a registered charity)

Hymns Ancient & Modern® is a registered trademark of
Hymns Ancient & Modern Ltd
13A Hellesdon Park Road, Norwich,
Norfolk NR6 5DR, UK

All rights reserved. No part of this publication may be reproduced,
stored in a retrieval system, or transmitted,
in any form or by any means, electronic, mechanical,
photocopying or otherwise, without the prior permission of
the publisher, SCM Press.

The editor and contributors have asserted their right under the Copyright,
Designs and Patents Act 1988 to be identified as the Authors of this Work

Scripture quotations marked NRSVA are from New Revised Standard Version Bible:
Anglicized Edition, copyright © 1989, 1995 National Council of the Churches of Christ in
the United States of America. Used by permission. All rights reserved worldwide.
Scripture quotations marked NIV are taken from the Holy Bible, New International
Version®, NIV®. Copyright © 1973, 1978, 1984, 2011 by Biblica, Inc.™
Used by permission of Zondervan. All rights reserved worldwide. www.zondervan.com
The "NIV" and "New International Version" are trademarks registered in the
United States Patent and Trademark Office by Biblica, Inc.™
Scripture quotations marked ESV are from The ESV® Bible (The Holy Bible,
English Standard Version®), copyright © 2001 by Crossway, a publishing ministry of
Good News Publishers. Used by permission. All rights reserved.

British Library Cataloguing in Publication data
A catalogue record for this book is available
from the British Library

ISBN: 978-0-334-06617-0

EU GPSR Authorised Representative
LOGOS EUROPE, 9 rue Nicolas Poussin, 17000, LA ROCHELLE, France
E-mail: Contact@logoseurope.eu

Typeset by Regent Typesetting
Printed and bound by
CPI Group (UK) Ltd

Contents

List of Contributors	vii
Acknowledgements	xi
Introduction Alexander Chow	1

Part I: Re-examining the Past and the Present

1. The Making of British Chinese Christianity 11
   Alexander Chow

2. Chinese History in English Churches: Monuments, Memorials and the Questions they Raise 29
   Renie Chow Choy

3. Contemporary British Chinese Christianity: Religious and Social Characteristics 48
   Yinxuan Huang

Part II: Re-forming Identity and Spirituality

4. Forever Foreigners: *Missio Dei* for the British Born Chinese 73
   James So

5. Called by Name: A British Born Chinese Perspective on Identity and Calling in the Church of England 92
   Mark Nam

6. Beyond the Lion Rock Spirit: A New Expression of British Hong Kongese Christianity 112
   Calida Chu

Part III: Re-imagining Community and Church

7 Beyond the Balance Sheet: A Ministry Reflection on
  Mainland Chinese Student Ministry in the UK   131
  Candy Zhang

8 Be Not Conformed To This Land: A Pastoral Theology for
  Migrants   145
  Kan Yu

9 Beyond the Immigrant Church vs Local Church Dichotomy:
  Towards an Internetworked Church   164
  Alexander Chow

10 A New Family: Pauline Adoption and its Contribution
   Towards a British Chinese Christian Identity   180
   Josh Shek

Conclusion: The Journey Continues   195
Bert Han

Index of Names and Subjects   201

List of Contributors

Alexander Chow, a Chinese American, is Senior Lecturer in Theology and World Christianity and Co-Director of the Centre for the Study of World Christianity in the School of Divinity, University of Edinburgh. He is the author or editor of six books, including *Chinese Public Theology* (Oxford University Press, 2018) and *Ecclesial Diversity in Chinese Christianity* (with Easten Law; Palgrave Macmillan, 2021). He has lived in the United Kingdom for over a decade and a half and has served in several British Chinese churches during that time.

Renie Chow Choy is Public Historian at Westminster Abbey, and Associate Lecturer in Church History at Westcott House, Cambridge. Previously she was Community Engagement Manager for historic collections at St Paul's Cathedral, where she led the curation of two trails about monuments associated with the British Empire. Renie is author of *Ancestral Feeling: Postcolonial Thoughts on Western Christian Heritage* (SCM Press, 2021) and *Intercessory Prayer and the Monastic Ideal in the Time of the Carolingian Reforms* (Oxford University Press, 2016), a monograph on early medieval monasticism. She sits on a number of committees responsible for the conservation of the Church of England's historic buildings, and is Visiting Research Fellow at the University of Chester and Research Associate at the Centre for the Study of Christianity and Culture at the University of York.

Calida Chu, born and raised in Hong Kong, is Teaching Associate in Sociology of Religion at the Department of Theology and Religious Studies, University of Nottingham. She received her PhD in World Christianity at the School of Divinity, University of Edinburgh, in 2020, with a thesis about Hong Kong public theology after 1997. Baptized in a British Chinese church in her undergraduate years, she has served in Hong Kongese Christian communities in the UK for more than a decade.

Bert Han is a Chinese American who has served the British Chinese heritage churches for over 25 years. He is currently a pastor at the Birmingham Chinese Evangelical Church.

Yinxuan Huang is a research manager at the British and Foreign Bible Society. He completed his PhD in Social Change from the University of Manchester in 2016, and his main research interests are diasporic Chinese communities, global Christianity, sociology of religion, and survey methodology. His work on the Chinese Christian community in Britain has appeared in *The Times*, *The Guardian*, *Christianity Today*, Premier Christian Radio, TWR-UK, BBC 2 and BBC local radio.

Mark Nam is a British Born Chinese priest and vicar of St John the Evangelist, Woodley, in the Diocese of Oxford. He was previously a pastor at The Vine Church in Hong Kong and completed his theological studies at Trinity College Bristol. Mark and his wife are co-founders of The Teahouse and he is a trustee for SPCK and the Li Tim-Oi Foundation. Mark received an Archbishop of Canterbury's Lambeth Award in 2023 for his 'contribution to the community in accordance with the Church's teaching'. He is a regular contributor to BBC Radio, Premier Radio and UCB and has written for *The Church Times* and *The Canterbury Preacher's Companion*.

Josh Shek is a PhD candidate at the London School of Theology. Having worked for ten years with the Chinese Overseas Christian Mission, ministering to second-generation British Chinese Christians, he is now conducting research into the function of shame and honour in the doctrine of adoption. He is British Born Chinese himself, son to parents who migrated from Hong Kong to Portsmouth, where he grew up as a takeaway kid.

James So, a British Born Chinese, currently leads the English Ministry Department of the Chinese Overseas Christian Mission. Much of his work relates to second-generation British Chinese Christians in Chinese heritage churches. He received his theological training at Wycliffe Hall, University of Oxford, and he also holds an MPhil in World Christianities from the University of Cambridge.

LIST OF CONTRIBUTORS

Kan Yu, a British Chinese, is a presbyter of the Methodist Church in Britain. She has served various Methodist churches in the UK since her ordination in 2017. She has established an emerging church among the Hong Kong community in south-west London and is a co-founder of Hong Kong Well UK (CIC), a charitable organization that provides counselling services to Hong Kong children and young people who have recently migrated to the UK.

Candy Zhang is a missionary with the Chinese Overseas Christian Mission (COCM). Beginning in 2009, Candy regularly participated in short-term mission trips from the USA to support COCM's national Mandarin student conferences. She joined COCM as a full-time missionary on graduating from the London School of Theology in 2016. Her current ministries include coordinating the COCM Training Centre, supporting COCM's Mandarin student conferences and pastoring Oasis London, a Mandarin-speaking church for students.

Acknowledgements

This book has been formed by a journey embarked on with many companions. A good number of these fellow travellers need to be acknowledged. First, I would like to extend my appreciation to the chapter contributors. This may seem odd for the editor of a book to say. But so many of these authors are in active church or parachurch ministry and few have the luxury of research time built into their day jobs. Yet time and time again I was so grateful for their commitment to this project. I really enjoyed the emails, the instant messages, the Zoom meetings and the phone calls. They were not just another set of administrative tasks to do. They were times of discussing and hashing out with contributors the ideas they were testing out, the obscure references they were engaging with and the lived experiences they wanted to bring to light in their chapters. This has been a real labour of love – and one that we all felt was important to do. Furthermore, there have been so many people supporting the contributors in writing their chapters. I know my wife Betty and our children listened to far more than perhaps they wanted to. I very much appreciate their encouragement – as I'm sure all the contributors are likewise appreciative of family, friends and colleagues who have championed this work.

There are also many people who have contributed to this book in ways other than writing chapters. I am grateful to David Shervington of SCM Press for believing in the idea behind this book, for always making a point of connecting at academic conferences, and for shepherding the project from start to finish. I am thankful for Bert Han who, as a fellow Southern Californian, has been a sounding board for me and a wonderful role model to so many, including many of the book's contributors. He has been such an important exemplar who has served so many in this land for over a quarter of a century. Furthermore, in October 2023 Bert generously hosted the team of writers at the Birmingham Chinese Evangelical Church, offering us a place to meet so we could share ideas and experiences and have genuine Christian fellowship – including a delicious Chinese meal, of course! I'm indebted to Kiet Van, who designed the cover for the book. His own biography, as an ethnic Chinese who fled the Vietnam of his birth and grew up in Wales, is just another example of how British Chinese churches have been so important in offering refuge and support to immigrants from Asia. Kiet sent me countless cover-design mock-ups and had to deal with innumerable pernickety tweaks and my overall indecisiveness. Despite all of that, he has crafted such a beautiful and thought-provoking cover for the book.

Finally, there are those who need to be acknowledged who may never know of their impact on this book. This book could only exist – and indeed British Chinese Christianity could only exist – because of people like George A. Kirkham, who started the first British Chinese church in Liverpool in 1910, and Stephen Wang, who started the Chinese Overseas Christian Mission in 1950, which helped to start so many of the British Chinese churches that exist today. There are also many 'uncles' and 'aunties' in churches, or British Chinese friends and acquaintances we have encountered, whose lives and experiences have come to mind so many times while we were writing. They remind us of theological, pastoral and practical concerns that point to what really matters. But I also know others outside the United Kingdom who have been inspirations for many of the contributors – people like Florence Li Tim-Oi of Hong Kong, the first woman ordained to the priesthood in the Anglican Communion in 1944, and Asian American theologians like Kwok Pui-lan, Peter C. Phan and Daniel D. Lee.

We have been blessed by God in a journey begun by a great cloud of witnesses. It is our hope and our prayer that, as we run the race set before us, this book may continue to bless others as we journey forward together.

Introduction

ALEXANDER CHOW

This book has been written during an important moment in history. On the one hand, the largest churches in Britain have experienced an unprecedented decline in attendance. This record slump was confirmed in the 2021 United Kingdom census, in which the majority of those surveyed said they have no religion. On the other hand, British Chinese churches are among the fastest-growing churches in the United Kingdom today. This growth is largely due to the influx of immigrants after the Home Office introduced a new visa route in January 2021 for Hong Kong British National (Overseas) (BN(O)) passport holders. This period also coincided with the rise in blatant anti-Chinese racism during the Covid-19 pandemic – also problematically described as the 'Chinese Virus' or 'Kung Flu'. Of course, British Chinese Christianity has a much longer history. The first Chinese Christian on British soil, Michael Shen Fuzong SJ, dates to the seventeenth century. A sizeable Chinese population has existed in the country since the late nineteenth century, which led to the founding of the first Chinese church in Liverpool in 1910. Today we can find approximately 200 British Chinese churches in every major city throughout the United Kingdom, along with Christians of Chinese heritage in every major British denomination.

Given the historical and statistical realities around British Chinese Christianity, it is surprising that no book like this has yet been written. How are we to understand Chinese Christianity in the United Kingdom if we do not first recognize it as part of British Christianity? How can we speak of the experiences of British Chinese Christians without being aware of how they have been shaped by Britain's encounters with China – from the colonial exploits known as the Opium Wars to competition in the global economy? How do we appreciate the unique contributions of British Chinese Christianity, while not forgetting the diversity found within?

This book tells the story of the rise of British Chinese Christianity. It outlines some of the ways British Chinese Christians have been negotiating their relationships with the wider British population. It also speaks about how they are shaping and reshaping the future of British Christianity. This book demonstrates that Chinese heritage is an integral part of British Christianity.

Beginning a journey

The origins of this book can be traced to the years of the Covid-19 pandemic. In the early months of 2020, news reports highlighted a new coronavirus spreading from Wuhan, China. I remember seeing a video circulating on social media of a Chinese woman eating a cooked bat, giving fodder to early popular theories of the origins of the virus. It later turned out the video was filmed several years earlier in 2016 as part of a food travel blog covering Palau, a Micronesian archipelago in the Pacific Ocean.[1] Conspiracy theories like these were undoubtedly believable, despite being unproven.[2] Collectively they communicated a message to the world that Chinese people were dirty and disgusting and, because of this, were the source of a pandemic causing millions of deaths and strict lockdown measures around the globe. It did not help that the President of the United States at the time insisted on speaking of the 'Chinese Virus' on Twitter despite the World Health Organization's advice to use the name 'Covid-19'.[3] This sparked unprecedented levels of anti-Chinese and anti-Asian racism on both sides of the Atlantic, even resulting in a debate in the Westminster Parliament in October 2020.[4]

By January 2021, I joined an increasing number of online groups and gatherings where British Chinese Christians shared concerns and asked questions in safe spaces. These digital fora offered support for those negotiating their experiences and emotions with their Christian faith. Yet as an American Born Chinese who has wrestled with my own identity and faith, I frequently felt like a spectator looking in on the conversations of my British Chinese Christian friends. But I also have privilege, given that I am one of the few Chinese heritage scholars in the British theological academic establishment with a permanent post – the handful of others who are in post tend to be on temporary or part-time contracts. So even though my academic scholarship is predominantly in Mainland Chinese theology,[5] I was increasingly being invited to give talks about *British* Chinese Christianity. Here was I, a Chinese American scholar of Mainland Chinese theology, speaking on behalf of British Chinese Christians!

INTRODUCTION

My own view of the matter changed in April 2021, when the children's news programme *CBBC Newsround* ran an item entitled 'Chinese children in the UK talk about racism and the impact on their lives'. It highlighted children sharing their stories of being told that they were 'contagious' or a 'coronavirus spreader'. My wife and I talked about this report and it struck us that, while it tried to promote inclusion, the article's title used the phrase 'Chinese children in the UK'. On Twitter, we pointed out to the reporter that this underscored the foreignness of the children – and we were grateful that he listened and promptly changed the title.[6] Needless to say, the nationality of these children is unclear. Of course, if a person is born in the United Kingdom to a parent who is or becomes a British citizen or a permanent resident, the child is entitled to British citizenship. Furthermore, the overwhelming majority of those who have come from Hong Kong are *already* British nationals by virtue of holding a BN(O) passport. Regardless of their nationality status, these children and their parents are part of British society now, as they help to build the British economy and shape its culture and future. Hence, they *are* British Chinese.[7] Likewise, while not every Chinese Christian in the United Kingdom would self-describe as 'British', they contribute to a collective picture of British Christianity. Hence they *are* British Christians. As such, I am proud to be a Chinese American theologian speaking on behalf of British Chinese Christians. But I am even more proud to be lifting up some of their voices through this book to speak from the diverse experiences and expressions of British Chinese Christianity.

Coming together

Starting in 2022, I began discussing the idea of a book with other Chinese heritage theological educators in the United Kingdom, as well as those in church and parachurch ministries. A book project like this needed to bring together a range of perspectives – from ministerial to academic, and those associated with British Chinese churches and historic British churches like the Church of England and the Methodist Church. It also needed a breadth of Chinese heritage backgrounds – those born in Hong Kong and Mainland China, British Born Chinese (BBC) and the odd American Born Chinese. Furthermore, unlike other edited volumes that I have been a part of, this has been a collaborative project from its start, with several online meetings, an in-person meeting in Birmingham in October 2023 and numerous email exchanges and one-on-one conversations about each of the chapters. It is not just a writing project. It has been a journey we have taken together.

So often it was confirmed and reconfirmed how much a book like this was needed. Despite the substantial literature published on Chinese American and Asian American Christianity,[8] no such monograph or anthology has been written that looks at the British Chinese situation. In fact, the main writings about Global Majority expressions of Christianity in Britain have focused on a Black and White binary,[9] with a few strides being made by those of South Asian heritage.[10] One of the first books with a more direct relevance to British Chinese Christians is Renie Choy's *Ancestral Feeling*, published in 2021, which grapples with the tension between a British spiritual inheritance and a Chinese familial ancestry.[11] Choy was born in Hong Kong, raised in Canada and eventually moved to England. So like myself, her situatedness still leaves her thoughts somewhat on the margins of British Chinese conversations.

Overall, British Chinese Christians wrestling with their faiths have had no option but to turn to those *beyond* their context, whether to Asia or America or among other groups in the United Kingdom. Hence several of the contributors in this volume have lamented that their theological education in the United Kingdom has been left wanting due to the dearth of such resources. Furthermore, it shouldn't just be British Chinese who are concerned about this lack of literature. It should also concern those leading churches and ministries with people of Chinese heritage in their pews and parishes.

As contributors offered their ideas for chapters, the structure of the book very quickly developed around three major parts. Part I, entitled 'Re-examining the Past and the Present', includes historical and sociological contributions as a foundation. Alexander Chow writes Chapter 1, which gives a historical sketch of British Chinese Christianity from the Opium Wars until the present and explores how this century and a half has been shaped by experiences of anti-Chinese racism. Whereas he focuses on the development of British Chinese Christianity, Renie Choy's Chapter 2 turns our attention to the portrayal of Sino-British relations through the monuments of British churches. She examines the church monuments commemorating British military officers and commanders, who are glorified with Christian scriptures, themes and values. The chapter narrates the fraught history of Sino-British relations while raising questions around how this may be experienced by Chinese Christians visiting these buildings. In Chapter 3, Yinxuan Huang shifts us away from history to the contemporary situation, based on a sociological survey of 1,179 participants between 2021 and

INTRODUCTION

2022, demonstrating the dynamics and the diversity of British Chinese Christianity today.

Following these foundational chapters, Part II looks at 'Re-forming Identity and Spirituality'. Chapters 4 and 5 are written by two BBCs, James So and Mark Nam respectively. Drawing on postcolonial theories, So argues that BBCs need to move away from 'strategic essentialism' and attempts at trying to fit into quintessentially 'British' or 'Chinese' cultural profiles. Instead, they need to recognize that their identities are ultimately grounded in Christ, to serve God's mission in this world in whatever situation they find themselves. Mark Nam also speaks about the limitations of 'strategic essentialism'. But as a third-generation BBC, he notes the distance he feels from his ancestral Chinese heritage and culture. He shares his story of being called by God to be a priest in the Church of England and also to support other Chinese heritage clergy in the denomination. Chapter 6, by Calida Chu, speaks about Christianity among the most recent influx of Hong Kongese who, she argues, have a different cultural and experiential background from earlier waves of Hong Kongese. As such, she challenges the conceptualization of 'British Chinese Christianity', arguing for a new identity and a new spirituality being birthed around 'British Hong Kongese Christianity'.

The final section, Part III, entitled 'Re-imagining Community and Church', offers theological, ministerial and missional reflections. In Chapter 7, Candy Zhang explains how ministry work with Mainland Chinese students can be seen as a low return on investment, given their short time in the United Kingdom before returning to China. She argues that this should not diminish the importance of serving these transient students but, instead, encourages local churches to aspire to become spiritual homes to the students God brings into their midst. In Chapter 8, Kan Yu speaks about the challenges she has experienced leading a group of Hong Kongese Christians in the journey to create a new church. In particular, she testifies to the blessings and challenges associated with relating to a local, historic English-speaking church, and offers pastoral theological recommendations for migrant Christians learning to adapt their discipleship in a new land. Like Yu, Alexander Chow's Chapter 9 picks up on the tension that exists between historic British churches and the growth of British Chinese and British Hong Kongese churches. Rather than focusing on which one is 'British' or 'immigrant', he suggests they should all be seen as 'native' British churches. Chow argues that migration and the advent of digital technologies have created the need for new ecclesiological understandings – what he calls an 'inter-networked' church, within and beyond British Christianity. Whereas

Chow advocates for an expanded ecclesiology, Josh Shek speaks of an expanded soteriology in Chapter 10. So much of the evangelical understanding of salvation dominant among British Chinese Christians is shaped by a penal substitutionary view of atonement. Shek argues that British Chinese Christians would benefit from considering the Pauline theme of adoption, because it underscores a culturally relevant, familial dimension to the doctrine of salvation.

Journeying forward

In this book's Conclusion, Bert Han explains how this collection of essays points to the start of a journey. Indeed, in bringing together theological educators, church ministers and parachurch workers, we have endeavoured to commence a conversation around the historical and contemporary situation, highlight some of the concerns of British Chinese Christians and suggest prospects moving forward. There are many voices that are still needed – especially from those with migration histories from Malaysia, Singapore and Taiwan, those of mixed heritage and those within Pentecostal and Catholic traditions. As this is the first work of its kind, we hope that many more books will follow and go beyond the points and themes it has introduced.

As Han rightly explains: 'the joy of the journey [is] not the destination but the adventure itself.' Taken together, the chapters in this book introduces readers to the ways Chinese heritage shapes and reshapes British Christianity. We look forward to this book stimulating more conversations among British Chinese Christians. We also hope it brings to the foreground another dimension of the diversity of British Christianity. But in order to do that, we must contest the common perception that those of Chinese heritage are 'forever foreigners' or 'perpetual foreigners'. Rather, this book points to the ways British Chinese Christians are *more than foreigners* and contribute to a richer vision of what God is doing in and through his church in the United Kingdom and beyond.

Notes

1 Laura Zhou, '"Sorry about the tasty bat": Chinese online host apologises for travel show dining advice as Wuhan virus spreads', *SCMP* (26 January 2020), available at https://www.scmp.com/news/china/society/article/3047683/sorry-about-tasty-bat-chinese-online-host-apologises-travel-show.

INTRODUCTION

2 See 'China coronavirus: Misinformation spreads online about origin and scale', *BBC News* (30 January 2020), available at https://www.bbc.co.uk/news/blogs-trending-51271037.

3 Donald J. Trump (@realDonaldTrump), 'The United States will be powerfully supporting those industries, like Airlines and others, that are particularly affected by the Chinese Virus. We will be stronger than ever before!', *Twitter* (16 March 2020), https://www.twitter.com/realDonaldTrump/status/1239685852093169664. In fewer than 160 characters, Trump juxtaposed American businesses against the 'Chinese Virus', thereby making an economic, political and racial statement.

4 Hansard Parliamentary Debates, 'Chinese and East Asian Communities: Racism during Covid-19', *House of Commons* 682 (13 October 2020), https://hansard.parliament.uk/Commons/2020-10-13/debates/858E78B5-1049-4480-A1A7-5362FC12F47E/ChineseAndEastAsianCommunitiesRacismDuring Covid-19. See Yulin Hswen, Xiang Xu, Anna Hing, Jared B. Hawkins, John S. Brownstein and Gilbert C. Gee, 'Association of "#covid19" versus "#chinesevirus" with Anti-Asian Sentiments on Twitter: March 9–23, 2020', *American Journal of Public Health* 111, no. 5 (May 2021), pp. 956–64, https://doi.org/10.2105/AJPH.2021.306154.

5 By this time I had already published two academic works on Mainland Chinese theology: Alexander Chow, *Theosis, Sino-Christian Theology and the Second Chinese Enlightenment: Heaven and Humanity in Unity* (New York: Palgrave Macmillan, 2013); Alexander Chow, *Chinese Public Theology: Generational Shifts and Confucian Imagination in Chinese Christianity* (Oxford: Oxford University Press, 2018).

6 Alexander Chow (@caorongjin), 'Important coverage by @BBCNewsround on anti-#BESEA racism in the UK. But @TRWBURROWS, your story's title of "Chinese children in the UK" implies foreigners in the UK. Please use "British Chinese" in your reporting. #BritishChinese', *Twitter* (15 April 2021), https://www.twitter.com/caorongjin/status/1382757495488188425.

7 A similar idea can be found in Scotland whereby all immigrants are considered 'New Scots' from the moment they move to the nation, because of their contributions to Scotland.

8 See Jonathan Y. Tan, *Introducing Asian American Theologies* (Maryknoll, NY: Orbis Books, 2008); Viji Nakka-Cammauf and Timothy Tseng, eds, *Asian American Christianity: A Reader* (Castro Valley, CA: Institute for the Study of Asian American Christianity, 2009); Daniel D. Lee, *Doing Asian American Theology: A Contextual Framework for Faith and Practice* (Downers Grove, IL: IVP Academic, 2022).

9 See Michael N. Jagessar and Anthony G. Reddie, eds, *Black Theology in Britain: A Reader* (London: Equinox, 2007).

10 See Inderjit Bhogal, *A Table for All: A Challenge to Church and Nation* (Sheffield: Penistone, 2000); Mukti Barton, *Rejection, Resistance and Resurrection: Speaking out Against Racism in the Church* (London: Darton, Longman & Todd, 2005). We must remember that, in the British context, 'Asian' usually refers to those of South Asian heritage and those of Chinese heritage tend to be referred to as 'Chinese' or 'Oriental'. Historically, the main collective term used to speak of those of non-White backgrounds has been BME (Black and Minority Ethnic)

or BAME (Black, Asian and Minority Ethnic) – thereby leaving those of Chinese heritage in a catch-all category of an anonymous 'Minority Ethnic'. This is one reason why BME and BAME have, since 2021, been left out of the official style guide of the Westminster government. See Race Disparity Unit, Cabinet Office, 'Writing about ethnicity', *Ethnicity facts and figures* (December 2021), https://www.ethnicity-facts-figures.service.gov.uk/style-guide/writing-about-ethnicity/, archived at https://archive.is/S2HD0.

11 Renie Chow Choy, *Ancestral Feeling: Postcolonial Thoughts on Western Christian Heritage* (London: SCM Press, 2021).

PART I

Re-examining the Past and the Present

I

The Making of British Chinese Christianity

ALEXANDER CHOW

Introduction

In February 2021 we were just beginning a second UK-wide lockdown for the Covid-19 pandemic. I was at home, futilely attempting to manage work while supporting home learning for my primary-school-aged children. I was helping my son with the materials offered by his school to learn about the Victorian era (1837–1901) and its many inventions and innovations – the harnessing of electricity, the telegraph and the steamship. It struck me that my son was being taught a glossy picture of this period. It overlooked how these niceties enabled Victorian Britain to become a major imperial force: creating the British Raj, Cecil Rhodes' Cape to Cairo railway initiative and the Opium Wars.

It was particularly important for me to teach my son about the last of these, the two Opium Wars (1839–42 and 1856–60). This was less a matter of explaining the complex role that Victorian Britain had in trafficking narcotics, its efforts to push the drug on Chinese lives despite the Middle Kingdom's campaign to prohibit its trade, or the unequal Treaty of Nanking (1842), which ended the war by forcing China to open five trading ports and to cede Hong Kong. Rather, this history is important because it is part of my son's heritage. My wife was born into British Hong Kong – a land she and her family left after the signing of the Sino-British Joint Declaration (1984), which planned for the end of one of Britain's last colonies in 1997. For myself, the First Opium War caused an economic crisis in Canton, forcing members of my grandparents' and great-grandparents' generations, who came from the so-called 'four counties' or *seiyap* of Canton province (also known in Mandarin as *siyi*), to migrate in order to survive – running small businesses in South East Asia, working as labourers for the California Gold Rush and running the merchant navy for the United Kingdom.[1]

This chapter is not about me or my family. But I begin with this story to highlight the importance of the inextricably linked nature of Britain and China/Hong Kong since at least the nineteenth century. Few British Chinese are aware of this history – and even fewer people within the wider British population. Yet it has had an immense impact on what we may today call 'British Chinese Christianity' and how it is perceived within and outside. This chapter begins with a brief overview of British Chinese history and the ways that Chinese in the country have related to Christianity.[2] This is followed by two sections on the most significant sociological changes in recent decades among the Chinese in the United Kingdom: first, the surge in Hong Kongese migrants since the January 2021 introduction of the Hong Kong British Nationality (Overseas) visa route;[3] and second, the steady growth of bicultural British Chinese – 1.5-generation migrants who came to the United Kingdom during their formative years and second-, third- or subsequent-generation British Born Chinese.[4] As a whole, this chapter will argue that the British Chinese cannot be easily dismissed as some 'foreign' factor, but must be regarded as *British*, because this subsector of the British population has had an important role in British society and British Christianity as a whole, regardless of nationality status.[5]

Four periods of changing demographics

We can consider the demographic shifts among the British Chinese across four major historical periods (see Table 1). Each of these is demarcated by significant sociopolitical events related to Sino-British relations and the upsurges in migratory flows that they produced. These inflows and outflows of Chinese often coincided with reactions from the broader British public – both somewhat positive, such as exotic interests in British Chinese cuisine, and clearly negative, such as forms of blatant anti-Chinese racism. Importantly for our purposes, each of these periods saw Christianity offering both blessings and challenges for the British Chinese.

Napoleonic and World Wars (1800s–1940s)

The first period started with the Napoleonic Wars (1803–15) but was accelerated by the First Opium War, which, as mentioned, created an economic crisis in the southern Chinese province of Canton. Due to British imperial interests in Asia and other parts of the world, there was an increased need for cheap labourers. Chinese from Canton province were a major source of this workforce, filling the need for seamen, including work on behalf of the British merchant navy during the two World Wars. Many of these seamen were discharged in ports such as Liverpool, London, Cardiff and Glasgow, and often married local women and had children. Despite their services and wartime sacrifices, shortly after both World Wars (1914–18 and 1939–45), British officials illegally deported Chinese men in 1919 (around 800) and 1945–6 (around 1,300) because they were seen as taking valuable jobs and housing from the mainstream population. Even more disheartening was that many husbands and fathers were dragged on to ships headed to Asia without their families' knowledge, leaving wives and children wondering if they had been abandoned.[6]

The vast majority of these Chinese labourers were not Christians prior to their arrival in the United Kingdom. In Liverpool, some of the earliest Christian work with Chinese was started by George A. Kirkham, who created a Sunday School in 1907 to teach Chinese working in local laundries, stores and lodging houses the English language and about Christianity. This evolved to become the first Chinese church in 1910, the 'undenominational' Gospel Hall Chinese Mission on 24 Village St in the Liverpool district of Everton.[7] The church was known for not only addressing the spiritual needs of the Chinese but also various social ills that they experienced. For instance, several members of the church collaborated with others in campaigning for the end of the opium trade. And when there were questions raised about whether the Chinese posed a social problem in Liverpool, Kirkham wrote to the then Home Secretary, Winston Churchill, in 1911, attempting to quash any perception that they were a nuisance and underscoring that the 'Chinese never enter our workhouses' – meaning that they were never a burden on the social welfare system of the day.[8]

Another example can be found in St Michael's Church on Pitt Street in Liverpool's Chinatown, which in the 1920s and 1930s became a social centre for families formed through marriages between Chinese men and local women. In a 1935 article that appeared in the *Liverpool Diocesan Review* with the eschatologically significant subtitle 'The Church of Many Nations', its minister, J. H. G. Bates, was described as a 'specialist in ethnology'. Concerning mixed marriages, it explained:

The mating of the yellow races with the white is eugenically good, and produces a fine physical type ... The children present a special problem ... They speak English, but their mode of thought is Eastern. Their real ego is wrapped in an impenetrable silence, and whilst the lips speak, the face is a mask, so different from the spontaneous frankness so delightful in English children.

Racial difficulties develop at the marriage age. 'If God had only made me white!' is the bitter cry of the half-caste girl in love with the decent white man, and this bitterness is accentuated by the great urge to motherhood ...[9]

This same article in the church periodical went on to speak about the 'special problem' with Chinese men, who have a 'curious fascination for some white girls', and the need to convince them to avoid the 'irreparable wrong done to these girls'.[10] Needless to say, this reveals the complex role of British Christians, on the one hand addressing some of the social needs of Chinese in Liverpool and, on the other, at times perpetuating racialized stereotypes.

This period witnessed the growth of another population of Chinese in the United Kingdom: Chinese students. The Opium Wars were a wake-up call that China needed to pursue modernization. They began sending their brightest students to Western destinations like Britain and the United States to pursue studies in navigation and shipbuilding – key to China's nation-building interests – but, eventually, to study law, economics and medicine. Before they left China, many of these students were already exposed to Christianity through education in Christian missionary schools. In 1908, Andrew Wai-tak Woo, a student from Hong Kong studying medicine in London, started an organization known as the Chinese Students' Christian Union of Great Britain and Ireland, which networked Chinese studying in British universities and sought to spread Christianity to other Chinese – students, seamen and shopkeepers.[11]

Post-war British appetite for Chinese food (1950s–70s)

The second major period came about after the end of the Second World War, when the British government issued a series of Acts between 1948 and 1981 that opened up immigration, initially for those born in colonies such as Hong Kong and Malaya (later Malaysia and Singapore). These individuals also included those who fled from the cultural revolution in Mainland China through the New Territories of Hong Kong, and those who fled war-torn northern Vietnam. Of course, for those who are forced to flee their homeland (whether in this second period or in the present day), finding work becomes a major practical concern. It so happened that the post-war period was also a time when the wider British population began to have more money to spend and a growing interest in British Chinese food. While there were a number of Chinese students and nurses who migrated to the United Kingdom during this time, by 1985 a whopping 90 per cent of British Chinese were employed in the catering business.[12]

As in the first period, most of the Chinese coming into the United Kingdom at this time were not Christians. The main efforts for Christian work were started by a man named Stephen Wang, formerly the headmaster of a Methodist school outside Beijing, who came to England in 1948 for further studies and as the William Paton Lecturer in the Selly Oak Colleges in Birmingham from 1949 to 1950. However, after the establishment of the People's Republic of China in 1949, Wang was not able to return to China and was separated from his wife and children for the rest of his life. Shortly after arriving in England, Wang attended a Methodist meeting in Liverpool that discussed the state of British missions to China and the shifting political situation. Outside the meeting, he encountered many Chinese in the streets of Liverpool who had never heard of Jesus Christ or the local church. Dismayed by the oversight of the British church, Wang eventually moved to London and in 1951 established one of the first British Chinese churches of the time, the Chinese Church in London, and in 1950 the Chinese Overseas Christian Mission (COCM). Through the latter organization, Wang and various partners travelled throughout the United Kingdom and helped to establish Christian work among the Chinese they encountered.[13]

Rise of China and Sino-British relations (1980s–2010s)

A third period can be identified from the 1980s to the early 2010s. First, the 1984 signing of the Sino-British Joint Declaration signalled Hong Kong's eventual return to China in 1997. This created an exodus from Hong Kong to many Western countries, including the United Kingdom. Second, Deng Xiaoping's reform and opening-up period and pursuit of a socialist market economy created a complex reality that encouraged migration from Mainland China. On the one hand, China once again began to send their brightest to be educated in Western countries. On the other hand, there was economic and political uncertainty coming out of the 4 June 1989 Tiananmen Square democracy protests. While a growing number of Mainland Chinese students came to British universities, this period also saw a sizeable population of Mainland Chinese seeking illegal migration.[14]

Despite these migratory inflows, Britain during this period was growing in blatant anti-Chinese racism. Racialized discourses became publicly debated in Parliament in 1989 around the British Nationality (Hong Kong) Act of 1990.[15] Furthermore, the 2001 foot-and-mouth disease outbreak was blamed on food supposedly destined for Chinese catering establishments, resulting in a downturn in these businesses of as much as 40 per cent.[16]

While the broader British public was unwelcoming to those of Chinese heritage, this period also experienced a tremendous growth of nearly 200 British Chinese churches. Most were non-denominational and started through partnerships with COCM. This also included 15 Methodist churches and a handful of churches associated with the Christian and Missionary Alliance and the Elim Pentecostal Church. Overall, these British Chinese churches tended to be built through ministries focused on students and restaurant workers. Likewise, a number of mainstream British churches attracted some Chinese, especially those who had more fluent English, such as British Born Chinese or those from Singapore and Malaysia. Some of these have also created international fellowships and English language classes to minister to transient Mainland Chinese students. While many of these latter ministries led by mainstream Brits have been in English, most of the British Chinese churches created ministries based in three languages: Cantonese, Mandarin and English.

New exodus and promised land? (2014–present)

We are currently in the midst of a fourth period that can be dated roughly from 2014 to the present. During this period, the Beijing and Hong Kong governments decided that the Sino-British Joint Declaration of 1984 was no longer legally binding, resulting in social unrest in Hong Kong, including protests related to the Umbrella Movement (2014) and opposing the amendment to the extradition law (2019–20). In 2021 the British Foreign Secretary, Dominic Raab, stated that the 'UK considers Beijing to be in a state of ongoing non-compliance with the Joint Declaration'[17] and the Home Office created a new visa route for Hong Kong British National (Overseas) (BN(O)) passport holders.[18] As will be discussed in greater detail in the next section, this has resulted in a tremendous growth in the British Chinese population, during a time of unprecedented levels of blatant anti-Chinese racism due to Covid-19's origins in Wuhan, China, and its description as the 'China virus'.

Table 1: Four periods of sociopolitical and Christian change

	1800s–1940s: Napoleonic and World Wars	1950s–70s: Post-war British appetite for Chinese food	1980s–2010s: Rise of China and Sino-British relations	2014–present: New exodus and promised land?
Sino–British relations	Opium Wars (1839–42, 1856–60) China's need for modernization and education ('self-strengthening movement', 1861–95) UK's need for cheap seafarers	British Nationality Act (1948); Commonwealth Immigrants Act (1962, 1968) Cultural Revolution (1966–76) causing refugee and economic crisis in HK Chinese Vietnamese refugees (esp. after 1979)	China's economic reforms ('reform and opening up period', est. 1978) British Nationality Act (1981) Sino–British Joint Declaration (1984) for return of HK in 1997 Tiananmen Square protests (1989)	Umbrella Movement (2014) Anti-Extradition Law protests (2019–20) Hong Kong BN(O) Visa route (2021)
Blatant anti-Chinese racism	Home Office's forced deportations: 1919 labour disputes (approx. 800 people) 1945–6 labour and housing shortage (approx. 1,300 people)	Minimal blatant anti-Chinese racism due to growth in Chinese catering, because: Geographically dispersed populations to avoid competition in catering Not recruited into wider labour market	Debate around British Nationality (Hong Kong) Act (1990) Foot-and-mouth outbreak (2001) blamed on Chinese catering	Rise of anti-Chinese racism connected to Covid-19 as 'China virus' Mainland Chinese–Hong Kong Chinese intra-ethnic tensions transplanted to UK
Christianity	Chinese Students' Christian Union of Great Britain and Ireland (1908–30s?) Gospel Hall Chinese Mission, Liverpool (1910–38)	Chinese Overseas Christian Mission (est. 1950) Chinese Church in London (est. 1951) Liverpool Chinese Gospel Church (est. 1953)	Creation of around 200 new British Chinese churches: Mostly non-denominational and independent Includes Methodist, Christian and Missionary Alliance and Elim Pentecostal	Growth of pre-existing British Chinese churches New Hong Kongese churches in UK New Cantonese fellowships in mainstream churches (esp. CofE and Roman Catholic)

In each of these periods, events shaping Sino–British relations have had knock-on effects on those of Chinese heritage who have come to or grown up in the United Kingdom. All have experienced some form of racial microaggressions. Most of these periods have also had some form of blatant anti-Chinese racism – with the one exception of the 1950s–70s. In all other instances, such racism was most dramatically experienced when those of Chinese heritage were perceived as taking away livelihood from mainstream populations – jobs, housing and health, the basic physiological and safety needs in Maslow's hierarchy of needs. In the one period of the 1950s–70s, when the wider British public had extra financial means and were intrigued by exotic British Chinese food, things were more or less calm. Ninety per cent of the Chinese employed in the country were in the catering business and, as a consequence, they weren't generally seen as competing in the wider workforce with the mainstream population.

I highlight these details in part to demonstrate the ways racism in the United Kingdom, contrary to the dominant discourse, is not just Black and White.[19] But furthermore, and especially for our purposes, it demonstrates how Christianity in the United Kingdom is not just Black and White. Each of these four periods has witnessed waves of new Chinese migrants, most of whom are probably not Christians. At the same time, they have also witnessed waves of creation of new churches and networks to minister to the changing British Chinese demographics. A small minority of these ministries were started by mainstream British Christians and churches, often with mixed understandings of British Chinese languages, cultures and experiences. The vast majority have been Chinese-led and created out of a need to address the spiritual and social needs of other Chinese.

Hong Kong Ready

When speaking of Christianity and Hong Kongese migration since January 2021, we should begin by recognizing the very positive contributions made by an organization like Welcome Churches, whose UKHK initiative encourages British churches to be 'Hong Kong Ready'. Krish Kandiah has held high-level conversations with the British government, the Home Office and the Prime Minister, and secured government funding to benefit the transition of many Hong Kongese to the United Kingdom. This has also heightened the profile of Hong Kongese migration for the average British Christian. Over 600 British churches have since signed up to their efforts and been given training related to Hong Kongese culture and the situation in Hong Kong that resulted in this migration. This has been a monumental task in itself, including training British Christians about cross-cultural ministry to Hong Kongese as they arrive on their doorsteps. Indeed, if something like this had existed in the 1950s, there would probably have been fewer British Chinese churches today, because mainstream British churches could have been far better equipped so much earlier.

Mindful of this, I am hesitant about some of the language employed when speaking about recent Hong Kongese migrants. For instance, Kandiah has juxtaposed this wave of migration with that of Windrush, noting the failures of the British church in 'making people from the Caribbean feel welcome in our nation and in our churches'.[20] First, while past failings should be acknowledged, this language underscores guilt and regret as motivating factors in responding. That is, we should welcome Hong Kongese now because we were unwelcoming to Caribbeans in the past. While I think Kandiah is rightly mindful of the past as a source for lessons learnt, this can lead to a faulty logic whereby we care for newcomers as a way to atone for our past sins. Second, the focus on Windrush misses the historic patterns of anti-Chinese racism. What about the 800 Chinese men illegally deported in 1919 or the 1,300 in 1945–6: husbands and fathers dragged on to ships without their families' knowledge because they were seen as taking valuable jobs and housing from the mainstream population? Or we could consider the ways many mainstream British churches have overlooked or, worse, discriminated against Chinese populations that came in waves since the nineteenth century. To put it simply, the British Chinese churches exist today because mainstream British populations didn't welcome or engage these earlier generations.

Another limitation has been in the language of 'integration'. Kandiah explains that UKHK encourages integration in three areas: social, educational and professional.[21] Likewise, the British government has published guidance for local authorities 'to support integration and promote community cohesion', especially given that 'new arrivals to the UK can struggle to find opportunities to interact and spend meaningful time with British people and other UK residents beyond their own migrant community'.[22] While integration is quite important for the immediate practical concerns of any migrant, Hong Kongese notwithstanding, it does not consider the longer-term implications of migration. Problematically, the language implies a one-directional flow of change, of the foreigner integrating with the domestic society. There seems to be little discussion of how British society, culture or, indeed, Christianity are shaped by the mass migration of Hong Kongese. How is British society integrating with these newcomers? How are 'British people and other UK residents' reaching out to new arrivals to the UK? How is British Christianity evolving with the evolving population? Is Britain willing to be transformed by these changes or, several years or decades down the line, will these migrants eventually be seen as a liability or a nuisance and, therefore, once again expelled?

We should consider the magnitude of the Hong Kong BN(O) visa route for the British social and religious landscape. From January 2021 to December 2023, the UK government issued 163,850 out-of-country visas for Hong Kong BN(O) passport holders, with 140,300 having already arrived.[23] According to the 2011 census figures, this is about 32.4 per cent of the pre-existing 433,150 Chinese heritage population. Furthermore, conservative estimates suggest that 21.6 per cent of the new arrivals are Christians.[24] This figure is higher than both the Christian population among the pre-existing British Chinese (approx. 18.9 per cent in 2011) and the Christian population within Hong Kong (approx. 16 per cent in 2020).[25]

This development comes at a particularly complex time for British Christianity in general. For one thing, we are at a stage in British history when the national churches of the four nations of the United Kingdom have all reported record declines in church attendance. These are churches that have historically maintained a significant amount of resources ('old money', if you will) and a strong sense of British Christian heritage, and continue to maintain a considerable role in British civic life. We need only to look at the passing of Queen Elizabeth II and the ascent to the throne of King Charles III to notice the intertwined relationship that exists between British Christianity and the state – from the various ceremonies presided over by archbishops to the King's oath in St James's Palace in London in September 2022, in which he proclaimed his willingness to protect the Church of Scotland and Presbyterianism. Despite the prominence of these churches, as already suggested, few of them have historically shown interest in those of Chinese heritage in the United Kingdom.[26] This is beginning to change for some, as we witness the creation of Cantonese-speaking sub-congregations within some mainstream British churches. But there is clearly more work needed here.

In contrast to the historic national churches, the British Chinese churches have comparatively fewer financial and human resources at their disposal and an inconsequential sense of British or British Chinese

Christian heritage, and have had little noticeable involvement with British civic life. The last of these is perhaps due to lack of opportunity and lack of theological or practical motivation. Yet with the influx of new Hong Kongese migrants, most British Chinese churches have at least doubled in size, with at least one that has grown from 200 congregants to 2,000 in the first year of the new visa. Much of this should be considered as transfer growth that will eventually plateau. While these churches are very happy to welcome the newcomers, this is a phenomenal increase in ministry load for already stretched churches, placing tremendous strains on human and financial resources and redirecting the ministry focus away from Mandarin and English ministries.

What is particularly important to remember with the new Hong Kongese migration is that the 21.6 per cent Christians in their number come from a wide range of denominations in Hong Kong – Anglican, Baptist, Christian and Missionary Alliance, Methodist and Roman Catholic – many of which have parallel denominations in the United Kingdom. But denominational affiliation does not always translate across a migratory movement. Other factors related to language and culture play a role in decision-making.

Furthermore, geopolitical conflict in Asia often gets transplanted elsewhere – both in actual and in perceived terms, and has proved to cause intra-Chinese tensions in the United Kingdom.[27] We see this historically in the United States, with the development of separate language-based congregations and denominations in Mandarin and Taiwanese. The latter can be seen in the formation of Taiwanese-speaking denominations, such as the Evangelical Formosan Church founded in Los Angeles in the 1970s. While many of these congregations have taken an apolitical stance, their linguistic and cultural expressions often convey perceived political affiliation, intentional or not.[28] In the United Kingdom, testament to this can already be seen in the nearly two dozen new congregations established by, and ministering to, new Hong Kongese, rather than working with pre-existing British Chinese churches.

A final factor to be mindful of is that many Hong Kongese have chosen to migrate not as individuals but as family units. They migrate to provide opportunities for themselves and for future generations. This is why many of the British Chinese churches have had to rethink children and youth ministries to accommodate the influx of these migratory families. The children have had less say on the matter – less agency if you will – and they have yet to fully realize the liminal space they occupy as a new 1.5 generation (that is, someone who immigrates to a new country before or during their early teens). They are wrestling with an in-betweenness in terms of cultural, linguistic and geopolitical identities. We must seriously consider how Christianity fits into this equation and who will serve as partners and role models in a pilgrimage of discovery and rediscovery – not just today but ten, 20, 30 years down the road.

Bicultural ready

This leads to the other focus of this chapter: pre-existing 1.5 generation British Chinese and British Born Chinese. As with the current situation, the earlier waves of migration included children who left Asia with their parents or who were born in the United Kingdom as part of the second, third or subsequent generations. The self-understanding of this group is *less* as a 'diaspora', given that 'home' is more to be found in the United Kingdom.

The vast majority of these individuals were introduced to Christianity as children and effectively grew up in the faith alongside their parents. British Chinese churches have served as sites where family, culture and religion have intersected and maintained shared values. But as they are Chinese Christians *in Britain*, the bicultural reality of their faith becomes increasingly sharp as they are faced with the wider contours of British society. Comparatively, many American Born Chinese become Christians in high school and university settings. In part, this is connected to the proliferation of evangelical parachurch organizations in American universities, such as InterVarsity Christian Fellowship, Navigators, Cru and Asian American Christian Fellowship – all of which have developed ministries focused on Asian Americans. Furthermore, since the 1990s the publishing arm of InterVarsity Christian Fellowship has produced books for bicultural Asian American Christians such as *Following Jesus Without Dishonoring Your Parents* (1998) and *More Than Serving Tea* (2006), the latter concerned with Asian American Christian women. This is quite different from the British context: most British universities will have, at most, a Christian Union with a White British focus or, in some London universities, an organization like the Overseas Christian Fellowship, which tends to focus on transient students from Singapore or Malaysia.

Another dynamic is the historic tendency for Chinese to be Britain's most regionally dispersed Global Majority group. To a large extent, this is due to the catering work and the need to be geographically scattered to minimize competition between Chinese restaurants and takeaways.

Many 1.5-generation and second-generation British Chinese have been 'takeaway kids', often helping with food preparation after school before working in the evenings at the front counters while their parents are cooking in the kitchen. They take the orders and, as children, often become translators for their parents with limited English. The counter becomes the meeting place with a world that offers everything from friendly banter to racialized or sexualized encounters.[29] Furthermore, few of these takeaway kids continue in the family business, but are generally instructed by their parents to study hard and take up white-collar professions.

Given the dispersed population, most British Chinese children grew up without ever encountering another British Chinese in their schools or neighbourhoods, and therefore lacking any sense of strong collective identity – let alone social or political voice. Terms like 'Chinese' or 'Oriental' still remain standard for referring to anyone of East Asian heritage, whereas the term 'Asian' is reserved for those of South Asian heritage. There has long been the designation of 'British Born Chinese' – but some see this as describing someone who is basically ethnically or culturally Chinese but was incidentally born in the United Kingdom. It was only in the 1990s that the term 'British Chinese' began to emerge for these newer generations to underscore a complex hybrid identity drawing from both British and Chinese cultures and experiences.[30] At the height of the anti-Chinese racism experienced during the Covid-19 pandemic, another term has gained currency: 'British East and South East Asian' (BESEA) or 'East and South East Asian' (ESEA). This term is meant to capture the complexities of Chineseness coming from Mainland China, Taiwan and Hong Kong, as well as to include other Asians with roots in Korea, Singapore, Malaysia and so forth. It is a way to highlight solidarity across those of Asian background who see themselves quite differently from South Asians, although it tends to still be dominated by those of Chinese heritage.[31]

While the terms 'British Chinese' and 'BESEA' came about in the 1990s and the 2020s, they are comparative latecomers when compared to the term 'Asian American', coined in the 1960s at the height of the US civil rights movement as an alternative to the derogatory terms 'Oriental' or 'Asiatic'. In other words, this kind of solidarity is still very much at an early stage in the United Kingdom. While these developments have mainly begun in the British arts sector,[32] British Christianity has been much slower in finding ways to offer solidarity for British Chinese or BESEA Christians. There are limits to what British Chinese churches can do, because Chinese ministries (often in Cantonese and Mandarin) are created in parallel with English ministries, the latter being uncritical evolutions of children's and youth ministries. Of around 200 British Chinese churches, few have full-time ordained English ministry staff and few of the staff are British Born Chinese themselves. Ironically, because of the intersection of family, culture and religion, few of the British Chinese churches are readily equipped to go further and engage with the complex concerns that shape the Christian faith, such as questions around bicultural identity and experiences of racism. And given that no British theological institution has anything comparable to Fuller or Princeton Theological Seminaries, with their centres of Asian American Christianity, there is virtually no substantial formal teaching on British Chinese Christianity. Thankfully, attempts have been made to develop spaces for solidarity, such as the COCM's PHAT Camp for secondary school youth, the Doxa conference for English ministry leaders organized by the Birmingham Chinese Evangelical Church, or The Teahouse for Chinese heritage clergy in the Church of England.

We also need to recognize that the 1.5-generation and British Born Chinese do not always attend British Chinese churches. This is particularly true of the second and third generations, who tend to be the most culturally and linguistically distant from Asia. It goes without saying that even with around 200 British Chinese churches, this doesn't come near the number of cities with British Chinese in the United Kingdom. Even if these individuals attended British Chinese churches as children, if they continue in the church they may find spiritual homes elsewhere as they become adults, find partners who may not be British Chinese, and move around the country.

It is useful to compare this with how many Asian American migrant churches in the 1990s were experiencing what was called a 'silent exodus' from their English ministries.[33] While Chinese American church leaders worried about this phenomenon, several decades later they found that departure from the migrant church did not necessarily mean departure from the Christian faith. Rather, it was an exodus to a new promised land in multiethnic churches – often large pan-Asian American congregations.[34] Today, Asian Americans have become integral to the shape of American Christianity. Many lead American Christian organizations as presidents of parachurches (such as InterVarsity Christian Fellowship and the Gospel Coalition) and deans and presidents of seminaries (such as Fuller Theological Seminary, Trinity Evangelical Divinity School and Claremont School of Theology). This is quite different from the United Kingdom, where British Chinese are welcome in the pews but not the pulpits, as theological students but not as theological educators.

In 2020, even Archbishop Justin Welby openly acknowledged that the Church of England was 'still deeply institutionally racist'.[35]

While we cannot simply universalize this to all British Christian institutions, it comes as little surprise that there are only a select number of Chinese heritage ministers in mainstream British churches and even fewer Chinese heritage theological educators on permanent contracts in British theological institutions. English ministries in British Chinese churches have sometimes added to their numbers those of BESEA, White British or other backgrounds and, conversely, mainstream British churches may include clusters of British Chinese. But the space for British Chinese or BESEA to find solidarity and critically engage and nurture the faith mindful of their contextual experiences and challenges is still much lacking within British Christianity.

Conclusion

In conclusion, a few things are worth briefly mentioning. First, in contrast with what is seen from the outside, there is a tremendous amount of diversity within British Chinese churches. It is hardly as homogeneous as some missiologists may claim. And with this variety have come, at times, intra-Chinese tensions.

Second, British Chinese churches tend to be broadly evangelical and have historically focused on gospel proclamation rather than a major focus on the broader society. This should not take away from the very important civic function of these churches in helping migrant populations to settle and orientate themselves to living in a foreign land. As second and later generations develop, British Chinese Christians increasingly support one another in wrestling with questions about how the Christian faith speaks into racial and social experiences. They are faced with a British context that often dismisses them as 'Chinese' or 'Oriental' – foreigners who are told to 'go home'. Rather, most British Chinese Christians are, rightly, *British nationals* – especially those who are British Born Chinese or hold Hong Kong BN(O) passports. They are *British* Christians.

This leads to the final point: it would be wrong to name British Chinese churches in the United Kingdom as mainly 'migrant' or 'diaspora' churches. They are changing the landscape of British Christianity. These are rightly *British churches*.[36] They are contributors to the making of *British* Christianity.

Notes

1 My family story is quite typical of this period. For a helpful discussion of why the *seiyap* fled China in the nineteenth century, see Madeline Y. Hsu's *Dreaming of Gold, Dreaming of Home: Transnationalism and Migration Between the United States and South China, 1882–1943* (Stanford, CA: Stanford University Press, 2000), pp. 18–29.

2 For a fuller account, see Alexander Chow, 'British Immigration Policies and British Chinese Christianity', in *Ecclesial Diversity in Chinese Christianity*, ed. Alexander Chow and Easten Law (New York: Palgrave Macmillan, 2021), pp. 99–120, https://doi.org/10.1007/978-3-030-73069-7_5.

3 In this chapter I will refer to Hong Kong British Nationality (Overseas) as Hong Kong BN(O). Also during this period there has been a growing emphasis on Hong Kong identity and the usage of terms such as 'Hong Konger' or 'Hong Kongese'.

4 As will be discussed later, 'British Born Chinese', as well as its Scottish and Irish equivalents ('Scottish Born Chinese' and 'Irish Born Chinese'), is an imperfect term. Nevertheless, for the purposes of this chapter, I will use it as a general umbrella term for those of Chinese heritage born in the United Kingdom.

5 Throughout this chapter I unashamedly employ the term 'British' and 'British Chinese'. See Ashley Thorpe and Diana Yeh, eds, *Contesting British Chinese Culture* (London: Palgrave Macmillan, 2018). For a different perspective that underscores how most Global Majority Christians are inheritors of Western Christianity, see Renie Chow Choy, *Ancestral Feeling: Postcolonial Thoughts on Western Christian Heritage* (London: SCM Press, 2021).

6 See Gregor Benton and Edmund Terence Gomez, *The Chinese in Britain, 1800–Present: Economy, Transnationalism, Identity* (Basingstoke: Palgrave Macmillan, 2008), pp. 26–31. Details for the latter can be found in Home Office 213/926 in the British National Archives, entitled 'Compulsory repatriation of undesirable Chinese seamen'.

7 After Kirkham died in 1920, the church continued to thrive until it held its last Sunday service on 10 April 1938, on Sidney Place in the Liverpool district of Edge Hill. 'Chinese Church to Go', *Liverpool Echo* (12 April 1938), p. 12.

8 George A. Kirkham to Winston Churchill, 8 April 1911, National Archives, Home Office 45/11843, pt. 2, fol. 80.

9 'St Michael's Pitt Street: The Church of Many Nations', *Liverpool Diocesan Review* 10, no. 8 (August 1935), p. 590.

10 'St Michael's Pitt Street', p. 590.

11 See Chow, 'British Immigration Policies and British Chinese Christianity', pp. 106–8.

12 Home Affairs Committee, 'Chinese Community in Britain: Volume I, Report Together with Proceedings of the Committee', House of Commons 102 (1984–85), p. xi.

13 Stephen Wang, 'The Chinese on Our Doorstep', *World Dominion* (September–October 1952), pp. 265–8.

14 See Hsiao-Hung Pai, *Chinese Whispers: The True Story Behind Britain's Hidden Army of Labour* (London: Penguin Books, 2008).

15 Benton and Gomez, *The Chinese in Britain*, pp. 314–15.

16 Paul Kelso, 'Chinese restaurants feel the pinch', *Guardian* (2 April 2001), https://www.theguardian.com/uk/2001/apr/02/footandmouth.paulkelso; Cindi John, 'Chinese fight foot-and-mouth claims', *BBC News* (5 April 2001), http://news.bbc.co.uk/1/hi/uk/1260861.stm.

17 Foreign, Commonwealth and Development Office, 'Radical changes to Hong Kong's electoral system: Foreign Secretary's statement', *Gov.uk* (13 March 2021), https://www.gov.uk/government/news/foreign-secretary-statement-on-radical-changes-to-hong-kongs-electoral-system, archived at https://archive.is/Lfs5q.

18 Home Office, 'British National (Overseas) factsheet', *Gov.uk* (2 March 2022), https://www.gov.uk/government/publications/nationality-and-borders-bill-british-national-overseas-factsheet/british-national-overseas, archived at https://archive.is/a7RCP.

19 While the discourse on racism in the United Kingdom is still very focused on Black and White issues, a classic discussion of anti-Chinese racism in America is Frank H. Wu's *Yellow: Race in America Beyond Black and White* (New York: Basic Books, 2002). A recent attempt at producing a Christian engagement with Asian American identity and racism is Jonathan Tran's *Asian Americans and the Spirit of Racial Capitalism* (New York: Oxford University Press, 2022).

20 OMF International, 'Krish Kandiah on Welcoming Hong Kongers', *OMF Billions* (September–December 2022), https://omf.org/uk/billions/articles/krish-kandiah-and-welcoming-hong-kongers/, archived at http://archive.ph/bMTDo.

21 OMF International, 'Krish Kandiah on Welcoming Hong Kongers'.

22 Ministry of Housing, Communities and Local Government, 'Hong Kong UK welcome programme – guidance for local authorities', *Gov.uk* (8 April 2021), https://www.gov.uk/guidance/hong-kong-uk-welcome-programme-guidance-for-local-authorities, archived at https://archive.ph/8Ndks.

23 National Statistics, 'Safe and Legal (Humanitarian) routes to the UK', *Gov.uk* (29 February 2024), https://www.gov.uk/government/statistics/immigration-system-statistics-year-ending-december-2023/safe-and-legal-humanitarian-routes-to-the-uk, archived at https://archive.is/s8Nij.

24 See Chapter 3 of this volume, endnote 12.

25 See Stuart M. I. Stoker, ed., *Hong Kong 2020* (Hong Kong: Information Services Department of the Hong Kong Special Administrative Region Government, 2021), p. 313.

26 A select number of parishes or dioceses in the Church of England and the Catholic Church have created Chinese communities within their churches. In the Church of England, there is the Bishop Ho Ming Wah Association and Community Centre established in 1964 as a Chinese congregation within St Martin-in-the-Fields in London. Chinese Catholic communities have existed for a number of years in Our Lady of the Assumption (London), the Cathedral Church of St John the Evangelist (Manchester) and in St Gregory's Church (Glasgow). With the rise in Hong Kongese migration, there has been some effort to create more periodic opportunities for Mass in Cantonese, including in the Cluster of St Barnabas (Milton Keynes), St Catherine of Siena (Birmingham), Our Lady of Lourdes (Sawston, Cambridge) and St Mary's Catholic Cathedral (Edinburgh).

27 This was already the case prior to the new visa route at the height of the Covid-19 pandemic, since the social problems that resulted were often associated with Mainland China. See Yinxuan Huang, Kristin Aune and Mathew Guest,

'COVID-19 and the Chinese Christian Community in Britain: Changing Patterns of Belonging and Division', *Studies in World Christianity* 27, no. 1 (March 2021), pp. 18–21, https://doi.org/10.3366/swc.2021.0323.

28 See Carolyn Chen, *Getting Saved in America: Taiwanese Immigration and Religious Experience* (Princeton, NJ: Princeton University Press, 2008), pp. 28–32, esp. p. 30, n.13.

29 For first-hand accounts of this, see Angela Hui, *Takeaway: Stories from a Childhood Behind the Counter* (London: Trapeze, 2022).

30 See David Parker, *Through Different Eyes: The Cultural Identities of Young Chinese People in Britain* (Aldershot: Avebury, 1995).

31 Diana Yeh, 'Becoming "British East Asian and Southeast Asian": Anti-racism, Chineseness, and Political Love in the Creative and Cultural Industries', *British Journal of Chinese Studies* 11 (July 2021), pp. 53–70.

32 See Helena Lee, ed., *East Side Voices: Essays Celebrating East and Southeast Asian Identity in Britain* (London: Sceptre, 2022).

33 Helen Lee, 'Silent Exodus', *Christianity Today*, August 1996, pp. 50–53.

34 Helen Lee, 'Silent No More', *Christianity Today*, October 2014, pp. 38–47. In his important study of pan-Asian American churches, Russell Jeung makes the insightful observation that 'Asian American ministers cannot simply start a church as whites can establish a local church. Instead, if they want to reach out to their neighborhood, they must start a *multiethnic* congregation because their racial presence in the pulpit obviously makes the church different from the European American norm.' Russell Jeung, *Faithful Generations: Race and new Asian American Churches* (New Brunswick, NJ: Rutgers University Press, 2005), p. 161.

35 This was in the context of Windrush and doesn't even come near to touching the nuanced reality that racism is more than Black and White. Justin Welby, 'Archbishop Justin Welby's remarks during Windrush debate at General Synod', *The Archbishop of Canterbury: Justin Welby*, 11 February 2020, https://www.archbishopofcanterbury.org/speaking-writing/speeches/archbishop-justin-welbys-remarks-during-windrush-debate-general-synod.

36 See Chapter 9 of this volume.

2

Chinese History in English Churches: Monuments, Memorials and the Questions they Raise

RENIE CHOW CHOY

Introduction

Aside from Chinese Christian churches and organizations (as outlined in Alexander Chow's opening Chapter 1), further indication of the existence of a Chinese dimension in British Christianity can be found in monuments and memorials in churches around Britain. These objects tell us that the 'Chinese heritage in British Christianity' is not only about the presence of Chinese Christians in Britain but also about the complex history of British involvement in China and vis-à-vis Chinese people, largely as it relates to military encounters. From the 1840s until 1943, Britain possessed extraterritorial rights in China, occupying a number of treaty ports. The British Empire also, at its height, held direct colonial possessions in Singapore, Malaysia, Hong Kong and Myanmar – all places with large populations of people of Chinese descent. Furthermore, the trade in indentured labourers, which emerged after the abolition of transatlantic slavery forced European colonial powers to seek cheap labour elsewhere, brought Chinese people to North America, Latin America, the Caribbean, South East Asia, Africa and Oceania. All of these developments were the direct result of military activities carried out by the British to expand commercial interests. The expansion of Christianity in East Asia is closely related to such military activities. According to the last available Pew Forum statistical report, *Global Christianity*, China in 2010 already had over 67 million Christians, and the former British possessions in East and South East Asia (Singapore, Malaysia, Myanmar, Hong Kong) a further 8 million in total.[1] These statistics do not include the large number of Christians belonging to the Chinese diaspora in the United Kingdom and Europe, the United States,

Canada, Australia and New Zealand. The 'opening up of China' to Christianity in the nineteenth and twentieth centuries is usually attributed to the entry of missionaries, but this in itself was only achieved through the aggressive military battles in the region.

Such battles are commemorated in the monuments found today in British churches; many might be considered 'contested heritage' as currently defined by both the Department for Culture, Media and Sport and the Church of England.[2] Much has changed since the nineteenth century, when the vast majority of the military memorials related to British activity in East Asia were installed: today, a large number of the viewers encountering the memorials will be of Chinese descent, and many of these will identify as Christians. The memorials now speak to a demographic their original commissioners would never have anticipated.

This chapter will 1) provide an overview of the key types of monuments related to British activity in China, focusing on the particular story they tell about Britain's relationship with China, and with Christianity in China; and 2) observe the tensions and dilemmas this story creates for the contemporary Chinese Christian viewer in Britain today. I wish to suggest that the monuments present an unsettling perspective about the relationship between Christianity, China and Britain, because they overemphasize British Christianity's national, military and commercial interests in China while overlooking the inextricable linkages with Chinese Christianity. Collectively these monuments fail to represent the Christianity many Chinese would recognize as 'theirs', and therefore make little room for the 'Chinese heritage in British Christianity'. As such, efforts should be made to insert the Chinese dimension more explicitly into the visual culture of British Christianity.

In describing memorials in British churches related to activity in China, I have relied primarily on the Imperial War Museum War Memorials database, though this overview is by no means exhaustive.

The history of Chinese–British relations as told by church monuments

The East India Company (EIC) was established in 1600 by a charter from Elizabeth I granting it the exclusive right to trade in the East. The EIC grew into a formidable commercial and military power, trading in high-value Indian commodities such as spices, saltpetre, cotton textiles, silk, indigo dye, tea and opium. To protect this trade, the Crown also gave the Company permission to raise its own armies and fortify territorial possessions. Most of the monuments related to the East India Company in Britain's churches point to the heavily militarized nature of the Company's rule, commemorating army officers and commanders. The EIC armies comprised units of British soldiers who served alongside Indian regiments under British commanders, and the monuments tell of key wars waged by the Company spanning vast swathes of land on the Indian subcontinent and in Central Asia and East Asia. For example, many monuments commemorate key battles that took place from the 1790s to the 1860s against the kingdom of Mysore, the Maratha Confederacy, the kingdom of Nepal, the Burmese empires and in the Punjab and Afghanistan. Britain's lengthy rule over large parts of Asia, especially in India, was made possible by the East India Company's defeat or subduing of all these regimes, events commemorated by many monuments in English churches. At St Paul's Cathedral in London, monuments were installed to (just to name a few) the Marquis of Cornwallis, Arthur Wellesley the Duke of Wellington, Charles James Napier and Henry Montgomery Lawrence, all officers who fought key battles to extend EIC territory on the Indian subcontinent.

In China the East India Company operated within the Canton system to engage in three-way trade, exporting Indian cotton and opium as well as British silver to China, and importing Chinese tea and other goods to Britain.[3] The opium that the British sold in China was made from the sap of poppy plants and had been used for medicinal purposes in China and Eurasia for centuries. The EIC established a monopoly in the cultivation, processing and production of opium, especially in the eastern Indian province of Bengal. With large numbers of Chinese becoming ill or indisposed from addiction to opium, the Chinese government saw the import of the opiate as a serious social and fiscal problem, banning its trade in 1800 and outlawing the smoking of opium outright in 1813. In response, the British East India Company hired private British and American traders to transport the drug to China, and smugglers distributed it through a network of middlemen. To address the large numbers of smugglers' boats working the opium trade by 1830, the Chinese government hired Lin Zexu to supervise the crackdown on the opium trade and consumption from Canton (Guangzhou) in 1839. Lin Zexu took several measures, including writing an open letter to Queen Victoria challenging Britain's support for the trade and its moral position, arresting Chinese dealers, seizing and destroying over 2,500,000 lb of opium and confining foreign merchants to a restricted area. These actions outraged British traders, most prominently Jardine Matheson & Co (the primary British opium producer) as well as the City of London:

they lobbied the Foreign Secretary, Viscount Palmerston, for military intervention to force China to reverse its position on opium imports. Palmerston, arguing for the right to free trade, persuaded Parliament to deploy 16 warships and 4,000 troops in China. What happened next can be told through the many monuments found in Britain's churches.

In June 1840, the British warships arrived at Canton (Guangzhou); over the next two years, British forces bombarded the coasts of China in a series of campaigns commonly referred to as the First Opium War (1839–42). Steam power was introduced to British naval warfare in this period and one such steam warship was the *Samarang*, commanded by James Scott. He led an attack at the Humen strait (Bogue) and the island of Taikoktow (west of Chuenpi), successfully capturing the fort. A series of similar victories, which resulted in the disabling of Chinese ships, burning of junks and dismantling of their forts, enabled the British Plenipotentiary, Charles Elliot, to negotiate with the Chinese Imperial Commissioner, Qishan, and led to the Convention of Chuenpi on 20 January 1841. Under this Convention, the island of Hong Kong was ceded in perpetuity to Great Britain, and an indemnity of $6,000,000 was to be paid and official trade reopened. Hong Kong officially became a British possession on 26 January under a royal salute. But when the Chinese failed to reopen the port of Canton to trade, the British resumed attack, this time capturing the forts on islands in the Pearl River Delta in Guangdong. James Scott, commanding the *Nemesis*, travelled towards the city of Canton (Guangzhou) to capture the fort there and demand ratification of the convention. For his services in command of a squadron that 'carried the Bogue forts in China', Scott was made a Commander of the Order of the Bath, and on his death a memorial was installed in St Paul's Cathedral. The plaque in the crypt lists his service in the 'Chinese' wars, in addition to the French and American wars, enumerating the capitals, towns, cities, batteries and forts seized, and the ships, frigates, gunboats and merchant vessels captured.

These events are also referred to in St Mary's Church in Gosforth in Cumbria, where Humphrey Le Fleming Senhouse, a senior naval officer during the First Opium War, is commemorated in a memorial 'erected by officers of the army and navy, belonging to the Chinese expedition'. He had led 300 seamen and Royal Marines against Humen in Guangdong, killing the Chinese admiral and taking the fort. Having died of fever, his memorial refers to him as one who 'lost his life in consequence of great mental and bodily exertions after the taking of the heights of Canton'.

With the Pearl River cleared of Chinese defences and Guangzhou secured, the British advanced on Central China. On 10 October 1841, a British naval force bombarded and captured a fort on the outskirts of Ningbo in central China. Shortly thereafter, Chinese authorities evacuated Ningpo (Ningbo) and the empty city was taken by the British on 13 October. This event is commemorated in the memorial to Sir Harry Rawson in St Paul's Cathedral.

With many Chinese ports now blockaded or under British occupation, the British sought to cripple the finances of the Qing Empire. Assembling 25 warships and 10,000 men at Ningbo and Zhapu in May 1841, they advanced into the Chinese interior, blocked Chinese logistics, captured royal tax barges and severely reduced the revenue of the imperial court in Beijing. Captain Granville Loch – commemorated by a marble relief and inscription at St Paul's – was present when China finally capitulated and surrendered to Britain's demands. He served as an aide-de-camp to General Sir Hugh Gough at the capture of Chinkiang (Zhenjiang), the last major battle of the First Opium War, which brought about the end of the conflict but led to mass suicide in the city. Loch, who was present at the surrender of the Chinese and the signing of the Treaty of Nanking, afterwards published an account called *The Closing Events of the Campaign in China*:

> The naval portion of the party returned to the ships early on the 29th, to be in time to see the Commissioners sign the treaty on board the Cornwallis. ... [I] saw the [Chinese] Emperor's letters, which had arrived the evening before, assenting (with the exception of free trade with Foo-choo-foo, and which Sir Henry overruled) to all the articles in the rough draft which had been forwarded for his inspection. Although there were perhaps a few objectionable expressions, showing that the leaven of ancient arrogance was not extinct, it nevertheless, from the first word to the last, evinced deep consciousness of fallen power ... There were four copies of the treaty written in both languages, under separate covers: the ends of the riband which tied them together were sealed to the paper; so that, without cutting it, no sheet could be abstracted – not an unlikely thing to be attempted by these slippery gentlemen to blind the eyes of their Imperial master. From a square box covered with yellow silk the Treasurer Whang took his writing-pencils, ink and the official seal of the Viceroy: it was an agate about three and a half inches long by two broad: this was pressed against a pad saturated with red lead, and then applied to the paper. The three Commissioners signed their names under the impression, and thus ratified the Plenipotentiary's first and last demands. It was a glorious spectacle for all who saw it. Two hundred miles within their

greatest river, under the walls of their ancient capital, in the cabin of a British 74, the first treaty China was ever forced to make was signed by three of her highest nobles under England's flag.[4]

This treaty – the Treaty of Nanking – provided extraordinary benefits to the British, including: the continued possession of Hong Kong; a huge indemnity (compensation) to be paid to the British government and merchants; five new Chinese treaty ports at Canton (Guangzhou), Shanghai, Amoy (Xiamen), Ningpo (Ningbo) and Foochow (Fuzhou), where British merchants and their families could reside; extraterritoriality for British citizens residing in these treaty ports, such that they were subject to British, not Chinese, law; and a 'most favoured nation' clause stipulating that any rights gained by other foreign countries would automatically apply to Great Britain as well. By 1879, not only had the Chinese been unable to stamp out the trade in opium but Chinese imports of opium had risen to 87,000 chests.

However, Britain was still dissatisfied. The Treaty of Nanking did not give privileges to missionaries, or Britain the right to conduct diplomatic relations with China as an equal sovereign state rather than via what was perceived as an outdated tributary-state ritual. And crucially, it had not legalized the trade in opium. Soon a pretext was found for reigniting war.

The Second Opium War, or the Arrow War as it is often termed in English, was sparked by a minor incident that was then escalated by the acting British consul in Canton, Harry Parkes, who is memorialized by a bust and plaque with inscription in the crypt of St Paul's Cathedral.[5] On 8 October 1856, Chinese officers boarded what was said to be a sailing vessel called the *Arrow*, suspecting that it was engaged in smuggling. Parkes claimed that Qing officers disregarded its registration as a British vessel, ignored the English captain, arrested the Chinese crew independently and hauled down the British flag. Parkes' claims turned out to be grave misrepresentations: the ship was owned by the Chinese but had been registered under a fake British owner in Hong Kong to avoid Chinese law; moreover, this registration had expired prior to the incident, and witnesses observed that no British flag had been flying. Nevertheless, spinning the incident as a major affront to British honour, Parkes asked Sir John Bowring (the governor of Hong Kong and the British Plenipotentiary to the Qing Empire) to call the British navy to bombard Canton in retaliation. On 23 October, even after the Chinese Governor-General Ye Mingchen had returned all the arrested crewmen to British custody, Royal Navy ships bombarded the forts in Guangzhou. The city of Guangzhou itself was fired on and Governor-General Ye's residence destroyed. Lord Palmerston, now prime minister, decided to support a new war in China, arguing that war was needed in order to expand trading opportunities for British merchants (through the legalization of opium), to transform the framework of diplomacy from China's traditional tribute system to the Western model of free trade based on diplomatic equality, to allow greater freedom of entry to and travel within China and to standardize taxes on imports and exports to China at a low level. Palmerston fought – and won – a general election on this platform (the 'Chinese election' of 1857); he is commemorated in Westminster Abbey by a large marble statue. Joint French-British forces launched attacks and captured Guangzhou before moving north to the city of Tientsin (Tianjin).

With Guangzhou bombarded and the Taku (Dagu) forts further north seized, the joint Anglo-French expedition was able to force negotiations, which led to the Treaty of Tientsin (Tianjin) in 1858. This expanded the number of treaty ports (ports open to foreign trade and residence) from five to 16, opened the Yangtze River to foreign navigation, granted a large indemnity to the British and French from the revenues of the Chinese customs, established foreign legations in Beijing and legalized Christian missionary work. Deeply embittered by the treaty, the young Qing emperor Xianfeng instructed the Chinese army to drive off the British fleet arriving to ratify the treaty. When a large Anglo-French expeditionary force arrived in Tianjin in the summer of 1860, the emperor was forced to flee and English and French troops looted and burned the imperial Summer Palace outside Beijing.

These events are commemorated in a number of memorials in English churches. Harry Rawson, commemorated by a bronze plaque in the crypt at St Paul's, was present at the capture of the Taku (Dagu) forts in 1858 before becoming an aide-de-camp on HMS *Encounter* in 1860, and so was present at the second recapture of the forts as well as at the battle of Palikiao (Baliqiao), the taking of Peking (Beijing) and the capture of Ningpo (Ningbo). The inscription on his memorial reads: 'Served in China war 1851–61, was present at capture of Peiho, Taku forts, and Pekin. Commanded thirteen hundred Chinese troops at defence of Ningpo, was severely wounded, and several times mentioned in dispatches.'

Major-General Charles George 'Chinese' Gordon likewise has a large memorial effigy on the floor of St Paul's. Gordon was present at the occupation of Peking; on winning the Second Opium war in 1860, he and his comrades looted the Summer Palace in Peking (Beijing) and burnt it down.⁶ Gordon criticized the burning and looting as 'vandal-like' in a letter home, but he also benefited from the loot and reported: 'I have done well.' Among the many objects he brought back to England was a Chinese imperial throne, which he placed in his regimental headquarters at Chatham (and is now in the Royal Engineers Museum in Gillingham). Gordon remained in the international settlement in Shanghai after the war, joining the British, French and imperial Chinese troops to help protect Western interests. During the Taiping rebellion against the Qing emperor, which sought to end exploitation by European trade and to install a more equitable system of taxation, Gordon commanded around 4,000 Chinese troops to suppress the rebels. Gordon's success propped up the Qing emperor, who conferred on him the position of mandarin in the Chinese army, an honourable title, a Peking medal and the right to wear the yellow jacket (the highest Chinese military rank). This earned him the nickname 'Chinese Gordon'.

Reflecting on these decades of intensive warfare in China, which at once exposed and exploited the weaknesses of an imperial nation that had seen 5,000 years of dynastic rule, Captain William King Hall – commemorated in a tablet at St Anne's Church in Sutton Bonnington, Nottinghamshire – wrote in his diary:

> [W]e forced a Treaty out of a weak and divided nation ... The Treaty was conceived by vanity and ambition, and obtained from them by mighty wrong and piracy ... We have spared when we should have struck, and struck unjustly without a cause except the power of doing so. We have forced a Treaty from a nation at peace with us.⁷

The unequal treaties imposed by western powers disrupted China's methods of conducting foreign relations and managing its maritime trade. The continuation of the opium trade and its social consequences prevented the Chinese government from paying its tax and huge indemnity obligations. Britain's wars of aggression and the 'century of humiliation' that followed shaped the rationale for the later Chinese Communist Revolution against imperialism and feudalism.⁸

What church monuments imply about the relationship between the British military, the Chinese and Christianity

The memorials tell a troubling story about the relationship between the British army, the Chinese and Christian ideals. Richard Blake's assessment helpfully anticipates the sense of confusion that may be experienced by a Chinese viewer when confronted with these memorials:

> The suppression of the Atlantic slave trade has largely retained its reputation as an altruistic blend of commerce, Christianity and sea power. By contrast, the opening of China to trade and western influence ... wears a different aspect. The same Admiralty which sacrificed men's lives and spent money in a humane cause in the Atlantic was apparently prepared to wage aggressive warfare to advance commercial profits in the Far East. In the words of Niall Ferguson, 'It is indeed one of the richer ironies of the Victorian value-system that the same navy that was deployed to abolish the slave trade was also active in expanding the narcotics trade.'[9]

In commemorating the officers, the monuments explicitly sanction the aggressive advancement of British commercial interests through war. They go a step further, asserting a very particular message about the role of Christianity in this warfare. For example, in St Peter and St Paul Church, Wadhurst, East Sussex, there is a memorial to Lieutenant Standish Haly of the Royal Irish Infantry, describing him as 'youngest son of Major and Mrs Aylmer Haly, both of this parish, who died the 12th of May 1841 off the island of Junkcylon [i.e. Phuket], on his way to China with his regiment, aged 25 years'. He did not have any noteworthy military achievements – he hadn't even made it to China, having died en route. Yet a memorial has been erected to him by his bereaved parents because of his tragic death at a young age. A similar memorial is found in St James Church, Arlington, North Devon, to a lieutenant of the Royal Navy, Louis Chichester, who 'died at the Cape of Good Hope on his way home from the war in China, December 8th 1858, at the early age of 24'. The tablet was 'erected by his affectionate father, to the memory of one greatly beloved and esteemed, and in sorrow for his early death', and includes the scripture 'The grass withereth, the flower fadeth, but the word of our God shall stand for ever.'

These are moving monuments and no one would ever blame a parent for erecting a memorial to their child so tragically taken at a young age. But the ideals of Victorian family domesticity and scriptural ideals on which the tablets depend are only applied to certain (English) lives and not others, and as such offer an incomplete representation of the nature of the loss caused by these wars. Frequently the memorials to British officers who served in the Opium Wars hold them up as examples of Christian virtue. For instance, the memorial to Brigadier-General Sir W. W. Turner at the Royal Garrison Church, Portsmouth, praises his military talents, which 'were conspicuously brought to notice' during the wars in the Crimea, in suppressing the Indian Mutiny, as well as in the Second Opium War. The memorial explains that the reredos in the church was 'erected to the glory of God' in his memory, and that 'he has left the noble example of a Christian soldier' and was a 'gentle upright honourable man'. Lieutenant C. H. B. Turner also lost his life, dying at Tianjin in the Second Opium War, and is commemorated at St Andrew's Church in Banwell, Avon, in a stained glass window: he is memorialized with the phrase 'Blessed are the dead who died in the Lord'. These explicit references to Christian Scripture and values, not to mention their placement in a place of worship, point to Christian providence and blessing underwriting these wars. Even a man as controversial as Harry Smith Parkes is praised, in a monument in St Paul's, for his 'lifelong service and unfailing courage, devotion to duty, and singleness of purpose'. These commemorations highlight the close collusion between Christianity and Britain's imperial military activities and victories. In the nineteenth century this would not have merited much notice, but this chapter concerns the effect it has on Chinese viewers who have adopted Christianity and uphold Christian values, who must then encounter the ascription of Christian blessing and exemplary living to individuals who waged war against their homeland.

Into this dynamic we need to remember how Protestant Christianity in China grew into such a formidable and significant movement at all. After bitter fighting in Guangdong province, the taking of forts in Tianjin, the occupation of Beijing and the destruction of the Summer Palace (all events related to the memorials discussed), the Treaty of Tientsin gave missionaries the right of travel and residence and protection from harassment. Contemporaries hailed this as the 'opening up' of inland China – now at long last open to foreign trade, opium and Christianity.[10] The wars of aggression definitively enabled the growth of Protestant Christianity in China: 'The navy was linked with the beginning of the Protestant missionary movement,' Blake argues, 'first by setting the context in which it operated and then by facilitating its expansion.' As the Naval Chronicle asserted: 'Nelson and his followers would have harassed our enemies beyond their resources by carrying a

British army from place to place with ease and rapidity ... and by proper attention we might spread the power of the gospel to all nations and languages by the same means.'[11]

Thus, while the memorials portray British military activity as a divinely sanctioned errand carried out under the hand of providence, in fact the relationship between the military and religion would highly complicate things for the cause of Christianity. Indeed, the ease with which these memorials make the connection between Christianity and military warfare conceals how this dynamic seriously complicated the situation on the ground in China. The 12th Duke of Somerset, Edward Adolphus Seymour, expressed this problematic state of affairs most clearly in a question debated in the House of Lords in March 1869 regarding missionaries in China. The immediate controversy was whether the navy should be deployed to support missionaries. The Duke of Somerset observed the complications in China caused by the presence of missionaries, who provoked anger and needed to be rescued by gunboats – gunboats that in turn complicated relations between China and England:

> every missionary almost requires a gunboat. The fact is, we are propagating Christianity with gunboats; for the authorities of inland towns know perfectly well that if they get into trouble with the missionary a gunboat will soon come up. In pursuing a course towards a weak country which we could not possibly take towards a more powerful one, it seems to me we are entirely wrong ... Suppose a Chinaman asks what effect this new religion has upon the people, and goes to Shanghai to see, what does he behold? Naval and civil officers who are acquainted with all the chief ports in Europe, America, and Asia inform me that, though seaport towns are not usually very moral places, there is no such sink of iniquity as Shanghai. And yet you expect that, having seen your example, and how you force Christianity on by gunboats and Armstrong guns, the Chinese will embrace Christianity!

Henry George Grey, the third Earl Grey, agreed:

> Nobody can be more anxious for the success of the missionaries than I am; but I am certain that in relying on an appeal to force when their own imprudence has brought them into difficulties, they are doing more harm than good to the cause of Christianity ... The most satisfactory statement made by the noble Earl (the Earl of Clarendon) was his intention to reduce the number of gunboats, for such is the pressure of British influence that if a strong naval force is at hand it is extremely

likely to be used; while, on the other hand, if we have not enough gunboats to bully the Chinese, both merchants and missionaries will show greater prudence, discretion, and fairness than if they saw themselves supported by a powerful force.[12]

The debate is most instructive because this dynamic remains entirely hidden in the memorials. Indeed, these finer nuances were lost on the Chinese, who could only see the correlation between aggressive military and commercial policies and those of the missionaries. This resentment led directly to the Boxer Rebellion of 1900, which treated missionaries and traders equally as the emissaries of foreign colonialism.

Violent uprisings in the north of the country targeted foreigners, Christian missionaries and Chinese Christian converts. The uprising was initiated by a Chinese secret society called the Yihequan (Righteous and Harmonious Fists), which practised a form of martial arts resembling boxing. The 'Boxers', as they became known, pursued a violent campaign to drive all foreigners out of China. Though initially a peasant movement, it was soon supported by the Imperial Chinese government and armed troops. Growing violence against foreign diplomats, missionaries, soldiers and Chinese Christians forced them to take refuge in the Legation Quarter of the capital, Beijing, and issue a call for international help. An alliance was formed between eight nations, which quickly dispatched a force of 20,000 commanded by a British general to relieve foreign legations in Beijing. The Chinese Empress Dowager perceived this as a foreign invasion and ordered the 'Boxers' and imperial troops to block the advance and attack the Legation Quarter. The international forces breached Beijing's defences, ended the siege of the Legation Quarter and pillaged and looted the Forbidden City, the imperial palace complex used by dynastic courts since the fifteenth century. The foreign alliance imposed harsh terms on the imperial court through the Peking Protocol of 1901: China was prohibited from importing arms for two years, agreed to permit foreign troops to be stationed in Beijing, and was made to pay $330 million in compensation. This humiliation, which exposed the weakness of the Qing dynasty and further increased Chinese indignation over foreign interference, contributed to the rise of the nationalist and republican movement.[13]

These include memorials to Edward Jeffries Esdaile (St Thomas of Canterbury, Cothelstone, Somerset), Commander P. N. Wright (St Nicholas Church, Churchstoke, Powys), Captain R. O. M. Doig (Assumption of the Blessed Virgin Mary, Lillingstone Lovell, Buckinghamshire), David Oliphant (St Nicholas Cathedral, Newcastle upon Tyne, Tyne and Wear), Captain Arthur Joseph Hill (St Peter's Church, Wimblington, Cambridgeshire), Townsend and Townsend (St Peter's Church, Aisthorpe, Lincolnshire) and Captain Henry Rotherham (St Giles Church, Wrexham, Clwyd). There are also memorials to those who fought to suppress the rebellion but were not killed, and who are commemorated for other military actions: Sir Vere Bonamy Fane (St Nicholas' Church, Fulbeck, Lincolnshire), Colonel O. S. Flower (St Eadburgha's Church, Broadway, Worcestershire), John Jellicoe and David Beatty (both St Paul's Cathedral, London).

Many of the memorials explicitly underscore the foreignness and enemy status of the Chinese, using language that is jarring today. For example, the memorial for T. Smith in St John the Baptist Churchyard, Derbyshire, literally refers to China as a 'foreign country'. The memorial to A. R. Higgins in St Mary's Church, Funtington, West Sussex, refers to his death 'whilst rescuing fellow countrymen from the Chinese'. Several memorials explicitly call the slain British men and women 'martyrs'. These commemorations of British missionaries are not great in number and are found in non-conformist churches, from which the largest numbers of missionaries had gone to China. The memorial to Mr and Mrs Nathan in Loughton Baptist Church in Loughton, Essex, describes their deaths as 'martyrdom', as does the memorial in the former Baptist Church in Rochdale, Greater Manchester, for Emily Jessie Pigott, Thomas Wellesley Pigott and their son William Wellesley Pigott, who are described as having 'suffered martyrdom' in Shanxi, China, in the summer of 1900, joining 'the noble army of martyrs'.

For the Chinese Christian viewer, alongside sorrow and even embarrassment for the ruthless murder of missionaries, the memorials may pose further discomfort. While the uprising of 1900 saw the deaths of around 250 Westerners, more than 30,000 Chinese Christians were massacred in a campaign to banish Western imperialism.[14] The vast majority of their identities remain unknown, their deaths uncommemorated.

Thus although the conflict in 1900 did occur between two opposing sides, today this 'us vs them' mentality is jarring, especially given the vast numbers of Chinese Christians who were caught in between. The us vs them language of the memorials is especially difficult because the allure of heritage is the opportunity for visitors to come face to face with their own places of origin, to enhance a sense of connectedness and rootedness in the past. However, while monuments related to Britain's imperial activities present plenty of opportunity for the Chinese to see names of places familiar to them, these references do not enhance connectedness but rather a deep sense of unease. From a personal perspective, I write as someone from Hong Kong whose ancestral village is in Guangdong. What should I feel seeing these place names listed in the plaques below? The memorials to Lieutenant Keith Stewart at St Ann's Church in Portsmouth, Hampshire, who died commanding the gunboat *Plover* in Hong Kong in 1857; to Rear Admiral Sir Francis Collier in St Nicholas Church in Wickham, Hampshire, who died 'whilst in command at Hong Kong' in 1849; to Captain Humphrey Le Fleming Senhouse in St Mary's Church in Gosforth, Cumbria, who 'lost his life in consequence of great mental and bodily exertions after taking the heights of Canton' in 1841; to Robert William Danvers in the King's Chapel of the Savoy, London, who was buried in 1858 in Hong Kong ... these memorials all bring my mind back to my ancestral homeland and city of my birth, but the images they conjure up are of British soldiers in uniform and gunboats. William Thornton Bate's memorial in St Ann's Church in Portsmouth offers the most dramatic example of an object that ought to inspire a sense of connectedness but instead alienates: it invokes Christian virtue and scriptural ideals while at the same time referencing the storming of a city of significance to my family history:

> Sacred to the memory of Captain William Thornton Bate R.N. who was killed under the walls of Canton, at the storming of the city December 29th 1857, in the 37th year of his age. His distinguished career of professional service, the conspicuous gallantry, consistent piety and Christian virtues which adorned both his public and private life, warmly endeared him to a wide circle of relatives and friends, who deeply mourn the loss occasioned to them and to his country by his untimely death. His friends in China add to a monument which they have erected at Hong Kong, this simple memorial of their respect and affection for his memory.
> To me to live is Christ, and to die is gain. Philippians Ch. 1. Ver. 21.[15]

What, then, to make of these contradictions?

Concluding thoughts

In the face of these contradictions, I would like to bring in the story of Robert Morrison, popularly acknowledged as the 'Father of Protestant Christianity' in China. In Hong Kong and Taiwan there are streets, colleges and other places named for Morrison; his life and legacy are well known among Chinese Protestants and his grave in Macau has become an important site of pilgrimage. Yet in Britain, Robert Morrison is not a widely known figure and there is no commemoration of him in British churches.

Prompted by a call to be a missionary in China, Robert Morrison set sail and arrived in Guangzhou in 1807, the only place where foreigners were at that time permitted in China. Aided by the contacts of George Staunton (an officer in the East India Company), he embarked on a programme of intensive Chinese language learning. The East India Company's objective was not Christian evangelism but trade, and evangelism was explicitly prohibited by the Chinese government. Yet the EIC needed Morrison's linguistic skills and hired him as an interpreter and translator; Morrison likewise needed a salary and, crucially, an affiliation with the EIC in order to remain in Guangzhou and Macau so that he could carry out his religious objectives. China's prohibition against Christianity and the EIC's own official policy against proselytizing on the one hand and Christian missionary criticism of the opium trade on the other were mutually disregarded by the EIC and Morrison, who worked reluctantly with one another so that each party could further its own aims. This is what Kristin Bayer has referred to as the 'model of disguise'.[16] Under this guise and within nine years, Morrison was able to produce a Chinese grammar book, a six-volume dictionary of Chinese and the Bible in 21 volumes. Nevertheless, even to the end of his life Morrison worried about how much his religious work was noticed or mattered, having converted fewer than a dozen people, and his journals reflect the discomfort he felt about his association with both the opium trade and the EIC itself: 'The society is not congenial to my mind. Obliged to sit and hear the Lord's name often profaned, I feel myself out of my place.'[17]

Nevertheless, Morrison was a trailblazer in forging the relationship between missionaries and the EIC that eventually led to the Company hiring more missionaries to work at the factory in Guangzhou. After he died, missionaries started to arrive in China in large numbers. The most renowned is James Hudson Taylor, who founded the China Inland Mission in 1865 and lived in China for 51 years. By the time of his death, the number of CIM missionaries, schools and converts in China was significant. Christopher Daily opens his monograph on Robert Morrison with this paragraph, full of superlatives and a narrative of origination:

> Robert Morrison (1782–1834), the first Protestant missionary to operate in China, was sent alone to his East Asian post by the London Missionary Society (LMS) in 1807. He spent more than half of his life (he died at his station in Guangzhou, China) planting a foothold in China for the benefit of the Protestant missionary movement, and, consequently, established the foundation upon which all subsequent Protestant missions to China rested. To list but a few of his achievements, Morrison composed the first Chinese–English dictionary and grammar, recorded the first conversions of Chinese to Protestantism, translated the first version of the Confucian Classics directly to English, established the first Anglo-Chinese educational institution. Subsequently, his pioneering mission planted Protestantism in China and his translations provided the foundation for the emergence of Anglophone sinology ... [He] remains one of the most important western figures in the history of Chinese Protestant Christianity.[18]

In Mark O'Neill's assessment in a public podcast, 'Time would tend to accept ... Now we have tens of millions of Chinese Protestants in the mainland, Hong Kong, Taiwan, and overseas, and they are all sons and daughters of Robert Morrison. So in that respect we have to say he did a remarkable thing.'[19]

The absence of memorialization to this missionary dimension of Christian heritage in the British ecclesiastical landscape is therefore notable. Official commemorations give the impression that we are still awed and captivated by the East India Company and the imperial endeavours, acquisitions and defences of its armies. Indeed, the only commemoration of Robert Morrison is in East Asia. And while a heritage trail and a commemorative plaque have been set up in Hudson Taylor's hometown of Barnsley, there are no memorials to him in British churches – presumably because he was not Anglican but a Congregationalist. Eighty-one of the missionaries working with the China Inland Mission and 21 of their children were killed in the Boxer Rebellion. However, as we saw above, the memorials in British churches predominantly commemorate army officers who served in suppressing the rebellion. The missionaries in China – a direct legacy of Morrison and Taylor's pioneering work – who were killed in this rebellion are barely commemorated: to my knowledge, none at all in Anglican churches, and only three in total in non-conformist churches within the UK, of which one is missing and cannot be located.[20]

We can summarize the tension regarding Christianity, the Chinese and the memorialization in British churches in this way. First, it was Britain's overt acts of mercantile pursuit and military aggression that brought Robert Morrison – and after him seminal missionaries like Hudson Taylor and the China Inland Mission – into China, leading to the 'planting of Protestantism' in East Asia. This is the reason for the vast number of Chinese Christians globally today. Thus, Britain's military ventures are central to the topic of 'Chinese heritage in British Christianity', and the military memorials are relevant because they commemorate events that explain the entry of missionaries into China, and themselves evoke Christianity.

Second, the memorials evoke a distinctively military-style Christianity which, in conflating Christian ideals with British military victories, has little to do with the personal faith and spirituality of many Chinese Christians.[21] In other words, though the commemorations have been installed inside churches and are religious in character, they take no interest in the actual story of Christianity as it developed in the meeting of the Chinese–British worlds. They ignore the Christian heritage in China and among the Chinese diaspora (Taiwan, Macau, Hong Kong, Singapore, Malaysia, not to mention other places of global migration) that emerged as a result of these historic military activities.

Finally, the memorials give a skewed picture. They overplay the importance of establishment (Anglican) Christianity. They ignore the contribution of non-conformist Christianity, which was tied less to the military and commercial aims. They focus only on military commemorations which, in invoking Christianity, give an unbalanced picture about the alliance between the military and Christianity, one that Chinese Christian visitors would probably not adopt themselves. They present themselves as 'Christian memorials' having relevance to the Chinese story but overlook the history of Chinese Christianity itself.

These monuments therefore do not make room for the 'Chinese heritage in British Christianity' – though, as they make clear in no uncertain terms, British Christianity had very much to do with affairs in China. And so the monuments present a one-sided story that highlights strength, heroism, loyalty, service, bravery and providence under the banner of British Christianity.

As this volume makes clear, Chinese heritage is a significant component of British Christianity today. The ever-growing number of Christians from the Chinese diaspora living in Britain means that the heavily militarized nature of Christian commemoration in British churches needs contextualization, explanation, engagement and expansion. We must more explicitly insert the Chinese dimension into the visual culture of British ecclesiastical spaces, in order to acknowledge the presence of Chinese Christians in Britain and to demonstrate that we are 'more than foreigners'.[22]

Notes

1 Pew Research Centre, *Global Christianity: A Report on the Size and Distribution of the World's Christian Population* (Washington, DC: Pew Research Center, 2011), pp. 75–6.

2 Department for Culture, Media and Sport, 'Guidance for custodians on how to deal with commemorative heritage assets that have become contested', https://www.gov.uk/government/publications/guidance-for-custodians-on-how-to-deal-with-commemorative-heritage-assets-that-have-become-contested/guidance-for-custodians-on-how-to-deal-with-commemorative-heritage-assets-that-have-become-contested; Church of England, 'Contested Heritage in Cathedrals and Churches', https://www.churchofengland.org/resources/churchcare/advice-and-guidance-church-buildings/contested-heritage.

3 The historical overview regarding the Opium Wars is drawn from various sources, including the educational material developed by Asia Pacific Curriculum (https://asiapacificcurriculum.ca/learning-module/opium-wars-china), the National Army Museum (https://www.nam.ac.uk/explore/first-china-war-1839-1842) and Massachusetts Institute of Technology, 'Visualizing Cultures', https://visualizingcultures.mit.edu/opium_wars_01/index.html; R. S. Horowitz, 'The Opium Wars of 1839–1860', in S. Haggard and D. C. Kang, eds, *East Asia in the World: Twelve Events That Shaped the Modern International Order* (Cambridge: Cambridge University Press, 2020), pp. 164–87; Julia Lovell, *The Opium War: Drugs, Dreams and the Making of China* (Basingstoke/Oxford: Picador, 2011).

4 Granville G. Loch, *The Closing Events of the Campaign in China: The Operations in the Yang-Tze-Kiang and the Treaty of Nanking* (London: J. Murray, 1843), p. 212.

5 Historical overview is drawn from John Y. W. Wong, *Deadly Dreams: Opium and the Arrow War (1856–1860) in China* (Cambridge: Cambridge University Press, 2002); Massachusetts Institute of Technology, 'Visualizing Cultures', https://visualizingcultures.mit.edu/opium_wars_02/ow2_essay01.html.

6 This section draws from the entry written by Amrita Shodhan for 'The East India Company at St Paul's' digital trail, www.stpauls.co.uk/east-india-company-st-pauls, accessed 14.05.2024.

7 Quoted in Richard Blake, *Religion in the British Navy 1815–1879: Piety and Professionalism* (Woodbridge: Boydell Press, 2014), p. 229.

8 See again Asia Pacific Curriculum, https://asiapacificcurriculum.ca/learning-module/opium-wars-china.

9 Blake, *Religion in the British Navy*, p. 159. The Ferguson quote is from

Niall Ferguson, *Empire: How Britain Made the Modern World* (London: Penguin, 2003), p. 167.

10 Ambrose Mong, *Guns and Gospel: Imperialism and Evangelism in China* (Cambridge: James Clarke & Co., 2016).

11 Quoted from 'The Naval Chronicle' XXIX, 1813, pp. 475ff., quoted in Blake, *Religion in the British Navy*, p. 156.

12 Hansard Parliamentary Debates, 'Lord Napier's Annuity Bill—No 15', *House of Lords* 194 (9 March 1869), https://hansard.parliament.uk/Lords/1869-03-09/debates/4e552b5d-874e-4497-a3c4-363d93028b84/LordsChamber.

13 For an accessible overview, see National Army Museum: https://www.nam.ac.uk/explore/boxer-rebellion. See also Robert Bickers and R. G. Tiedemann, eds, *The Boxers, China, and the World* (Lanham, MD: Rowman & Littlefield, 2007), and Robert A. Bickers, *The Scramble for China: Foreign Devils in the Qing Empire, 1800–1914* (London: Allen Lane, 2011).

14 Miikka Ruokanen and Chen Yongtao, 'Christianity in Chinese Soil', in Kirsteen Kim, Knud Jørgensen and Alison Fitchett-Climenhaga, eds, *The Oxford Handbook of Mission Studies* (Oxford: Oxford University Press, 2022), pp. 456–74 at p. 460.

15 His grave in the Chapel of the Protestant Cemetery, now Hong Kong Cemetery, has the headstone: 'Sacred to the memory of Captain William Thornton Bate R. N. who was killed at the storming of Canton on December 29th 1857 in the 37th year of his age. Mark the perfect man and behold the upright for the end of that man is peace.' He is also commemorated in a memorial tablet in St John's Cathedral in Hong Kong along the north wall.

16 Kristin Bayer, 'Desire, Disguise, and Distaste: Robert Morrison, the British East India Company, and Early Missionary and Merchant Negotiations in Guangzhou, China', *Journal of World History* 32, no. 4 (2021), pp. 581–600.

17 Quote in Bayer, 'Desire, Disguise, and Distaste', pp. 594–5.

18 Christopher Daily, *Robert Morrison and the Protestant Plan for China* (Hong Kong: Hong Kong University Press, 2013), p. 1.

19 RHTK-HK Hong Kong Heritage Podcast, 'Missionary Robert Morrison', 22 January 2017, https://podcast.rthk.hk/podcast/item.php?pid=164&eid=86229&lang=en-US, accessed 26.01.2023.

20 See memorials to Mr and Mrs Nathan at Loughton Baptist Church in Essex and to Rev. and Mrs Underwood at Manvers Street Baptist Church in Bath. The memorial to the Pigott family was located in the former Baptist Church in Rochdale, Greater Manchester but cannot, according to the Imperial War Museum database, be located.

21 On Chinese Christian spirituality, see Yinxuan Huang's Chapter 3 in this volume.

22 See Alexander Chow's Introduction in this volume.

3

Contemporary British Chinese Christianity: Religious and Social Characteristics

YINXUAN HUANG

Although more than a century has passed since the Liverpool Gospel Hall Chinese Mission became in 1910 the first Chinese[1] church to be established in modern Britain,[2] there is a notable lack of systematic, empirical research focused on this expanding community. This research gap is particularly glaring given the significant influx of migrants from Hong Kong since early 2021. More recently, however, there has been a burgeoning body of literature that delineates the historical context of Chinese churches in the UK, explores their faith characteristics and discusses the impact of Covid-19 and British Nationality (Overseas) or BN(O) immigration from Hong Kong (see for example Li et al., 2020; Chow, 2021; Huang et al., 2021; To and Chan, 2023).

This chapter aims to enhance the conversation by providing a comprehensive, data-driven viewpoint. Data is not just for statisticians. Numbers can help us to understand landscapes, trends and characteristics on an aggregated level: How big, how often and how different? Following a sociological approach, it addresses these questions in the British Chinese Christian community by utilizing official data, including the Census 2021 and the largest survey conducted on the Chinese Christian community in Europe. Empirically, this chapter outlines the three fundamental aspects commonly employed by sociologists to interpret religion: *believing*, *belonging* and *behaving* (McAndrew, 2020). In this framework, 'Christianity' is examined not just as a personal belief system but also as a multifaceted construct encompassing various attitudes and practices within both church and societal contexts. Combined, this exploration is instrumental in revealing the unique dynamics and the underlying religious and social constructs of the British Chinese Christian community.

The bricolage of diasporic Chinese Christian communities

While empirical research on Chinese churches in Western societies can be traced back to the United States in the 1980s, the lag in research on Chinese churches in Europe may not be surprising. As compared to America, the number of Chinese immigrants and churches in any European country is historically much smaller. Moreover, in terms of religious culture and sentiments, European nations appear not to be as 'religiously observant' as the United States (Putnam, 2000, p. 65). The value of these studies in America also lies in their provision of references and benchmarks for research on diasporic Chinese Christian communities in other places.

These studies convey a crucial message: the bricolage of diasporic Chinese Christian communities is far more than just a spiritual or religious phenomenon. First, the movement of immigration creates transnationalism, the 'processes by which immigrants forge and sustain multi-stranded social relations that link together their society of origin and settlement' (Basch et al., 1994, p. 7). Research in various regions such as North America, Western Europe and the Middle East shows that the faith life of local Chinese Christians, both individually and at the church level, is not only rooted in their surrounding community but also intricately linked with the social and cultural capital they possess in their sending countries (Guest, 2003; Kalir, 2009; Rao, 2017). In this regard, discussions about Chinese churches in the UK need to go beyond the static presumption of being 'replanted permanently in the UK' and instead be based on a dynamic understanding, one that envisions a continuous social migration back and forth. Second, the diasporic Chinese Christian community represents a complex tapestry woven from varied secular threads, which 'syncretize' into the construction of individual faith and church. Social scientists use the term 'adhesive patterns of adoption' to describe how East Asian immigrants tend to adopt some aspects of local culture and social life, while simultaneously preserving or reinforcing their ethnic social capital and identities (Kim and Hurh, 1993). This phenomenon was observed in both American and British Chinese Christian communities, in which the formation of diasporic Chinese Christian communities was accompanied by ongoing contestation and negotiation between Christian, Chinese and American/British values and identities (Yang, 1999; Li et al., 2020).

When the observation of Chinese churches in the UK extends to both sacred and secular domains, we often find that Chinese Christians are not a homogeneous group. Other chapters of this book also illustrate from different perspectives how the faith life of Chinese Christians in the UK is deeply connected to their transnational backgrounds, such as Mainland China, Hong Kong or being UK-born. These distinctive backgrounds lead to vastly different perceptions, formations and expressions of faith (Li et al., 2020; To and Chan, 2023). Existing qualitative research has revealed that such distinctions may result in divisions and even segregations within the Chinese church. For example, it was shown that young Chinese Christians in the UK from Mainland and Hong Kong backgrounds experienced conflicts during the 2019–20 Hong Kong protests and the Covid-19 pandemic due to differing political views (Huang et al., 2021). The arrival of BN(O) immigrants is also subtly transforming the landscape of Chinese churches. Unlike the pre-2021 Cantonese congregations in Britain, the new BN(O) immigrants from Hong Kong, while demonstrating a strong dedication to their Christian identity, also possess resolute and uncompromising political stances and identities, putting them at odds with other Chinese Christians in Britain (To and Chan, 2023). Moreover, all Chinese churches are part of the broader British social and Christian communities. Compared to Chinese churches in other European countries, the English-speaking environment and a relatively higher level of educational occupation enable Chinese Christians and seekers to have more frequent and deeper contact with local English-speaking churches (Yu, 2020). This form of engagement facilitates greater exposure of Chinese churches to the doctrinal teachings and secular applications of other non-Chinese congregations and Christian groups, thereby prompting a process of either adopt or reject. Consequently, the interaction contributes to the bright and blurred boundaries between them.

Gauging religion and the Chinese Christian community in Britain

Statistical records of religion in the UK can be traced back to as early as 1851. The 1851 religious census was an unprecedented survey encompassing known places of worship at the time, which included not only Church of England congregations but also Nonconformist and Catholic churches, as well as Jewish synagogues. However, it was not until 2001 that the UK introduced a voluntary question on religion in its modern census. Additionally, there are a few organizations in the UK that specialize in conducting statistical work for Christian churches.[3]

While we discuss the potential revival of British Chinese churches due to immigration, the 2021 census of England and Wales showed that for the first time in history the proportion of Christians fell below 50%. Notwithstanding this seemingly robust trend, sociologists of religion over the past two decades have rarely used the term 'decline' to conclude the development of Christianity in the UK. The key point to grasp is that the constituencies comprising the church today, such as denominations, political leanings and ethnicity, are more complex than at any previous time in history. Against the backdrop of an overall decline there also exists evidence supporting church growth. Among the most significant are those church communities formed by new arrivals, especially in the context of Britain's increasing net immigration numbers (Goodhew, 2012; Davie, 2015). In this regard, post-2021 the Chinese Christian community in Britain has provided us with an invaluable and timely case study.

The few empirical studies on Chinese churches in the UK have, as previously mentioned, all adopted qualitative research methods based on observation and interviews. There is a complete absence of quantitative records based on numbers and statistics, which strongly motivated the present research. It is particularly worth noting again that quantitative measurement of Chinese churches should not be limited to church attendance or self-reported religious affiliation. Like many other Western societies, Britain, in the neo-liberal, post-truth era, has witnessed its Christian community becoming increasingly decentralized and diverse (Guest, 2022). Therefore, when analysing the Chinese Christian community, it is essential to assess not only its intra-group variations but also how its narrative aligns with the broader British and transnational social, cultural and political contexts.

In the light of this vision, the remaining part of this chapter's empirical discussion will be divided into three sections. At the outset, I will introduce the design, data collection and methodology of this study. The empirical research then focuses initially on the religious and faith dimensions of the Chinese Christian community. This includes the demographics and trends at the church level, as well as patterns of private and communal practices on the individual level. The final section of this chapter examines the social domain of Chinese Christianity in Britain. It utilizes three distinct indicators that illuminate how Chinese Christians in the British and transnational contexts are either united or divided in their perspectives on key sociocultural issues.

Data and method

The data used in this study is from two sources. The first comprises secondary data derived from official records, predominantly the 2011 and 2021 population censuses, the 2021-22 Annual Population Survey and data from the Home Office regarding BN(O) immigrants. These large-scale datasets were also employed to calculate statistical weights to enhance the validity of subsequent analyses.

The primary data of the study is from a survey specifically targeting adult ethnic Chinese residents aged 18 and above from both British-born and immigrant backgrounds. The survey, entitled 'The Bible and the Chinese Community in Britain' (BCCB), was conducted between November 2021 and March 2022.

Data collection in ethnic minority or immigrant populations is usually more challenging than in a general population. These challenges – from lack of appropriate sampling frames to limited access to minority networks – often make it difficult to define and collect reliable data. To address this issue, the BCCB adopted the Centre Sample Technique (CST), which offers significant advantages especially in researching minority groups (Baio et al., 2011). CST circumvents the challenge of securing an accessible sampling frame by focusing on intercept or aggregation points instead of individual networks.

The BCCB identified a variety of locations and platforms popular among the Chinese population in Britain to serve as central aggregation points.[4] Initially, the web-based questionnaire was disseminated across both the physical and digital realms of these centres, encompassing four Chinese supermarkets, three community centres, three language schools, two cultural associations and one business association. A supplementary 'booster sample' was subsequently obtained with assistance from 27 Chinese churches, five non-Chinese churches and a number of key church and mission organizations that cater to the Chinese community.[5] This booster sample aimed to augment the representation of Christian participants in the study.

With a sample size of 1,179, the BCCB is the largest sample of a Chinese Christian community in Europe. The initial general sample comprised data from 797 individuals, 152 (19%) of whom identified as Christians. The booster sample, collected from predominantly Christian settings, consisted of 382 individuals, with 352 (67%) identifying as Christians. In total, the survey included 504 Christian respondents, predominantly Protestant (N=502) with only two Catholics.[6]

Chinese Christianity in Britain's religious data: the big picture

According to the 2021 census for England and Wales, 17.3% of Chinese residents (N=76,918) identified themselves as 'Christian' (Figure 1).[7] Nearly two in three Chinese respondents reported having no religious affiliation. Buddhists constitute the second-largest religious group among the Chinese, accounting for 9.3%. Within these 76,918 Christians, 17.4% are first-generation immigrants, while 16.8% are second-generation British Born Chinese. This generational decline in the proportion of Christians is in fact discernible across all minority ethnic groups in the census. Interestingly, the generational decline among the Chinese is the second smallest of all these groups, only slightly more than Bangladeshis (0.3%).

Figure 1: Religious affiliation of ethnic Chinese in England and Wales

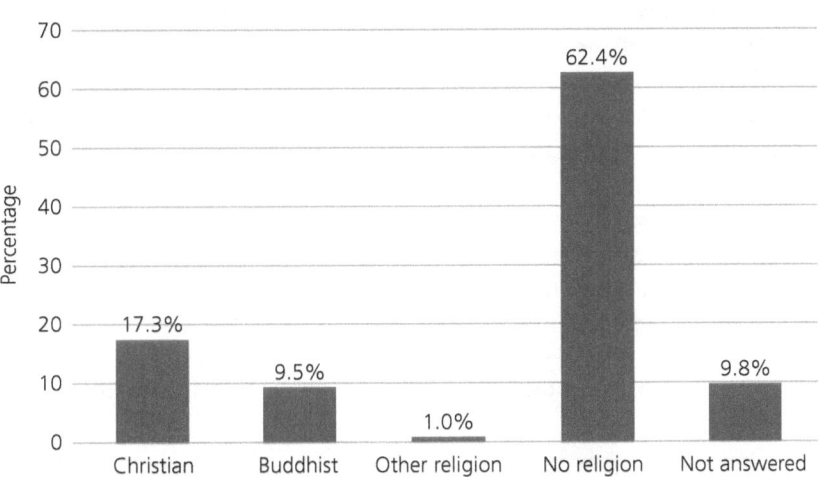

Source: 2021 England and Wales census.

In general, due to its rigour and breadth the census is the most reliable among all demographic data sources. However, it must be noted that the 2021 UK census exhibits two significant flaws in measuring the Chinese Christian community. First, since the BN(O) visa route was only opened by the government at the beginning of 2021, the influx of immigrants from Hong Kong to the UK did not take place until mid to late 2021. The peak of this wave was also not in 2021 but between 2022 and early 2023. Consequently, Census 2021 has largely failed to capture these newly arrived Hong Kongers.

Second, the ethnic category appears to inadequately capture the full diversity of the Chinese population. Among individuals born in China, 97% identify with 'Chinese' ethnicity, whereas this figure stands at 86% for those born in Hong Kong.[8] The percentage significantly decreases to only 55% among individuals born in Taiwan, with 40% opting for 'Other Asian'.[9] The gaps probably stem from contestation over Chinese identities, especially as the term 'Chinese' in English does not distinguish between Chinese nationality and Chinese ethnicity. Despite clarifications in the original questionnaire, this evidently did not fully resolve the linguistic ambiguity. Elsewhere, research on Hong Kong and Taiwan indicates that local people, especially the younger generation, are increasingly distancing themselves in their identity from aspects associated with 'Chinese' or 'Mainland China' (Stockton, 2002; Corichi and Huang, 2023).

A series of measures were implemented to address these two issues. First, an optimized projection of the Chinese Christian population in Britain required making use of statistics from the Home Office on BN(O) Hong Kongers entering the UK during the same period, to better delineate the contours of this newly arriving group in the statistics. Second, the numbers for ethnic Chinese in the census were recalibrated. This new approach went beyond considering just the 'ethnicity' question; it also incorporated 'place of birth', 'first language' and 'national identity' as three additional criteria to redefine the scope of Chinese and Chinese Christian populations.[10] Combined, these measures considerably enhanced the reliability of the data.

Table 1: Rates of change in the Chinese Christian community in Britain, 2011–2023

	Chinese congregations and Christian organizations[11]	Chinese Christians
2011 total number	138	83,072
2021 total number	174	89,475
Total change (N)	+36	+6,403
Mean annual change (%)	2.6%	0.7%
2021 total number	174	89,475
2023 total number	201	115,290*
Total change (N)	+27	25,815
Annual change (%)	7.8%	14.4%

* Projected number based on 2011 Scotland census, 2011 and 2021 England and Wales census 2021–22 Annual Population Survey, Home Office Border Control data, and BCCB.

When past and present are compared, what is the evolving landscape of Chinese Christianity in Britain over the last decade, particularly in the most recent two years? This story is summarized in Table 1, which presents a comparison of the number of Chinese congregations and Christian organizations and the population of Chinese Christians in 2011, 2021 and 2023. What stands out in Table 1 is the rapid expansion of the Chinese Christian community across both these categories, especially from 2021 to 2023. At the church level, there was an increase of 36 churches and organizations from 2011 to 2021, averaging an annual growth rate of 2.6%. However, the last year, 2023, has witnessed the establishment of an additional 27 churches and organizations, marking an average annual growth rate of 7.8%. On the individual level, the increase was 6,403 Chinese Christians from 2011 to 2021, equating to an average annual growth rate of 0.7%. The data for 2023 is from the revised dataset discussed in the previous paragraph. Compared to 2021, the figures jump to 25,815 and 14.4% in 2023. This rate of increase has reached 20 times the average of the previous decade.

There is an important caveat to note here. As previously mentioned, Chinese Christians are not a monolithic group, a fact that is especially evident in the post-BN(O) era. The growth rate of Hong Kong-background Christians, at 36.3%, is significantly higher than the average rate of 14.4%.[12] It is no exaggeration to state that the growth of Chinese churches between 2021 and 2023 is primarily a result of the immigration phenomenon brought about by the BN(O) visa scheme. In this context, the main driving force behind growth has perhaps been the social function of churches rather than evangelical ministries or any form of spiritual awakening. According to estimates from the Home Office, nearly 300,000 BN(O) immigrants are expected to arrive in the UK. However, while such growth may continue in the short term, its pace will eventually slow down over time.

Christian affiliation and identity

The previous section used macro-level data, including the census, to outline the position of Chinese churches within the broader religious society of the UK and their longitudinal changes. We now return to 'street level' to examine the characteristics and differences in denominations and traditions within the Chinese Christian community.

Figure 2 illustrates the denominational distribution of Chinese churches and organizations in the UK as of March 2023.[13] The crucial aspect to understand is that the structure of Chinese churches in the UK is highly decentralized. The majority of Chinese church organizations, including many of the early-established Chinese Christian Churches (CCCs), are non-denominational. Of the 181 items listed, 109 are non-denominational, accounting for exactly three-fifths of the total. Among all denominations, the Methodist Church is the most numerous, with 15 congregations. The Elim Pentecostal Church, founded in the early twentieth century, has 12 Chinese branches. Notably, the Elim Chinese Church is one of the fastest-growing Chinese denominations in the UK in recent years. It is worth noting that, even within the same denomination, congregations often operate independently in terms of finances and ministries.

The arrival of Hong Kong immigrants has also invigorated the Christian landscape. In 2021 and 2022 at least nine Hong Kong churches were established in the UK. A common characteristic of these churches is that they are predominantly composed of BN(O) immigrants and often these congregations or groups were already formed, established or operating in Hong Kong. Prominent examples include the Good Neighbour Church and the Christian Zheng Sheng Association. Another increasingly popular model could be termed 'nested congregations'. These are 11 Chinese sub-congregations within English-speaking churches, most of which are from Anglican or community church backgrounds. The vast majority of the nested congregations were formed after 2021.[14] A key characteristic of the nested congregations is that, unlike many other Chinese churches that merely rent space from local churches for gatherings, nested congregations are organically integrated into their parent churches. As such, they are part of the parent church, yet also hold regular gatherings or small group meetings conducted in Mandarin or Cantonese.

Among all individuals who have participated in any form of communal church activities in the past four weeks, 26.1% reported attending activities at English-speaking churches. Additionally, 15.0% indicated involvement in both Chinese and English-speaking church activities. Of these, British Born Chinese had the highest participation rate in English-speaking church activities (52.3%). Those born in Hong Kong were more actively involved in English-speaking church activities compared to those born in Mainland China (36.1% vs 12.3%).

Figure 2: Chinese congregations and groups in Britain

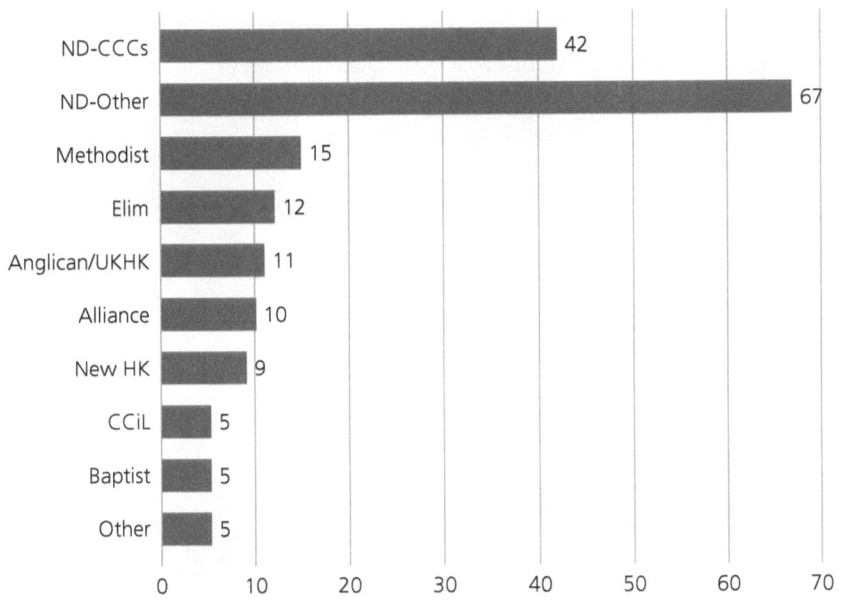

Source: BCCB.
Note: ND = non-denominational; CCC = 'Chinese Christian Church'; New HK = new Hong Kong churches established in 2021 and 2022; CCiL = Chinese Church in London.

Another issue of interest to the BCCB is discerning what Chinese people mean when they identify as Christians. A direct indicator is understanding the Christian tradition that they follow. Figure 3 reveals that exactly half of the Chinese Christians identify as evangelical, a proportion significantly higher than for other groups of evangelical Christians in the UK.[15] However, this is not unexpected, because overseas Chinese churches in Western countries have historically shown a marked preference for evangelical and independent congregational structures (Yang, 1999; Li et al., 2020). Notably, among all Chinese congregations only nine are members of prominent UK evangelical church networks, including the Evangelical Alliance and the Fellowship of Independent Evangelical Churches, indicating again the decentralized and independent nature of Chinese churches in terms of structure. Furthermore, 15.9% of Christians stated that they do not follow any specific tradition of Christianity. Besides these groups, nearly one-tenth of the total identified as Charismatic/Pentecostal. Reformed and liberal Christians each account for approximately 7.5%. Overall, Chinese Christians tend to lean towards conservative traditions. This tendency will be further exemplified in our subsequent discussion on the social attitudes of Christians.

Figure 3: Christian traditions followed by Chinese Christians

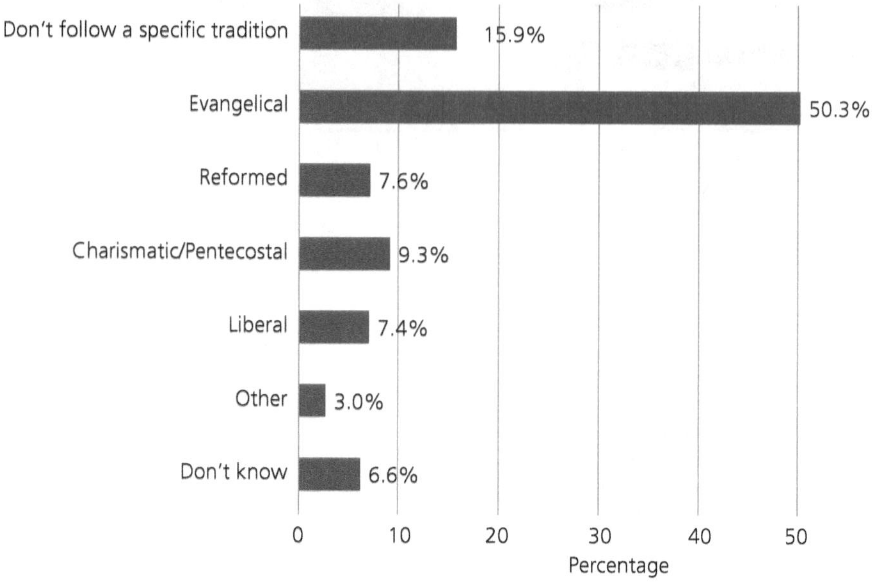

- Don't follow a specific tradition: 15.9%
- Evangelical: 50.3%
- Reformed: 7.6%
- Charismatic/Pentecostal: 9.3%
- Liberal: 7.4%
- Other: 3.0%
- Don't know: 6.6%

Source: BCCB.

Personal religiosity

The above-mentioned description of Chinese churches primarily focuses on religious affiliation, which is largely a nominal measure used to differentiate individuals from members of other Christian categories. In contrast, religiosity, another indicator often employed by sociologists of religion, concentrates on the extent of an individual's subjective commitment to their faith. While quantifying religiosity is feasible, as shown by extensive scholarly literature, there are no standardized criteria for measuring its specific aspects. This is due to the inherent diversity of religious life, with religiosity made up of multiple facets. A practical approach is to divide personal religiosity into two fundamental categories: *private* and *communal* (McAndrew and Voas, 2014). The former focuses on measuring individual practices, while the latter concerns participation in group religious activities.

This approach is also adopted by the BCCB. Questions related to private and communal practices included: 'How frequently have you prayed privately in the past 12 months?' and 'How often have you attended church gatherings (such as Sunday worship, Bible study or prayer meetings) in the past 12 months?' Additionally, a question about Bible interaction was specifically included: 'How frequently have you read or listened to the Bible in the past 12 months?' This inclusion was inspired by the emphasis on the importance of Bible engagement in church culture and the personal faith journey, as highlighted by many church leaders and lay Christians in follow-up interviews after the survey. Most interviewees agreed that active Bible engagement is one of the key indicators in discerning a Christian's level of commitment.

Descriptive statistics are summarized in Table 2.[16] Approximately one-third of Chinese Christians report praying 'daily/almost daily', while 30% indicate that they pray 'weekly/almost weekly'. In terms of communal practice, over half (50.7%) of respondents state that they participate in various church gatherings almost every week. Lastly, the proportions of Chinese Christians who read the Bible 'daily/almost daily' and 'weekly/almost weekly' are 21.1% and 31.6%, respectively. Using weekly participation as a threshold, Chinese Christians show active involvement across all three dimensions of religiosity.

Table 2: Personal religiosity among Chinese Christians

	Daily/ almost daily	Weekly/ almost weekly	Monthly/ almost monthly	Less often/ never
Private prayer	33.2%	30.1%	18.8%	17.9%
Communal gathering	2.2%	48.5%	27.8%	26.5%
Bible engagement	21.1%	31.6%	22.1%	25.2%

Source: BCCB.

Indeed, from an empirical standpoint Chinese Christians in the BCCB survey exhibit higher levels of religiosity compared to the general Christian population recorded in other prominent social surveys. Within the national representative sample of the Isaiah 2018 survey conducted by the British and Foreign Bible Society and YouGov, only 17.0% of Christians reported church attendance more frequent than once every two weeks. The disparity in Bible reading frequency is even more pronounced; in the Isaiah 2018 survey, just 14.8% of Christians read the Bible more frequently than once every two weeks. This survey did not include a question about the frequency of personal prayer; it only asked whether respondents prayed individually, with 26% responding 'yes'.

In every measure, the difference between Chinese Christians and their wider British counterparts is stark.

In descriptions of Christianity's transformation over recent decades, we often encounter terms like 'cultural Christian' and 'nominal Christian' used to describe non-practising Christians who identify with Christianity on certain personal and cultural levels (Davie, 2015). In quantitative research, these Christians are most notably characterized by lower levels of religiosity, a phenomenon some scholars have termed 'fuzzy fidelity' (Voas, 2009). However, Table 2 suggests that such 'fuzzy Christians' are rare in Chinese churches. Across the dimensions of private practice, communal practice and Bible engagement, those choosing 'less often/never' comprise a relatively small percentage. This higher level of devoutness is evident not only in absolute percentages but also in the noticeably higher relative level of devotion when Chinese Christians are placed in the broader context of the British landscape.

The social domain

It was noted a few times at the beginning of this chapter that religious participation for Chinese immigrants not only involves the construction of faith but also invariably entails the reconstruction of identity, value orientation and behaviour. Hence this section will focus on exploring the social implications within the Chinese church – examining the similarities and differences between Chinese Christians and other non-Christian Chinese individuals.

To make an accurate assessment it is imperative to re-emphasize the transnational characteristics of Chinese churches, which are embedded in the sociocultural contexts of both the host country (in this case, Britain) and the countries of origin. Within this framework, the measurement tool for assessing the social implications of being a Chinese Christian in Britain should consider two aspects: first, their social attitudes towards key issues in today's British society; and second, their ties to their country of origin. The first aspect will be measured by the BCCB respondents' attitudes towards same-sex marriage. The second aspect will be measured by individuals' perceptions of China.

A key aim of these analyses is to highlight the intra-group differences among Chinese populations based on faith, immigration experiences and birth backgrounds. Therefore we initially categorized all Chinese respondents in the BCCB (N=1,179) into five groups: Mainland Chinese, Hong Kong Chinese who moved to Britain before 2021, Hong Kong

Chinese who moved to Britain from 2021, British Born Chinese and all other Chinese. Each group was further divided into two subcategories: Christian and non-Christian. To achieve a more accurate estimation, a series of logistic regression models were constructed to incorporate additional control variables including age, gender, marriage and educational occupation.[17] The multivariate analyses will thus enable us to interpret how the interplay of Christian and transnational identities manifests in social effects when other prominent sociodemographic factors are held constant.

We first turn our attention to attitudes towards same-sex marriage, which can be regarded as a barometer used in British social surveys over the past two decades to measure the public's value orientation. In 2013 and 2014 the law was changed in England, Wales and Scotland to allow same-sex couples to get married. But a notable increase in the acceptance of same-sex marriage among both churches and the general public in the UK had started in the 1990s. Data from the British Social Attitudes survey, which has been tracking this trend over an extended period, shows that by 2021 two in three British Christians viewed sexual relations between two adults of the same sex as either 'rarely wrong' or 'not wrong at all'. This is a significant increase from approximately 30% in the early 2000s. A recent national public opinion poll suggests that 77% Britons say same-sex relationships are just as valid as heterosexual relationships.[18] In November 2023 the Church of England also experienced a watershed moment when the General Synod endorsed a proposal to conduct stand-alone blessing services for same-sex couples on an experimental basis. This arrangement enables gay Christians to organize a distinct ceremony, potentially on Saturdays, where they can invite family and friends to bless and celebrate their union.

All participants in the BCCB were asked whether they believe 'same-sex marriage can be justified'. Response options used a 5-point Likert scale ('strongly disagree', 'disagree', 'neutral', 'agree', 'strongly agree'). The results displayed in Figure 4 distinctly show that all five Chinese Christian groups tend to be more conservative in their attitudes towards same-sex marriage than their non-Christian counterparts. Furthermore, the gaps here are much wider than the difference between an average British Christian and the national average of Britain shown in the last paragraph.

It is also worth elaborating on the response of British Born Chinese Christians. Among all five Chinese Christian categories, they are the most positive towards same-sex marriage, indicating their closer alignment with broader British societal views. However, when comparing their predicted probability (25.1%) with other British Christians, it becomes apparent that British Born Chinese Christians are, on the whole, leaning much more towards the conservative end of value orientation.[19] In terms of social attitudes, it is clear that British Born Chinese Christians are influenced by the positions of their families and churches despite their stronger overall social connections and cultural identification with British society compared to their parents' generation. Figure 4 reveals that British Born Chinese may find themselves 'sandwiched' between the values of the Chinese church and mainstream British values.

Figure 4: Attitudes towards same-sex marriage (predicted probabilities)

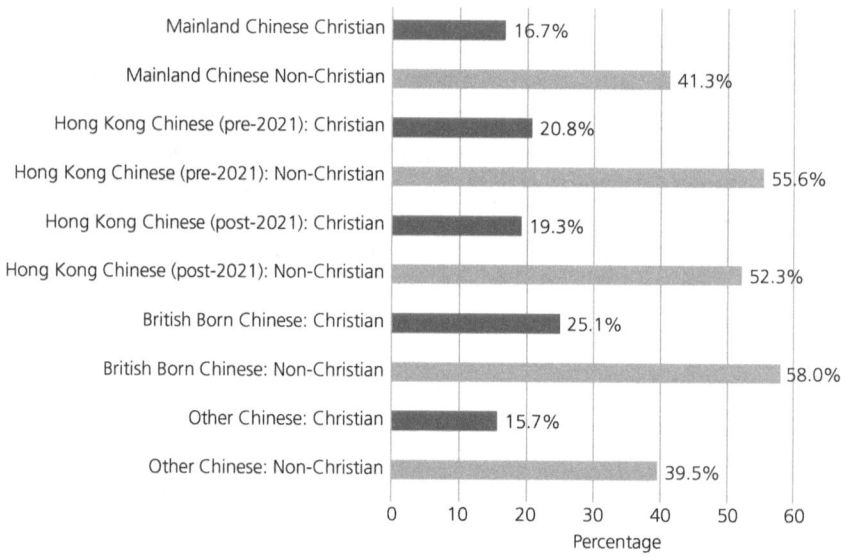

Data: BCCB.
Note: Results are derived from a series of logistic regression models. Control variables include age, gender, marriage and educational occupation.

The second area of interest has to do with the perception of China. While not all Chinese individuals come from a Mainland Chinese background, China and its geopolitical dynamics present a profound impact on the identity construction of British Chinese people, especially first-generation immigrants. While the BN(O) immigration per se is a direct consequence of larger sociopolitical changes centred around China, a recent study also found an association between the strong pro-democracy values among younger-generation Cantonese-speaking

Christians and the legacy of the 2019–20 Hong Kong protests against plans to allow extradition to Mainland China (To and Chan, 2023). As previously observed in the interpretation of the 2021 census, the identification with 'Chinese' varies significantly across different Chinese groups, particularly in the case of individuals born in Taiwan. Moreover, the addition of a Christian identity may further complicate these differences. Therefore there is ample reason to hypothesize that views on China can both unite and divide British Chinese, including Christians with varying opinions. This reshapes the 'Chineseness' of an ostensibly unified yet inherently and increasingly fragile 'Chinese' category.

As mentioned earlier, the term 'Chinese' in English can be ambiguous, referring both to Chinese nationality and Chinese ethnicity. To avoid such ambiguity, the BCCB purposefully focuses on respondents' feelings about the rise of China. The response options adhere to the same 5-point Likert scale employed in the preceding analysis. Figure 5 shows that the majority of Chinese individuals, whether Christian or non-Christian, exhibit predominantly negative views on China. Across the board, Christians display an even more negative perception. The only exception are Mainland Chinese respondents, who exhibit a much more positive reaction to the rise of China. The gap between them and others has reached an astonishing level of over 50% in most cases. As such, the perception of China has become a clear boundary dividing Mainland Chinese from other Chinese groups, and this is also evident within the church.[20] For Mainland Chinese Christians, the development of China and their Christian identity largely do not conflict. Conversely, within other Chinese communities, particularly among their Christian populations, a negative perception of China appears to have emerged as a prominent element shaping their collective identity.

Another interesting phenomenon is the subtle gap in the perceptions of China's rise among post-2021 Hong Kong immigrants, predominantly comprising new BN(O) arrivals. Within this category, 26.1% of non-Christians expressed a positive view, while only 14.1% of their Christian counterparts did the same. The reasons behind the 12.0% difference may be multifaceted, yet some newly established Hong Kong churches in the UK do present clear pro-democracy political stances, which is indicative of the impact of Hong Kong's sociopolitical changes on the identity of these new churches. For example, the Hong Kong Christian Church in the United Kingdom, which established four branches after its inception in May 2021, declares on its website:

After the year of 2019 in Hong Kong, we decided to dedicate ourselves to show our faith through our daily life: to do justly and to love mercy, to speak the truth and to reject every lie.

While the BN(O) immigration has significantly increased the numbers in Chinese churches, it is essential to recognize that this numerical growth conceals a diverse community – one marked by divisions over conflicting political views and collective memories regarding China's role in their identity. Often this diversity leads to fragmentation and conflict, and these conflicts are likely to persist within the British Chinese church community for an extended period.

Figure 5: Perception of China's influence (predicted probabilities)

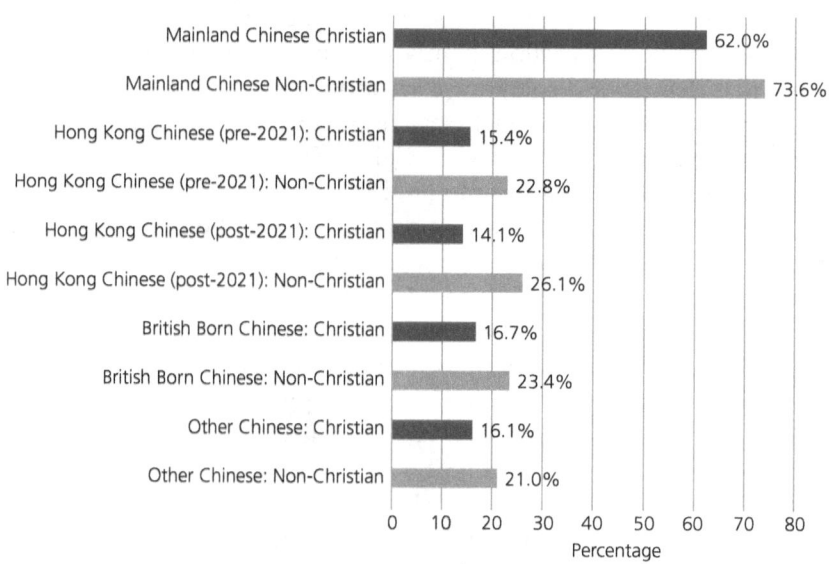

Data: BCCB.
Note: Results are derived from a series of logistic regression models. Control variables include age, gender, marriage and educational occupation.

Conclusion: the 4-D shape of the Chinese Christian community

In this chapter, I present various sacred and social aspects of the Chinese Christian community in Britain from a data-driven perspective. Statistics on both individual and church levels suggest that 'the Chinese church' is not a singular, static concept. It is filled with diversity, change and even conflict, although it also possesses unique aspects compared to other British churches. Taken together, we can broadly summarize the shape of today's British Chinese Christian community with a 4-D concept.

Due to the influx of Hong Kong BN(O) after 2021, the Chinese church has become one of the most *dynamic* Christian groups in Britain. However, two caveats need to be addressed before any attempt to give moral superiority to the growth rate of the Chinese Christian group. First, this growth is primarily a short-term social phenomenon resulting from the BN(O) policy and significant sociopolitical changes in Hong Kong. Second, it is by no means a type of spiritual revival and will cool down as the immigration wave slows.

The structure of the entire Chinese church is highly *decentralized*. Historically, the most popular form of institution within the Chinese Christian community has been independent churches. Yet to date, neither these independent congregations nor the denominational churches can claim to represent the voices and theological viewpoints of the Chinese church or Chinese Christians more than any other. Moreover, two products of the BN(O) immigration wave – new Hong Kong churches and nested churches – have increased the Christian options in the Christian market for Chinese people more than ever before. Previously dominant players, such as evangelical churches and Mandarin congregations, are facing new 'competitors' (e.g. Pentecostal churches and local English-speaking churches).

From the perspective of personal religiosity, the descriptive analysis shows Chinese Christians to be a *devoted* group of Christians. It is important to note that this conclusion is based on a relative rather than an absolute standard. Compared to Britain's general Christian population, Christian respondents in the BCCB display a discernibly higher level of religiosity in terms of private practice, communal practice and Bible engagement.

Lastly, Chinese Christians' beliefs tend toward conservatism, which is the most cohesive aspect of the entire study. However, in many respects, especially on the social level, it should not be neglected that the so-called 'Chinese church' is highly *diverse* as an entity. This is not only reflected in the division of Mandarin, Cantonese and English congregations under the Chinese church umbrella, based on language differences. The final analysis of this chapter shows the subtle boundaries within the church, which are especially apparent in the perception of China. Such socially and culturally defined boundaries will have long-term impacts on the future shape of the Chinese Christian population in Britain.

Notes

1 The term 'Chinese' needs further exploration. The English word 'Chinese' is often ambiguous and falls short of capturing the nuanced distinctions among the different identities of (diasporic) Chinese people. Within the Chinese diaspora, subtle distinctions are made between notions such as *huaqiao* (華僑, overseas Chinese sojourners), *huaren* (華人, people of Chinese ethnicity), *huayi* (華裔, people with Chinese heritage), and *zhongguo ren* (中國人, Chinese nationals of the People's Republic of China). In this chapter, unless otherwise specified, 'Chinese' is used as an ethnic concept and refers to *huaren*; that is, ethnic Chinese people, who were born in the UK or migrated from other parts of the world.

2 See Chapter 1 of this volume by Alexander Chow.

3 Some prominent examples include the British and Foreign Bible Society, the Data Services Unit of the Church of England, Brierley Consultancy, British Religion in Numbers and the Faith Survey. Since the late 2010s, the continuous decrease in the Christian population in the country seems to have somewhat dampened the enthusiasm for this statistical work, leading to a plateau in the pool of sources for Christian church statistical data.

4 The centres were selected from major British cities in terms of Chinese population and number of Chinese churches. Ten of these cities were assigned with more than two centres: London, Manchester, Birmingham, Leeds, Milton Keynes, Oxford, Bristol, Cardiff, Glasgow and Edinburgh.

5 These include the Chinese Overseas Christian Mission (COCM, the oldest and largest mission organization in the UK and Europe), The Teahouse (a Church of England group supporting clergy with Chinese heritage), the Anglican Minority Ethnic Network, OMF (UK) and the Christian Centre for Gambling Rehabilitation (London).

6 To validate the sample, it was compared with the Chinese demographic data (N=3,130) from the 2021-22 Annual Population Survey (APS), one of the UK's most extensive national representative surveys. This comparison revealed that the general sample from the BCCB survey mirrored the characteristics observed in the APS's Chinese sample. The four key demographic indicators include mean age (37.2 in BCCB vs 37.7 in APS), proportion of female (55% in BCCB vs 53% in APS), married (49% in BCCB vs 49% in APS) and self-reported Christian respondents (19% in BCCB vs 21% in APS).

7 The proportion of Chinese Christians decreased by 2.3% in the 2021 census relative to the 2011 census.

8 The 2021 Hong Kong census shows that 8.4% of Hong Kong residents were not of Chinese ethnicity. In recent years, the proportion of non-Chinese individuals born in Hong Kong has been steadily increasing – 75.3% and 52.5% of ethnic

minorities (excluding foreign domestic helpers) aged 0–14 and 15–24 respectively were born in Hong Kong. Nonetheless, if individuals not born in Hong Kong are excluded, the proportion of non-Chinese born in Hong Kong is notably less than 8.6%. Data in Taiwan regarding this aspect is not available.

9 The census data does not further differentiate 'Chinese ethnicity', such as distinguishing between Han Chinese and non-Han Chinese (e.g. Taiwanese indigenous peoples). However, this lack of classification is unlikely to significantly impact the comparisons made here. In mainland China, Hong Kong and Taiwan the Han ethnic group all constitute the absolute majority of the population, accounting for at least 90%.

10 Because the 2021 Scottish census data has not yet been released, the projection for Scotland was calculated based on the 2011 Scottish census and the Scottish sample in the 2021–22 Annual Population Survey.

11 Data is collected from three main sources in addition to author's own records. These include Christian Herald (UK), COCM and the Welcome Churches.

12 Cantonese-speaking Christians are statistically shown to be the only main contributor to the growth. Mandarin-speaking churches experienced a negative growth of 0.4% between 2021 and 2023, while English-speaking Chinese churches saw only a 1.1% increase. Meanwhile, using these statistics, it is estimated that just over one in five (21.6%) new Hong Kong arrivals are Christians.

13 In addition to Chinese churches, the 'congregations' here also include two other types of groups. In the UK, there are various Chinese 'fellowships'. These often lack full-time pastors or leaders but they may be guided by preachers or 'elders' and have regular meetings. The second type includes Chinese sub-congregations within non-Chinese English churches. This will be explained later when we discuss 'nested congregations'. Additionally, this list encompasses various 'groups', primarily missionary organizations and regional Christian associations. However, service-orientated or online institutions, such as Christian bookstores, are not included in this categorization.

14 A significant driver of this trend is the UKHK network established by the Welcome Churches organization, which encourages local English-speaking churches to collaborate in welcoming new arrivals from Hong Kong.

15 According to a national representative survey (Project Isaiah) conducted by the British and Foreign Bible Society and YouGov in 2018, involving nearly 20,000 participants, self-identified evangelical Christians represent 6.7% of all Christians in England and Wales. Additionally, independent evangelical congregations, which currently represent the most common form of church among the Chinese, account for just under 3% of all Protestant churches in the UK. Please contact the author of this chapter for detailed information about this survey.

16 All analyses that follow from this point will use the BCCB's full sample (N=504). Employing the full sample entails an evident bias: the booster sample's size exceeds that of the general sample, and the booster sample contains a higher proportion of practising Christians. To address this issue of inflation, a weight variable was computed to enhance the representativeness of the analyses by giving greater robustness to the impact of the general sample.

17 In each model, predicted probabilities will be calculated for each of the 10 Chinese groups based on the results of the full model. A predicted probability indicates the likelihood of respondents in the group selecting 'agree'/'strongly agree' in

response to the question of the dependent variable, after taking into account the effects of age, gender, marriage, educational attainment and occupation.

18 The poll was carried out by YouGov and can be accessed here: https://yougov.co.uk/topics/politics/trackers/support-for-marriage-of-same-sex-couple.

19 In the BCCB, 52.2% of British Born Chinese Christians attend Chinese churches, while 47.7% are members of non-Chinese churches. Interestingly, the responses between these two groups do not show a significant difference. Among the former, 22.3% 'agree' or 'strongly agree' that same-sex marriage can be justified, compared to 28.4% among the latter. On the other hand, the BCCB found that a majority of British Born Chinese were brought up in Chinese churches (69.3%). Those who were raised in Chinese churches exhibit observably more conservative views on same-sex marriage compared to others (18.9% vs 45.2%). Therefore it is plausible to hypothesize that, compared to current affiliation, church upbringing is a more powerful determinant in shaping the value orientation of Chinese Christians. This assertion requires further research for validation, as the BCCB has a relatively limited sample size for this particular population.

20 During the pilot interview phase of the BCCB, I heard more than once from church leaders about instances of conflict between Mandarin-speaking and Cantonese-speaking congregants within the church due to differing political views. Despite the prevalence of knowledge and news regarding China's religious policies and the persecution of Christians, the majority of Mandarin-speaking congregations mentioned that they would deliberately avoid such politically sensitive topics in sermons and other gatherings.

References

Baio, Gianluca, Gian Carlo Blangiardo and Marta Blangiardo (2011), 'Centre Sampling Technique in Foreign Migration Surveys: A Methodological Note', *Journal of Official Statistics* 27, no. 3, pp. 451–65.

Basch, Linda, Nina Glick Schiller and Christina Szanton Blanc (1994), *Nations Unbound: Transnational Projects, Postcolonial Predicaments and Deterritorialized Nation-States* (London: Gordon & Breach).

Brierley, Peter (2021), 'Where is the Church Going?', *Brierley Consultancy*, https://www.brierleyconsultancy.co.uk/where-is-the-church-going, accessed 21.01.2024.

Chow, Alexander (2021), 'From Takeaway to British Chinese: Christianity among Overseas Chinese in the United Kingdom', in Sam George (ed.), *Journeys of Asian Diaspora: Mapping Originations and Destinations, Volume 1* (Minneapolis, MN: Fortress Press), pp. 9–24.

Corichi, Manolo and Christine Huang (2023), 'How People in Hong Kong view Mainland China and their own Identity', *Pew Research Center*, https://www.pewresearch.org/short-reads/2023/12/05/how-people-in-hong-kong-view-mainland-china-and-their-own-identity/, accessed 10.01.2024.

Davie, Grace (2015), *Religion in Britain: A Persistent Paradox* (Oxford: Blackwell).

Goodhew, David (2012), *Church Growth in Britain: 1980 to the Present* (Farnham: Ashgate).

Guest, Kenneth J. (2003), *God in Chinatown: Religion and Survival in New York's Evolving Immigrant Community* (New York: New York University Press).

Guest, M. (2022), *Neoliberal Religion: Faith and Power in the Twenty-First Century* (London: Bloomsbury).

Huang, Yinxuan, Kristin Aune and Matthew Guest (2021), 'COVID-19 and the Chinese Christian Community in Britain: Changing Patterns of Belonging and Division', *Studies in World Christianity* 27, no. 1, pp. 7–25, https://doi.org/10.3366/swc.2021.0323.

Kalir, Barak (2009), 'Finding Jesus in the Holy Land and Taking him to China: Chinese Temporary Migrant Workers in Israel Converting to Evangelical Christianity', *Sociology of Religion* 70, no. 2, pp. 130–56, https://doi.org/10.1093/socrel/srp027.

Kim, Kwang Chung and Won Moo Hurh (1993), 'Beyond Assimilation and Pluralism: Syncretic Sociocultural Adaptation of Korean Immigrants in the US', *Ethnic and Racial Studies* 16, no. 4, pp. 696-713, https://doi.org/10.1080/01419870.1993.9993804.

Li, Xinan, Line Nyhagen and Thoralf Klein (2020), 'Encounter, Initiation, and Commitment: Christian Conversion Among New Chinese Migrants in Britain', in Nanlai Cao, Giuseppe Giordan and Fenggang Yang (eds), *Annual Review of the Sociology of Religion, Volume 11: Chinese Religions Going Global*, pp. 77–96 (Leiden: Brill).

McAndrew, Siobhan (2020), 'Belonging, Believing, Behaving, and Brexit: Channels of Religiosity and Religious Identity in Support for Leaving the European Union', *British Journal of Sociology* 71, no. 5, pp. 867–97.

McAndrew, Siobhan and David Voas (2014), 'Immigrant Generation, Religiosity and Civic Engagement in Britain', *Ethnic and Racial Studies* 37, no. 1, pp. 99–119.

Stockton, Hans (2002), 'National Identity on Taiwan: Causes and Consequences for Political Reunification', *American Journal of Chinese Studies* 9, no. 2, pp. 155–78.

Putnam, Robert D. (2000), *Bowling Alone: The Collapse and Revival of American Community* (New York: Simon & Schuster).

Rao, Xinzi (2017), 'Revisiting Chinese-ness: A transcultural Exploration of Chinese Christians in Germany', *Studies in World Christianity* 23, no. 2, pp. 122–40, https://doi.org/10.3366/swc.2017.0180.

To, Yvette and Yuk Wah Chan (2023), 'Same God but Different? Politico-Religious Dynamics and the New Hong Kong Christian Diaspora in the United Kingdom', *American Behavioral Scientist*, https://doi.org/10.1177/00027642231194189.

Voas, David (2009), 'The Rise and Fall of Fuzzy Fidelity in Europe', *European Sociological Review* 25, no. 2, pp. 155–68, https://doi.org/10.1093/esr/jcn044.

Yang, Fenggang (1999), *Chinese Christians in America: Conversion, Assimilation, and Adhesive Identities* (University Park, PA: Penn State University Press).

Yu, Yun (2020), 'From Universities to Christian Churches: Agency in the Intercultural Engagement of Non-Christian Chinese Students in the UK', *Higher Education* 80, pp. 197–213, https://doi.org/10.1007/s10734-019-00474-5.

PART II

Re-forming Identity and Spirituality

4

Forever Foreigners: *Missio Dei* for the British Born Chinese

JAMES SO

Introduction – 'Where are you from?'

'Where do you come from?' is perhaps a common question that most of us will have been asked at some point when meeting someone new. To many people, it is a simple question with a straightforward answer. 'I come from ... , I was born in ..., I grew up in ..., but now work in ....' However, ask this question of a British Born Chinese (BBC), or most British-born minority ethnic people for that matter, and the responses can be more varied and complex. For many BBCs the question of their identity can be a confusing one. Do they consider themselves Chinese, given their biological ethnicity and that their parents may originally hail from a Chinese-speaking country? Or are they to consider themselves British, given that the UK was their place of birth and upbringing and that English is likely to be their first language? Or do they consider themselves to be a mixture of the two? And if so, how do these two cultural heritages interact? Does one particular culture take priority over the other?

The complexity of these questions is also reflected in how many BBCs often find themselves giving different descriptions of their cultural identity depending on the person asking them. If a BBC was asked by a White Briton where they came from, they might feel inclined to emphasize their Chinese ethnic identity, sensing that, to a Caucasian, their Chinese appearance might not be typically associated with a British identity. Similarly, if a BBC found themselves in a Chinese speaking context like Mainland China or Hong Kong, and was asked the same question by a local, they might feel more inclined to stress their British identity, sensing that their limited skills in Chinese, dress sense or other cultural expressions might be perceived as more Western.

This simple illustration shows how the issue of cultural identity is a highly complex one for BBCs. Understanding one's cultural identity goes beyond simply describing one's race or the country one was raised in. Rather, it requires an assessment of a whole host of factors that they embody, including race, place of birth and education, family migration history, language and many others. Furthermore, this identity seems to be in a continual state of flux and changes and adapts according to the particular social setting and people that BBCs encounter. Though they may share some cultural affinity with certain groups, they never feel as if they completely belong to any of those groups because of other aspects of their cultural being that set them apart. Consequently, many BBCs can journey through life with a lost sense of identity, not knowing where they belong and who their 'people' are, and they can develop a sense being a perpetual foreigner, as this chapter title suggests.

Of course, British society has all too often contributed to these feelings of 'not belonging' among BBCs. Many BBCs have experienced some form of racial rejection in their lives, whether explicit and/or implicit, and the rise of Sinophobia in the West following the Covid-19 pandemic has only made matters worse. The re-emergence of far right-wing British Nationalism in some pockets of society has only reinforced the narrative that the true British people are Caucasian and that minority ethnic groups or those with a Global Majority Heritage (GMH), regardless of whether they were British-born or not, are better off returning to 'their countries' or taking their place as second-class citizens to Whites, should they remain in Britain. Thus, in a current sociopolitical climate that can place so much value on cultural and national belonging and which also states which races should make up those national groups, it is unsurprising that many BBCs can see their mixed cultural heritage as more of a curse than a blessing when they do not fit into the 'traditional' cultural and national categories that are set before them.

The purpose of this chapter is not simply to lament over the marginalization that many BBCs have experienced. Though we will further explore these experiences, this chapter is primarily a theological reflection on the purpose of the BBC's mixed cultural heritage, especially in relation to the issue of increasingly culturally segregated churches in the UK. Could BBCs, through their unique cultural experiences, play an important role in restoring God's purposes in British churches and society and in understanding national identity more broadly?

Cultural segregation in British churches and Chinese churches through the eyes of a BBC

Our main question is part of a wider discussion regarding cultural segregation between churches in the British context. The general landscape of British churches exhibits a collection of different homogeneous churches which, although existing in close proximity to each other, rarely share any significant interaction. In 2020, following the events of George Floyd's murder in the United States, Britain witnessed an increase in societal pressure challenging various forms of institutional racism. As part of this, British church communities were also challenged. This has gradually led to various British denominations and church groups confessing to the perpetuation of cultural biases and the implicit reinforcement of a monoculture (often a White, British, middle-class one) that marginalized those of different backgrounds and heritages. In response, many denominations, churches and parachurch organizations have pledged to start building more diverse Christian communities via various strategies.[1] Some have gone further and stated the need for multicultural churches to be formed. For example, the missiologist Harvey Kwiyani argues that British churches should be more intentional in becoming multicultural churches that bring together people of different ethnicities and reflect the diversity in wider British society.[2] While we await the progress and fulfilment of these promises, some remain sceptical on the basis that similar initiatives launched in past decades have often failed or been abandoned due to loss of momentum or lack of general concern. While these issues remain on the popular agenda for now, some still question what further action can be taken to help homogeneous churches in Britain towards a more heterogeneous picture that reflects the New Testament, eschatological vision. As part of this issue, British GMH-majority churches are also called into question. There is a growing realization that the task of cultural diversification should not just be reserved for the 'White' churches. Though some might argue that British denominational churches are culpable because they catalysed the formation of homogeneous churches in Britain in the first place through their actions during the Windrush period, there is also increasing concern for minority ethnic churches to rethink their homogeneous nature in the light of the New Testament vision.

Mindful of these challenges, this chapter will assess the experiences of BBCs in the contexts of both the British White-majority church and the Chinese heritage churches. This will help to shed light on the experience of rejection in churches, as well as to unearth its causes.

BBCs in the White-majority church

We begin by discussing the experience of those BBCs who choose to attend White-majority churches, which often include denominational churches such as the Church of England.[3] While there is little literature documenting the experiences of BBCs in White-majority churches specifically, there is literature written from the British GMH experience in White-majority churches, in particular from the Church of England, which resonates with the BBC experience. Like many other GMH individuals, BBCs find that cultural integration into these churches is not seamless. Many BBCs find that their identity is often mistaken on joining British churches. For example, in those churches that have an international student ministry, BBCs often find that they are wrongly assumed to be international students or mistaken for first-generation immigrants from East Asian countries. Most are not assumed to be locally born individuals with a British heritage and upbringing. Perhaps this dynamic is partly due to the fact that the national population of BBCs, and British Chinese generally, is still relatively small.[4] Unlike their British African, British Caribbean or British Indian counterparts, who make up far more substantial numbers and are better represented in the media and public awareness, BBCs find that there is a general lack of awareness that British Born Chinese individuals such as themselves even exist. As a result, BBCs are often misidentified by other church members. Even when BBCs take the opportunity to correct these misconceptions and explain their multicultural identity, they are still left feeling that their explanations only leave people with a conceptual understanding of their cultural identity and not a more experiential understanding that leads to a deeper empathy.

As a result of this, those BBCs who choose to remain in these churches often face a dilemma in their attempts to try and integrate. For some BBCs, the process of 'whitewashing' is the easiest means by which to find cultural acceptance. Having British heritage, BBCs possess the means to accentuate their British cultural expressions, and many BBCs become 'cultural chameleons', morphing themselves to fit the surroundings. However, to do this effectively, BBCs must also silence or mute other parts of their cultural being. Any aspects of their cultural being that are not 'White' or British are likely to be hidden, 'left at the door' so to speak.[5] Nevertheless, those BBCs who can do this effectively present themselves as being no different from the rest of the congregation apart from their physical appearance; thus they make themselves more culturally comprehensible and easily accepted into the White-majority culture. In doing this, however, BBCs need to continually deny parts of themselves or again risk being perceived as foreign.

For other BBCs, integration into the White churches may be achieved not through whitewashing but through 'orientalizing' themselves. Some British churches show some awareness of non-White cultures in their locality or congregations and have intentions to incorporate them. However, they may do this by using outdated 'colonial' and orientalist profiles for different cultural groups.[6] For example, in some churches African individuals may be commonly perceived as culturally 'lively' and 'enthusiastic', and thus well suited to worship-leading ministry and so on. BBCs can often be perceived as 'traditionally Chinese' individuals, who are steeped in Confucian tradition, generally submissive to their superiors and diligent hard workers, and who are unlikely to cause any problems. And so BBCs can be subconsciously ushered into roles that are 'suitable' for them, such as responsibility for more supportive and subservient roles behind the scenes, but overlooked for roles of leadership. As well as this, BBCs can sometimes be expected to serve as repositories of knowledge regarding East Asian affairs, histories and customs that can help inform and diversify the life of the church. The problem is that while BBCs may share some East Asian heritage, they will not embody this to the level expected of a person who is born and raised in the Asia. For example, some BBCs are asked about affairs in China and how the church might pray for China; but to their embarrassment they find themselves unable to offer much in response because they have limited connection or personal insight regarding China. Once again, BBCs are forced to adapt. But here, rather than whitewash themselves, BBCs are required to morph into the role of exoticized foreigners who can serve as cultural representatives of those 'exotic' places that are deemed to add diversity to the church. Once again, BBCs are made to feel foreign because they must play up to a role that does not embody their true selves. In pursuing this route, BBCs once again find that they receive no sympathy from others. Nevertheless, some BBCs feel the need to do this, as some role is better than no role. Better to play up to the role of a 'Chinese native' than attempt to re-educate the whole church on their BBC identity, which is still not comprehensible to many and risks leaving them off the church's 'global map' entirely.

BBCs in the Chinese heritage church

For many BBCs, attending a Chinese heritage church is a common choice. Statistics suggest that the number of Chinese heritage churches and congregations in the UK numbers around 200, with at least one Chinese church present in most of the major UK cities.[7] In more recent years, these numbers have been boosted by the swathes of Hong Kong immigrants entering the UK via the special Hong Kong British National (Overseas) ((BN(O)) visa route. Nevertheless, the presence of most of the Chinese heritage churches in the UK has been substantial for the past half century or more, with many of them sharing similar origin stories. Many other British GMH churches, such as those of African and Caribbean heritage, share a similar origin story of their original members of the Windrush Generation being explicitly rejected by local British denominational churches due to their race and so subsequently forming their own churches.[8] By contrast, many of the British Chinese churches were not necessarily formed as a result of Chinese people experiencing direct rejection at the doors of their local parishes. Rather, the historic lack of willingness by British churches to engage with Chinese-speaking people with limited English meant that Chinese individuals were the main missionaries to other Chinese and were forced to create their own Chinese Christian fellowships that could meet their spiritual, cultural and linguistic needs. Many of the current Chinese churches began life as small fellowship groups, many of which were set up for Chinese restaurant and takeaway workers or international students. Over time, many of these fellowships grew into fully-fledged churches, often under the guidance of White missionaries with experience of East Asian contexts or Chinese missionary organizations, most notably the Chinese Overseas Christian Mission (COCM). The result was the formation of Chinese heritage churches in most of the major cities of the UK, which conducted their ministries in Chinese and Mandarin.[9]

Most BBCs will find that their original attendance at Chinese heritage churches was mainly due to familial ties rather than personal choice. For many of them, their parents or relatives were among the original members that formed the Chinese churches. Interestingly, those BBCs who grew up in these churches, particularly during the 1980s, 1990s and early 2000s, found that while they enjoyed acceptance through familial bonds, they also experienced marginalization. Because many of these churches were primarily set up to accommodate overseas immigrant Chinese who spoke Cantonese or Mandarin, BBCs realized that they were poorly accommodated in them. The lack of English-speaking ministries in these churches during this time meant that for many BBCs, attendance at church required them simply to sit through services in which they understood very little due to their limited Chinese and in which they found very little cultural connection given their distinct British upbringing. Even when English-speaking youth groups were set up to accommodate some of the BBCs in their teenage years, these were primarily run by first-generation Chinese immigrants who could teach Bible studies in English but lacked the cultural experience to contextualize much of it to the specific experiences of BBCs growing up in the UK. And so, ironically, BBCs have also experienced foreignness in Chinese churches. Though they share a common physical appearance with other members of the church, they are still largely surrounded by people who do not completely understand them linguistically and culturally. Consequently, some BBCs have either left the Chinese churches to attend other British churches or have simply stopped attending church altogether. For many of those who remain, they do so largely due to familial and relational ties rather than as a result of successful cultural integration into the rest of the church.

BBCs in the Chinese church English ministries

Nevertheless, in the last decade or so some developments have started to emerge. With time, many of the BBCs who have remained in the Chinese churches have matured into leaders, with a growing number taking up lay leadership positions and a smaller number even going on to become fully trained ministers. The result of this has been the development of English ministries (EMs) in Chinese churches through the establishment of Sunday services, fellowship groups and other ministries in English. While these EMs still remain part of the Chinese church, they offer a sub-cultural worship space that allows some needs of the BBCs to be met. Consequently, in most of the major Chinese churches in the UK we now see more EMs with substantial BBC populations in attendance. To many BBCs, the establishment of these EMs has been welcome. In a societal and church context that has all too often rejected or misunderstood the BBC cultural identity, the EMs provide a worship space in which BBCs can simply 'come as they are' and also be with other BBCs who share and understand their common cultural struggles. Consequently, the EMs have provided a much-sought context in which BBCs can share their cultural challenges with those who truly understand and who can pray with them.

These EMs have also become important platforms for evangelism to non-Christian BBCs. Perhaps lending some truth to Donald McGavran's homogeneous unit principle,[10] EMs have been relatively effective in evangelizing BBCs who have not yet been churched. To non-Christian BBCs, EMs often provide one of the most immediately accessible spaces and communities where they can find cultural acceptance and familiarity. Thus, even though these individuals may initially join EMs primarily seeking community and friendship, as they share in these communities they also encounter the gospel message and are given an opportunity to accept the Christian faith. All things considered, the establishment of EMs has been important. They keep together and nurture a generation of BBC Christians who might otherwise already have left the church; they also serve as important communities to bring other BBCs into the faith; and they create a space in which BBCs do not feel 'foreign' and can discuss and process their specific cultural experiences in the light of God.

Yet while we may appreciate the development of the EMs, we still need to call into question the type of communities they may be creating and the cultural trajectory on which they could be headed. Though Chinese church EMs may be conducive to quickly building up BBC communities, they have the potential to form communities that are insular and closed in on themselves. To their advantage but perhaps also to their detriment, EMs largely serve two functions. On the one hand, as any church would, they form a Christian community that gathers people to worship God; on the other hand, they also serve the additional purpose of providing a safe haven for BBCs. However, problems begin if the latter purpose becomes the primary driver that gathers the EM community. When the decisions and formation of the community become predominantly focused on sustaining its BBC identity and safe space, then it is at risk of being exclusive. In reaction to their experiences of rejection, where they could not fit into the monoculture of other churches and the wider society, BBCs can be susceptible to building their own homogeneous churches through EMs that are just as exclusive as the original monocultures that rejected them in the first place. Certainly, a BBC culture is helpful in collating common experiences and grounding the BBCs in their own life experiences in relation to God. However, while this new identity may remove their sense of foreignness by rallying round other BBCs like themselves, if they accentuate their common identity too strongly they also can make foreigners out of others who are different from themselves. Some may think that because BBC is a heterogeneous culture it is therefore more naturally inclusive compared to more traditional British or Chinese monocultures. Yet although BBC culture may be heterogeneous or multicultural in composition, it can still be harnessed to become a new monoculture that is just as homogeneous and closed as the aforementioned cultures. Perhaps the key issue is that those who experience cultural rejection are not necessarily stirred to behave differently; rather, victims of cultural rejection often perpetuate further cultural rejection by creating their own impermeable culture bubble in self-defence.

Thus, if BBCs are in the process of establishing their identity through EMs, how can they go about it in a way that prevents them from committing the same forms of rejection that hurt them in the first place, and how can they use their particular cultural experiences to become a blessing to all instead?

Orientalism and the construction of culture and national identity

Having illustrated some of the cultural experiences of the BBCs in various church contexts, we need to seek some of the possible underlying factors that could be sustaining this cultural segregation. To this end, we can consider some perspectives offered by postcolonial theory from the last half century. In particular, the writings of Edward Said and Homi K. Bhabha are especially useful for our discussion.

Perhaps one of Said's most crucial contributions was in tracing how modern framings of cultures and nations can be attributed to 'orientalism', which was introduced during the age of Western colonization. As Said described it, during the period of colonization, as the colonizers encountered more and more new territories and their peoples, they started to categorize these people into various essentialistic cultural profiles, with the nineteenth century witnessing a particular distillation of these ideas in literature.[11] A particularly strong example of such profiling was the categorization of people in the Orient by their race. With the prevalence of Darwinism, racial classification of different peoples started to gain popularity. As part of this, biological classifications of different races of the Orient based on physical features were presented and, furthermore, ranked by their varying degrees of degeneracy in comparison to the Westerners.[12] Said highlighted how this cultural profiling was not conducted in a neutral way. Rather, it was done in a way that contrasted and juxtaposed the non-Western cultures of the Orient with that of the Western colonial nations or the Occident. The undertones of these comparisons were to highlight the superiority of the Occident and contrast the primitive and despotic nature of the Orient, which needed westernization and western enlightenment.[13] As Said shows in his work, such ideas were implicitly conveyed through much popular literature during the colonial period, which led to their seeping into public consciousness. Crucially, a major effect of orientalism was its ability to convince people of its ideas and its framing of other cultures in an undisputed and normative way.[14]

As history shows, these colonial and orientalist mindsets also permeated the British churches and were particularly evident during the age of missions in the nineteenth century. As Kwok Pui-lan states:

> Many Anglicans in the eighteenth and nineteenth centuries viewed the expansion of the British Empire in favourable terms because they thought God had chosen their country for a special mission. They believed in God's providential action in the world and that the English people were especially blessed because of their religion and culture.[15]

Such thoughts were held and even promoted by senior Christian leaders in Britain. For example, in 1840 the Bishop of Chichester, Philip Shuttleworth, stated that Britain had been: 'specially selected, and endowed by Providence, as an instrument for suffusing knowledge and civilization and social happiness throughout the world'.[16] What we witness during this period is that much of the Anglican church did not necessarily see the colonial conquest as something negative or anti-Christian. If anything, they saw it as divine providence: the growth of the empire provided opportunity for the spread of Anglicanism, and equally, Anglicanism could elevate the empire with a higher mission.[17] Thus, rather than challenge the orientalistic views of the colonial period, the church was in support of it, even furnishing some of these colonial concepts with a theological basis. For example, if a major argument from orientalism was that those of the Occident were biologically and socially superior to those of the Orient, many church leaders such as Bishop Shuttleworth hinted that such ideas were natural, given that God had specially blessed the Westerners with extra social graces that the Orient 'heathens' lacked. Thus the church imported a colonial theology that, as Kwok identifies, created a binary between the British Anglicans and the 'ignorant' and 'pitiful' heathens.[18] Furthermore, on this basis it also normalized the British expression of Christianity as the most superior and pristine form of Christian expression, which others needed to learn from and adapt to.

Much more can be said about orientalism and Said's extensive work. But in the light of some of these major concepts, do they explain some of the cultural segregation we observe in the UK churches today? Does the legacy of this colonial period still exist in the issues we are assessing? Arguably, we can perceive some influence of orientalism in how White-majority churches interact with GMH individuals who join them. One of the major by-products of orientalism is how it has created a binary demarcation between the Occident and the Orient, a divide between Western cultures and those of the GMH world.[19] Here, differences between these cultural groups are accentuated rather than trying to identify commonalities between the two. GMH cultures are construed as 'other' in relation to the Westerners. We observe traces of this sort of thinking in the initial experiences of GMH individuals joining White-majority churches. For many GMH individuals joining these churches, there is a feeling that they are immediately categorized by signifiers that are based on their skin colour, ethnicity, accent, country of origin and other factors that ultimately determine whether they belong to the West or not. If they are deemed to be an 'other', barriers of difference are immediately constructed, which White and GMH individuals must overcome before they can appreciate any commonality or shared heritage as fellow Christians. As Said also argued, orientalism does not just highlight differences between the West and GMH cultures but also organizes them into a hierarchy in which the West resides at the top as the ultimate model and the GMH cultures sit below in need of Westernization before they can progress upwards. As Kwok has argued, this sort of hierarchy was also translated into the church context by the church leaders of the colonial period, when they established Western Christian expression as the supreme form of Christianity.

Again, we can see hints of these dynamics at play in how GMH individuals often feel that their participation in the White-majority church is dependent on their adapting and learning the Western expression of Christianity and church. For example, while BBCs feel the urge to highlight their Western sensibilities, they may simultaneously feel the need to downplay their Chinese heritage out of fear that these cultural expressions may not be truly respected or, even worse, judged as inferior in comparison to the Western church culture. As mentioned, in a bid to make their churches more 'international', some churches can show awareness in wanting to appreciate and involve GMH cultures. Nevertheless, some of them go about this by 'exoticizing' GMH individuals. Here, GMH cultures may be incorporated into the church and displayed, but in a way that places them alongside the Western culture as a contrast but not necessarily to inform, change or challenge. Thus, GMH individuals may be included as exotic pieces of a multicultural mosaic but the White culture still forms the centrepiece untouched. Furthermore, the GMH individuals are expected to fit outdated and static colonial tropes that bear little resemblance to their actual cultural heritage. Ultimately, this unwillingness to allow other cultures to truly dialogue with Western culture in church continues to reveal the implicit belief that the British expression of church is sacrosanct and superior to others, an attitude that was at the heart of colonial orientalism.

Although the Chinese churches in the UK may not be responsible for constructing the orientalist framework, we can see that orientalism affects them when they subconsciously adopt it and through it perpetuate cultural segregation. Gayatri Spivak makes the interesting observation that in some post-colonial contexts, certain minority ethnic groups can engage in 'strategic essentialism' in which they may temporarily focus on their essential identity and form a group identity to achieve certain goals, even when they might consider the essentialist logic to be faulty.[20] Arguably, this bears much relevance to how UK Chinese churches were first created and how they continue to perceive their identity. Returning to the origin stories of many Chinese churches, because many Chinese individuals were not actively welcomed into British churches on the basis of their Chinese nationality, culture and language, Chinese Christians were driven to form their own Christian communities that centred around an essentialist Chinese cultural identity. To interpret this further, the earliest Chinese immigrants in the 1950s and 1960s might not have perceived such a strong 'Chinese' identity for themselves. But having these cultural labels placed on them by British society could have required them to adopt such labels and even use them to secure certain goals. We could suggest that the first Chinese Christian immigrants might not necessarily have wanted to create Chinese churches in the UK but nevertheless felt the need to do so because they soon recognized how their perceived Chinese identity was the key signifier in determining which churches they could or could not worship in. Thus, many early Chinese Christians took their essentialized identity to construct their own alternative church communities around it with the goal of securing a worship space for themselves. The overall outcome of this is that Chinese churches have also perpetuated this economy in which people are expected to attend a church of their given cultural identity or ethnicity as prescribed by the Western orientalist world view.

Overall, we see that the legacy of colonial orientalism still underpins much of the cultural segregation both within and between White-majority British churches and Chinese heritage churches. Orientalism continues to equip Christians in the British context with a lens by which to primarily categorize others and themselves according to race, national identity and other features that originate from the colonial period. These categorizations are then used to make value judgements regarding others, which are then further used to determine with whom one ought or ought not to be in a church community. If this is taken as the key issue that we are dealing with, then an important step in leading UK churches to become more intercultural might begin with deconstructing some of these old definitions of culture or ethnicity and proposing alternatives. In particular, we might question whether there are more biblical ways to define ethnic identity that transcend those colonial definitions that have proved to be divisive.

Towards new notions of ethnic identity in 1 Peter 2

When considering issues of ethnic identity in the Bible, 1 Peter 2 comes to the fore. Scholars have identified the second chapter in the first Epistle of Peter as one of the few scriptures that touch on the issue more directly. As David Horrell identifies, within 1 Peter 2.9, Peter uses the terms γένος (*genos*), ἔθνος (*ethnos*) and λαός (*laos*), which can be respectively translated as 'race', 'nation' and 'people'.[21] Nowhere else in Scripture do we find all the known terms of the time that relate to ideas of ethnic identity compressed together in a single verse or passage.[22] With regard to the literary context of 1 Peter, it is largely accepted that Peter was writing to Gentile Christians scattered across various diaspora churches in the Roman Empire.[23] Furthermore, Peter's purpose in writing the Epistle was to encourage these early Christians, who were enduring persecution for their faith, to persevere in that faith despite experiencing such suffering and trials. Crucially, the tactic Peter employed to do this was to describe a new Christian ethnic identity in which all of them were now a part. In the light of this, Peter wanted to reframe his reader's experiences of hostility and suffering from non-Christians as signs that they were part of a new Christian ethnicity that was foreign to the old pagan surroundings and peoples. The hope in doing this was, as Janette Ok describes, 'to build greater internal cohesion among the churches throughout Asia Minor and imbue them with confidence by giving them a separate system of honor by which they can better endure hostility and persecution'.[24]

Scholars have analysed what concepts of ethnic identity Peter was utilizing when making his case. Some modern-day readers might question the objectivity of Peter's proposed ethnic identity. Are Peter's ideas here to be interpreted as a new fictional ethnicity to help encourage those early Christians, but not to be taken as a true objective ethnic identity based on biological race? This in itself is situated in the wider discussion of what constitutes objective ethnic identities. For some scholars, the idea that we can have truly objective definitions of ethnic identity based on things such as race is unfounded. Max Weber argued, for example, that ethnic identities have always been formed by creating an overarching communal consciousness, taking on the form of a common ethnicity regardless of whether objective blood relationships exist.[25] Another important insight is, as John Barclay observes, that even the Judaic concepts of ethnic identity during Peter's time would have primarily focused on tradition and the criterion of religion, in which proselytes could also join.[26] What some of these arguments claim, then, is that ethnicity based on biological race might not need to be seen as the objective way of defining ethnicity. If anything, it is a modern construct. Rather, ethnicities have always been social constructs, conveyed through discourse to meet certain societal and community purposes. Thus, when we return to Peter's arguments, we may perceive him to be engaging in a creative constructionist approach, as Horrell describes: Peter created a new Christian ethnicity including features such as a new name of Χριστιανός (*Christianos*) – a shared common ancestry in God as the divine father, a shared historical memory in the heroic actions of Christ, a new pattern of living as believers, an idea of a homeland that is located in heaven rather than on earth and, finally, a shared sense of solidarity in their trials as Christians in the world.[27]

Nevertheless, when we read this we are not to see Peter as fashioning a fictional gimmick; rather, Peter's presentation of a new Christian ethnicity should be appreciated as a real ethnic identity in both ancient and modern-day terms.[28] Peter was presenting a genuine new ethnic identity that centred on the values and person of Christ, which could truly help his readers to understand their identity and situations better. In this way, the apostle Peter encourages Christian readers to be creative in perceiving their identity as centring around their faith; and more than that, to see how their new ethnic identity should lead to a missional identity that might also bring even non-believers into that new ethnic group. As J. Ramsey Michaels describes, the ultimate goal of 1 Peter in these opening passages is for Christians to change the mind of their accusers through exemplary Christian behaviour.[29]

Missio Dei as the basis for BBC ethnicity

Thus, returning to our original question of how to better understand BBC cultural identity in relation to segregation in UK churches, we ought to consider some key cues. First, a better understanding must deconstruct some of the orientalist and essentialist ways of framing BBC cultural identity. Though we may take note of factors such as biological race, national identity or the country from which one's ancestors originally hailed, we must lighten the emphasis on these things. Furthermore, we need to move away from employing quintessentially 'Chinese' or 'British' cultural profiles into which BBCs cannot fully fit and which also force BBCs to essentialize themselves into outdated static profiles. Instead, as 1 Peter 2 reminds us, our ethnic identities require us to search deeper for identities grounded in Christ that serve his ultimate purpose of mission.

In the light of this, perhaps a better way to define the ethnicity of Christian BBC in this time is not by their skin colour or chosen language but by their shared experience of growing up in a post-colonial British context in which their British and Chinese heritage makes them feel foreign. While this experience will vary between BBCs, all of them are born into this tension in some way that affects their self-identity. Furthermore, just as Peter created an ethnic identity that finds a teleological purpose in God's mission, we too argue that this new BBC ethnic identity might be grounded in a sense of mission or *missio Dei* in relation to their specific experiences of foreignness. Thus we need to explore the nature of this mission.

In his discussion of hybridity in post-colonial contexts, Homi Bhabha argues that it is those individuals who exist in the hybrid spaces where the colonizer and colonized cultures interact who can bring about new ways of perceiving culture. Hybrid individuals like BBCs on the one hand mimic the colonizer culture, wanting to be like them, yet on the other hand present themselves as a distinct recognizable other, the colonized.[30] It is this process of 'mimicry' that disrupts the authority of the colonizers and their normative narratives.[31] As Shehla Burney puts it, mimicry creates a hybrid culture that intermixes the colonizer's culture with that of the colonized, and which consequently displaces the history that creates it and sets up new structures of authority and political initiatives.[32] In this way, as those who live in the hybrid space of Chinese and British culture, BBCs could be particularly predisposed to become aware of, and break the spell of, the 'normative' orientalist perspectives that still bind many churches and society generally. As BBCs try to integrate into society but fail to do so because of the limited cultural categories that are laid out before them, they should realize that this is not due to a fault with themselves but with the presentation and existence of such profiles in the first place. In this way, BBCs might be predisposed to engage in a mission that leads their fellow church members to lay down these old colonial ideas, and to help them form new Christ-centred ethnic identities that transcend the old ones. In an increasingly globalized country, where the number of multicultural heritage individuals will only continue to grow, the British church's mission to these people depends on their ability to reform their way of perceiving ethnic identity; failure to do so runs the risk of alienating all these individuals. Thus, in this wider missiological need BBCs might serve as key pioneers in aiding the church in this way, to serve as 'Peters' who can guide the church by articulating more biblical and inclusive ways of seeing others.

Such a missional call must be extended to BBCs worshipping in both White-majority churches and Chinese heritage churches, as they help their respective churches to move beyond their homogeneous tendencies. Nevertheless, embracing such a missional call will not be easy and will require BBCs to expect certain resistances and pitfalls. Those BBCs in White-majority churches must expect their fellow church members to be slow or even unwilling to lay down their old ways of perceiving culture, even when they are presented with better biblical ones. In those moments, BBCs may be tempted to re-assimilate these old ways of thinking in order to find belonging by either exoticizing or whitewashing themselves again. However, just as Peter called the early Christians to embrace feelings of foreignness as a result of holding on to gospel values, BBCs must also be willing to remain 'foreigners' to their churches as they persist in advocating for more gospel-centred ideas of ethnicity, even when others may not agree, and even when they may feel alienated in the process.

For the BBCs in Chinese heritage churches, there could be a temptation to fall into the trap of more of the strategic essentialism that formed their churches in the first place. Though the EMs have provided a much-needed safe space for them, if not careful they too could essentialize themselves into an exclusive homogeneous space and define themselves with the same unhelpful signifiers based on race, language and national identity. Doing so will only perpetuate further exclusive homogeneous church spaces and shut them off from the world. Perhaps a unique opportunity has been granted to these EMs because they gather some of the largest BBC populations around the country. Furthermore, these populations will only grow with the mass arrival of more Hong Kong immigrants into the UK. Crucially, in these EM gatherings, rather than use these spaces primarily for self-protectionism, BBCs could use them to teach and explore with each other more Christ-centred ethnic identities. These communities must be used to encourage BBCs to embody such new identities together. In this way, EMs could be platforms to give birth to a generation of intercultural agents who could transform the attitude of their parent Chinese churches or even beyond. But to do this, BBCs from these Chinese churches must be willing to open their doors and step back into spaces that will bring them into contact with those who made foreigners out of them in the first place. However, rather than abandon those people who hurt them, BBCs should choose not to retaliate to rejection with equal rejection but to offer grace by reaching out to these people and showing them a more Christlike way to perceive others. Again, BBCs will run the risk of being perceived as foreign as they do this, but this is a necessary risk.

To conclude then, this chapter does not claim to define 'the' new ethnic identity for Christian BBCs; much further thought must be dedicated to understanding how the BBC experience can be rooted in Christ and used for the mission of God. Many more ideas and perspectives need to be shared and considered. Furthermore, the scope of this chapter does not cover the practicalities of what more multicultural churches in Britain might look like and how they might function. Nevertheless, this chapter hopes to encourage a first step towards that process by stimulating BBCs, or other multicultural individuals for that matter, to be the bridge builders and catalysing agents who can open up their churches to intercultural exchange through new discussions on Christian ethnicity.

Thus, should a stranger ask a BBC 'Where do you come from?', perhaps they will one day say, 'A foreigner to the British, a foreigner to the Chinese, but not a foreigner to Christ and certainly not a foreigner to you.'

Notes

1 Chine McDonald, 'Is the Church of England racist?', *Church Times* (3 July 2020), https://www.churchtimes.co.uk/articles/2020/3-july/features/features/is-the-church-of-england-racist, accessed 30.03.2024; Kang-San Tan, 'Overcoming racism: Through leadership diversity in the local church', *Baptists Together* (2020), https://www.baptist.org.uk/Articles/589082/Overcoming_racism_through.aspx, accessed 30.03.2024; '10-step roadmap to racial diversity and unity', *The Evangelical Alliance*, https://www.eauk.org/what-we-do/networks/one-people-commission/10-step-roadmap-to-racial-diversity-and-unity, accessed 30.03.2024.

2 Harvey Kwiyani, *Multicultural Kingdom: Ethnic Diversity, Mission and the Church* (London: SCM Press, 2020), pp. 133–6.

3 Archbishops' Anti-Racism Taskforce, *From Lament to Action* (London: Church of England, 2021), https://www.churchofengland.org/media/press-releases/lament-action-archbishops-anti-racism-taskforce-calls-urgent-changes-culture, accessed 8.10.2024.

4 Census 2021, 'Ethnic group, England and Wales', *Office for National Statistics* (29 November 2022), https://www.ons.gov.uk/peoplepopulationand community/culturalidentity/ethnicity/bulletins/ethnicgroupenglandandwales/ census2021.

5 Maurice Hobbs, *Better Will Come: A Pastoral Response to Institutional Racism in British Churches* (Nottingham: Grove Books Limited, 1991), p. 7.

6 Selina Stone, *'If it Wasn't for God': A Report on the Wellbeing of Global Majority Heritage Clergy in the Church of England* (London: The Archbishops' Council, 2022), p. 3.

7 Yinxuan Huang, *Chinese Christianity in Britain: A Booklet of Ten Vignettes* (Swindon: British and Foreign Bible Society, 2023), p. 9.

8 John Wilkinson, Renate Wilkinson and James H. Evans, *Inheritors Together: Black People in the Church of England* (London: Board of Social Responsibility of the Church of England, 1985), p. 13.

9 Alexander Chow, 'British Immigration Policies and British Chinese Christianity', in *Ecclesial Diversity in Chinese Christianity*, ed. Alexander Chow and Easten Law (New York: Palgrave Macmillan, 2021), pp. 99–120, https://doi.org/10.1007/978-3-030-73069-7_5.

10 Donald A. McGavran, *Understanding Church Growth*, 3rd edn (Grand Rapids, MI: Eerdmans, 1990), p. 163.

11 Edward Said, *Orientalism: Western Conceptions of the Orient* (New York: Vintage Books, 1979), p. 203.

12 Said, *Orientalism*, pp. 206–7.

13 Said, *Orientalism*, pp. 37–40.

14 Said, *Orientalism*, p. 202.

15 Kwok Pui-lan, *The Anglican Tradition from a Postcolonial Perspective* (New York: Seabury Books, 2023), p. 28.

16 Rowan Strong, *Anglicanism and the British Empire: c.1700–1850* (Oxford: Oxford University Press, 2007), p. 280.

17 Stewart J. Brown, 'Anglicanism in the British Empire, 1829–1910', in *The Oxford History of Anglicanism, vol. 3: Partisan Anglicanism and its Global Expansion, 1829–c.1914*, ed. Rowan Strong (Oxford: Oxford University Press, 2017), p. 66.

18 Kwok, *The Anglican Tradition from a Postcolonial Perspective*, p. 29.

19 Said, *Orientalism*, p. 201.

20 Gayatri Spivak, 'Subaltern Studies: Deconstructing Histography?', in *The Spivak Reader: Selected Works of Gayati Chakravorty Spivak*, ed. Donna Landry and Gerald MacLean (London: Routledge, 1996), p. 214.

21 David G. Horrell, '"Race", "Nation", "People": Ethnic Identity-Construction in 1 Peter 2.9', *New Testament Studies* 58, no. 1 (January 2012), p. 124, https://doi.org/10.1017/S0028688511000245.

22 Horrell, '"Race", "Nation", "People"', p. 129.

23 J. Ramsey Michaels, *1 Peter*, Word Biblical Commentary 49 (Dallas, TX: Word, 1988), p. xlvi.

24 Janette H. Ok, 'Always Ethnic, Never "American": Reading 1 Peter Through the Lens of the "Perpetual Foreigner" Stereotype', in *T&T Clark Handbook of Asian American Biblical Hermeneutics*, ed. Uriah Y. Kim and Seung Ai Yang (London: T&T Clark, 2019), p. 423, https://doi.org/10.5040/9780567672636.0044.

25 Max Weber, *Economy and Society: An Outline of Interpretive Sociology*, ed. Guenther Roth and Claus Wittich (New York: Bedminster Press, 1968), p. 389.

26 John M. G. Barclay, *Jews in the Mediterranean Diaspora from Alexander to Trajan (323 BCE – 117 CE)* (Edinburgh: T&T Clark, 1996), p. 408.

27 Horrell, '"Race", "Nation", "People"', pp. 139–40.

28 Horrell, '"Race", "Nation", "People"', p. 141.

29 Michaels, *1 Peter*, p. 120

30 Homi K. Bhabha, *The Location of Culture* (London and New York: Routledge, 1994), pp. 85–7.

31 Bhabha, *The Location of Culture*, p. 88.

32 Shehla Burney, 'Edward Said and Postcolonial Theory: Disjunctured Identities and the Subaltern Voice', *Counterpoints* 417 (2012), p. 59.

5

Called by Name: A British Born Chinese Perspective on Identity and Calling in the Church of England

MARK NAM 甄英深

For six months, a photograph hung in the mezzanine of the British Library in London featuring an Anglican priest in front of what might be described as a typical English parish church. A relatively unremarkable scene except for one small detail. The priest had a Chinese face, and that priest was me (Figure 1).

Figure 1: The Revd Mark Nam (from '8 Stories') by Jamie Lau (2023)

The photograph was part of a national exhibition that ran from November 2022 to May 2023, entitled 'Chinese and British', drawing on personal stories and moments of national significance to ask what it means to be Chinese and British.[1] One of the reasons the photo attracted attention was the way it challenged two cultural stereotypes, namely: a) what a typical English parish priest might look like; and b) what a Chinese heritage person might aspire to be. I intend to explore these two notions by returning to the photograph from time to time and examining some of the complexities that successive generations of British Born Chinese ('BBC') are required to navigate in determining their spiritual identity and calling in the UK.

In doing so, I will question whether existing models of bicultural spirituality – which enable first- and second-generation BBCs to construct a hybrid identity – are of any help to subsequent generations of BBCs, who have little or no affinity to their Chinese heritage or culture. I will look to Asian American scholarship to inform my reflections and then offer an alternative reading of Moses, which incorporates those whose Chinese heritage has been lost to them and yet affirms a connection to their ancestral heritage and British identity through the concept of divine encounter and covenant.

I will argue that using covenant to comprehend BBC identity is more biblically robust and inclusive than previous attempts at forming BBC identity through bicultural spirituality or hybridity. I will then conclude by putting forward an argument for why I believe the increased representation of BBCs in the Church of England is vital for the acceptance and flourishing of future generations of BBCs in the UK and the development of British Chinese spirituality in general.

Bicultural identity for Asian Americans and BBCs

The concepts of bicultural spirituality and hybridity in a theological framework for the East Asian diaspora is not new. In the United States, Chinese communities have had a larger and more established presence than in the UK. Shortly after the construction of the great American railroads in the mid-nineteenth century – which employed over 15,000 Chinese workers – the United States experienced large-scale Chinese immigration, which saw more than 300,000 Chinese descend on the West Coast during the California Gold Rush. The number of Asian Americans has grown most dramatically since 1965 due to the US government changing its immigration policies; and since 2010 Asian

Americans have become the fastest-growing racial group in the United States, by percentage growth.[2]

Within this context, a steady body of Asian American scholarship has formed and continues to grow, seeking to articulate the existential experience of Asian Americans, to the point that writers now refer to different generations of Asian American theologians. This is in stark contrast to the British context, where immigration has been relatively smaller in scale, and where the Chinese are much more dispersed geographically, as detailed in Alexander Chow's Chapter 1 in this volume. Accordingly, there has been little, if any, equivalent BBC scholarship, which is why a book of this kind is so necessary.

While it is outside the remit of this chapter to explain the development of Asian American history and consciousness in detail,[3] it is important for those of us in the British context to extrapolate what we can from Asian American scholarship to inform our own reflections. I will use the term 'Asian American' as it has been used in contemporary discourse; that is, as a generic and convenient shorthand to categorize all Americans of Asian ancestry and heritage.[4]

Within Asian American theological discourse, Jung Young Lee's theology of marginality is widely considered to be a seminal reflection on the quintessential Asian American experience.[5] In his book *Marginality: The Key to Multicultural Theology* (1995), Lee encourages Asian Americans to embrace living on the margins of society as a positive and self-affirming aspect of being Asian American. He constructs a contextual theology comprising three stages: in-between, in-both and in-beyond.[6] The first stage describes the feeling of being totally negated by both cultures (in-between), and the second stage describes the positive feeling of total affirmation from both cultures (in-both). By juxtaposing the two contrasting aspects of marginality, Lee proposes a third way (in-beyond), whereby Asian Americans integrate the negative aspects of being 'in-between' with the positive aspects of being 'in-both', creating a hybrid identity personified in the 'new marginal person'.[7]

This idea of bicultural identity and hybridity is an attractive prospect for second-generation BBCs who also find themselves on the margins. On 16 October 2023, Alexander Chow brought together Chinese heritage representatives from across different denominations and Chinese Churches to the Birmingham Chinese Evangelical Church (Figure 2).

Figure 2: Historic meeting of Chinese heritage church leaders and scholars from across the UK

Left to right: Dr Alexander Chow (University of Edinburgh), Revd Bert Han (Birmingham Chinese Evangelical Church), Josh Shek (London School of Theology), Revd Kan Yu (Methodist Church in Britain), Revd Mark Nam (Diocese of Oxford, Church of England), Dr Calida Chu (University of Nottingham), Dr Yinxuan Huang (British and Foreign Bible Society), Candy Zhang (Chinese Overseas Christian Mission) and James So (Chinese Overseas Christian Mission). Photo by Bert Han (2023).

The gathering was significant, not just because it included many of those who would be contributing to this volume but because it was the first time such an eclectic mix of Chinese heritage Christians – church leaders and scholars – had come together specifically to discuss British Chinese identity and spirituality. From the discussions that followed, it became apparent that notions of bicultural identity and hybridity occupied a central place in some of the thinking. According to one second-generation BBC leader: 'Perhaps BBCs, in their own experience of hybridity, can also find a particular purpose of eventually working towards justice, mercy and reconciliation between their two cultural heritages; a ministry that only they can perform in their specific sociological context.' Sentiments like these are found in the writings of Asian Americans like Sang Hyun Lee who, in *From a Liminal Place: An Asian American Theology* (2010), posits the idea that Asian Americans – because of their liminality – are uniquely positioned to take a prophetic stance and exercise a particular vocation towards God's justice and reconciliation.[8] While it is relatively straightforward to see how this framework can be applied to second-generation BBCs who have grown up in both British and Chinese cultures, it is less obvious how – or even *if* – it can be applied to successive generations of BBCs, who have little engagement with Chinese cultures, languages and traditions.

As someone who is a third-generation BBC – fourth-generation on my mother's side – I do not identify with a 'stereotypical BBC upbringing'. My parents did not emigrate from Asia; they were born and brought up in the Welsh valleys. My family did not work in a restaurant or takeaway; my father was a chemical engineer and my mother was a primary school teacher. We spoke only English at home, we ate predominantly Western food, and our friends were all White. I did not grow up on the margins. We attended a traditional Anglican church, and the only engagement I had with other Chinese people was through extended family, who on the whole were just as distant from their Chinese heritage and culture as I was. As a third-generation BBC, I am left asking, 'Why am I not captivated by the promises of bicultural identity and hybridity?'

I am not the only person to ask this question. In what I consider to be one of the most important books for BBCs navigating the Western church, *Ancestral Feeling: Postcolonial Thoughts on Western Christian Heritage* (2021), Renie Chow Choy considers Sang Hyun Lee's assertions on bicultural identity and liminality and remarks, 'His argument sought to make me feel better about my situation, but why (speaking for myself only) am I not convinced?'[9]

In October 2022, an independent report was commissioned by the Church of England looking into the well-being of Minority Ethnic and Global Majority Heritage (GMH) clergy.[10] In one of the findings, the report stated: 'It seems important therefore, that GMH clergy have the space to process how they integrate their ethnicity, culture and vocation, rather than this being *assumed by others*, especially those more senior.'[11] In a bid to scratch this existential itch – and influenced by the findings of the report – I took a trip to America in the spring of 2023 with the aim of engaging with Asian American scholars directly, so that I might process how to integrate my own ethnicity, culture and vocation, rather than it being assumed by others, including those already within the Chinese community.

A critique of bicultural identity and hybridity for BBCs

When I was in Los Angeles County I had the privilege of meeting Daniel D. Lee, the Academic Dean for the Center for Asian American Theology and Ministry, based at Fuller Theological Seminary in Pasadena. In his book *Doing Asian American Theology: A Contextual Framework for Faith and Practice* (2022), Lee considers bicultural and hybrid theological models, explaining that:

Early generations of Asian American theologians sought a common essentializing experience, looking, for example, to marginality, liminality, or community. This might be an example of 'strategic essentialism', where a common experience becomes a strategic core on which to build a political alliance. Obviously, there are benefits and limitations to such a strategy.[12]

The common essentializing experience adopted by earlier generations of Asian American theologians did not fully extend to address the experiences and perspectives of subsequent generations. According to Jonathan Y. Tan in *Introducing Asian American Theologies* (2008), this is because first-generation theologians expended their energy on attacking *external racism* and discrimination, while second-generation theologians were able to take a far more critical stance on *internal challenges* and shortcomings.[13]

It stands to reason, therefore, that unless the BBC theological community is open to incorporating the views and experiences of successive generations of BBCs, it will succumb to a similar type of 'strategic essentialism' associated with first-generation theologians, which alienates those who do not share their common experience but who nevertheless identify as BBC.

In his book *Grassroots Asian Theology: Thinking Faith from the Ground Up* (2014),[14] the Singaporean scholar Simon Chan points out that one of the problems of constructing a theology on cultural experiences is that they are limited in scope and reductionistic.[15] Simon Shui-Man Kwan – who identifies as Hong Kong Asian[16] – in his book *Postcolonial Resistance and Asian Theology* (2014), recognizes that an uncritical adoption of essentialist notions of hybridity 'could [itself] become oppressive by imposing a common denominator on all theologies that aim to be Asian'.[17]

Returning to the Asian American context, Daniel Lee demonstrates this problem when contemplating the growing number of multiethnic and multiracial Asian Americans.[18] I only have to consider my own BBC cousins – around half of whom are 'half-Chinese', and their children – my second cousins – who are 'quarter-Chinese' – to see how focusing identity formation on hybridity could potentially alienate them from laying claim to their Chinese heritage, as it has for me. Accordingly, Daniel Lee warns that 'we cannot draw our concepts of Asian American identity [and therefore BBC identity] so narrowly as to preclude them from belonging.'[19]

Even if this warning is heeded, there is a further obstacle that needs to be overcome, and that is a line of thinking that persists within Asian theology which seeks to discount the contribution of subsequent generations of Asian Americans/BBCs. This is perhaps most evident in the provokingly titled book *Mangoes or Bananas? The Quest for an Authentic Christian Theology* (2004), by the Bishop Emeritus of the Methodist Church in Malaysia, Hwa Yung, who says:

> Among the fruits commonly found in tropical Asia are the banana and the mango. The banana is of uncertain origins, whereas the mango is an authentic Asian fruit. Ripe bananas are yellow, but when peeled reveal a flesh off-white in colour. On the other hand, most species of mango when ripe are golden yellow on both the outside and inside ... Asians may love the banana, but there is no doubt that the sweet, succulent flesh of the mango is prized much more highly ... The agenda for Asian theology for the future therefore seems clear. What we need are more theological 'mangoes', and not 'bananas'.[20]

The term 'banana' is widely understood to be a pejorative term – along with 'coconut' and 'Twinkie' – to describe Asian Americans who are perceived to have been assimilated and acculturated into Western culture to such an extent, that they can no longer relate to their Asian heritage.[21] They are yellow (or brown) on the outside but white on the inside.

Distinctions like these are rarely helpful, inevitably generating divisions within Asian American and other Asian diasporic communities – creating a hierarchy of sorts – and dictating what is deemed authentically Asian and what is not. And yet as Daniel Lee points out, 'far too often that unsophisticated way of talking reinforces stereotypes and marginalises other Asian Americans who do not share such experiences.'[22]

When I was training for ordination, the library at my theological college had very few books – if any – that spoke to the contemporary East Asian experience. The books and resources that were available were predominantly written by first-generation Asian Americans or authors who sought to prioritize indigenous 'grassroots' Asian theologies over and above those written by Asians who were educated in the West, due to their perceived 'uncritical assimilation of Enlightenment epistemology' and 'resultant lack of theological discernment'.[23]

Looking back, and given what I was reading, it is no surprise that I began to believe that I had no meaningful connection to my Chinese heritage – I was merely a 'banana' after all – and presumably had nothing of value to offer due to my so-called 'uncritical assimilation' of Western categories of thought. It is no exaggeration to say that any theological enterprise I felt inside was rendered dead in the water – I was at a loss; which brings me back to the photograph in the British Library.

I had never stopped to contemplate the symbolism of the graves surrounding me – some so weathered that the names are no longer legible – until I received an email out of the blue from Steve Taylor, a missiologist based in New Zealand and co-editor of *Ecclesial Futures*,[24] who had seen the photograph and felt compelled to write:

> But I see a vicar, 'more tea vicar', yet of migrant descent (I presume from the art piece), standing outside a most English looking church. Is the vicar outside wanting to engage those outside the church? Or is the vicar outside because they don't feel included. The vicar stands among the graves. Again, a traditional stereotype – of vicar caring at hatch/match/dispatch? Or are the graves suggesting death, of standing in a place of discomfort and unwelcome ... The art piece is doing a lot of work theologically about identity and ministry.[25]

Taylor's words impacted me deeply. Up until that point I had not considered the presence of the graves before, but as I pondered their meaning, I wrote the following in my journal:

> Why am I standing among the graves? Have I become so anglicised, that I don't even recognise the graves that belong to my own ancestors? Am I so removed from my Chinese heritage that they no longer call out? Are they dead to me? Am I dead to them? I can no longer even read the names of my forebears anymore. I have forgotten who they are. Have I forsaken who I am?

These were the questions that haunted me, as I desperately tried to figure out how to reconcile the neglected aspects of my identity and history into a coherent whole – or what Daniel Lee describes as the challenge of self-integration into a divine shalom.[26] What is particularly helpful in his work is the way he incorporates interdisciplinary insights from interpersonal neurobiology and trauma theory. He proposes that Asian Americans often suffer a fragmented self because of microaggressive traumas. This is not only inflicted from majority-White spaces but from *within* Asian/Asian American contexts themselves, where the label of 'cultural heritage' is essentialized to exclude those who do not fit conveniently under the bicultural/hybridity frameworks[27] – in other words, BBC 'bananas' like me. And just like everyday racism, this everyday cultural stress can add up to create trauma.[28]

To remedy this situation, Daniel Lee argues that we must be willing to complexify our understandings of Asian Americans.[29] Similarly, Simon Kwan argues that a 'non-essentialist, hybrid notion of identity is best for understanding Asian identity if Asian theologians are to resist forces of homogenization and emphasize differences'.[30] It seems logical, therefore, that our goal in the UK should be to complexify our understanding of BBCs and to question the assumptions underpinning the theological reflections used to affirm essentialist bicultural and hybridity frameworks in the first place.

However, I believe it is necessary to go one step further: to move away from hybridity entirely – even 'non-essentialist' versions – and instead move towards a spiritual/supracultural approach that comes through divine encounter and re-adoption under God's covenant.

Divine encounters, not hybrid identities

> *To forget one's ancestors is to be a brook without a source, a tree without roots.* (Chinese proverb)

The language of hybridity continues to capture the imagination of scholars looking to develop a theological framework for an increasingly multicultural world. This is most notable in a recent volume entitled *A Hybrid World: Diaspora, Hybridity, and Missio Dei* (2020),[31] a compendium of papers from a hybridity in diaspora mission consultation held in 2018 and sponsored by the Lausanne Movement and Global Diaspora Network.[32] Resources like these point to diaspora and hybridity found throughout Scripture and history. One biblical character who is closely associated with hybridity is Moses.[33]

At the 2023 gathering of Chinese heritage church leaders and scholars in Birmingham (Figure 2), Moses was put forward by a second-generation Chinese church leader as an exemplar of hybridity, whom BBCs can relate to and identify with, thus providing meaning and purpose to their own bicultural identities. The presumption is that Moses was born and raised in a Hebrew family – speaking the language, learning the values and history of his people – while also being adopted and educated by the Egyptian aristocracy. It was argued that this reflects the experiences of BBCs who are raised in Chinese homes and grow up in the UK.

I question the validity of this presumption. At the beginning of the story in Exodus 2, we read that Moses' mother could only hide him for three months, before placing him in a basket to be later found among the reeds along the bank of the Nile (vv. 3–4). Moses was just a baby, and it is highly unlikely that he would have been able to remember anything about the first few months of his life in a Hebrew household. We do see Moses returned to his birth mother, so that she can nurse him (vv. 7–9), which creates the possibility that he might have been raised as a Hebrew. But as pointed out in *Ancient Near Eastern Texts Related to the Old Testament* (1974),[34] Moses' mother probably only nursed him until he was three years old, the usual age when a baby was weaned, before returning him to the princess, who raised him as a prince of the royal family.

While we are unable to infer an exact age, it cannot be said with any confidence that Moses experienced a bicultural upbringing, certainly not one that can be likened to second-generation BBCs. It is much more probable that Moses was raised predominantly as an Egyptian and was accustomed to Egyptian ways, having grown up in the palace. Consequently, Moses would have been cut off from his Hebrew identity, culture and heritage. He was, to all intents and purposes, and to quote the animation studio Dreamworks, a 'Prince of Egypt'.

That being the case, I would contend that Moses' upbringing more closely resembles the experience of subsequent generations of BBCs – third- and fourth-generations like myself – who have been severed almost completely from their Chinese heritage and cannot identify as bicultural in the way that earlier generations of Asian American and BBC scholars have presumed. The life experiences of Asian Americans and BBCs are diverse and multifaceted; they cannot be condensed into such simple terms or parameters.

Trauma is a reality in the bodies of those who suffer from a fragmented self. According to Daniel Lee, the constant self-editing, self-redacting and self-questioning that Asian Americans endure leads to 'emotional leakage'. Although the manner of leakage cannot be predicted, it is often visible when someone of a marginalized status interacts with someone with privilege, sometimes with violent or destructive consequences.[35] This might offer some insight into the incident where Moses, after having grown up, murders an Egyptian who was beating a Hebrew, 'one of his own people' (Exodus 2.11–12, NIV). Moses is experiencing emotional leakage, built on years of trauma and frustration stemming from his fragmented sense of self, and explodes destructively.

But this is not the end of the story. After Moses flees and accepts that he is a 'foreigner in a foreign land' (v. 22, NIV), we read that he has a significant encounter with God. This is the point at which I would like to suggest that Moses connects in a meaningful way with his Hebrew heritage – not because of hybridity per se but because of a divine encounter with God and his re-adoption under God's covenant.

Remembering the names of our ancestors

Falling leaves settle on their roots. Everything reverts to its original sources. (Chinese proverb)

When God finally chooses to introduce himself to Moses in Exodus 3, he does so by announcing in verse 6 that he was the God of Moses' father (*av*), meaning his Hebrew father. But later, in Exodus 3.13, Moses is commissioned by 'The God of your fathers (*avote*)' (NIV), in the plural. In doing so, God does something incredibly profound. He connects the dots of Moses' life to his ancestors (his forefathers), starting with his birth culture and naming himself from that point of reference. Moses does not reconnect with his Hebrew identity because he was brought up biculturally. Moses reconnects with his heritage because God awakens in him *the names* of his ancestors with whom he created a covenant.

The encounter between God and Moses takes place on holy ground (v. 5), which draws me back to the photograph in the British Library, where I am standing among graves (Figure 1). It is in this holy place that God connects me back to my Chinese heritage – my ancestors – who would otherwise be dead to me. By stepping into God's divine presence, Moses is incorporated back into the life of God's covenant people. Similarly, when I – as a third-generation BBC – bring my fragmented self into union with Christ, my identity is restored, including the parts that were previously beyond my grasp or even denied by others.

Approaching lineage in this way – what Daniel Lee calls a 'covenantal basis of contextuality'[36] – offers a much more compelling and theologically robust way forward for future generations of BBCs to contemplate their identity and calling, rather than relying on cultural constructs like biculturalism and hybridity on which to base their identity, which as we have seen, are limited in scope and potentially exclusionary.

Please note, I am not saying there are no benefits to contemplating hybridity. There are certainly occasions when BBCs can use their experiences to share about the virtues of Eastern 'collectivism' in relation to Western 'individualism' and how to navigate these two positions in a constructive way that benefits society. However, it is my contention that this cannot be the foundation on which to build or understand future BBC identity. If hybridity is to be utilized responsibly, then its proponents must situate it within a broader and stronger theological framework such as the one I am proposing for BBCs, based on divine presence and covenant.

Furthermore, focusing on God's covenant as the starting point of identity formation cuts across ethnic and cultural lines. Indeed, it cuts across hierarchies that have been created both from without and within communities. Irrespective of whether one might identify as Black, White, Asian (or any one of the numerous 'hyphenated' identities adopted by diasporic communities), each and every person can seek healing of their fractured selves in the presence of the Lord and enter into his covenant through the death and resurrection of Jesus Christ who grafts us into the story of God and his people, in whom we share a common history and heritage. It is through Christ that the dividing walls are broken down – internal and external – so that we can truly call one another brother and sister. This is the basis on which we now understand ourselves and relate to the world. It is through Christ's work on the cross and the ongoing ministry of the Holy Spirit that we can also better discern our unique callings and vocation.

Vocation: BBC identity and calling in the Church of England

The team at the Center for Asian American Theology and Ministry have found three core components to bringing healing to the personal fragmentation suffered by Asian Americans, namely: language, narrative and community.[37] Language is about finding the right vocabulary so that past and present experiences can be articulated and acknowledged fully. Narrative – or personal storytelling – is about developing a sense of coherence and understanding about what is going on, enabling the Spirit to reveal the truth of the matter. Community plays an important part in the healing process. These three components perform a cognitive, therapeutic and neurological role in the healing of fragmentation and dissociation within Asian American/BBC lives.[38]

For the purposes of this section, I will utilize narrative and personal storytelling to demonstrate how viewing my BBC identity through the lens of encounter and covenant has enabled me to discern a distinct calling in the Church of England, and why I believe increased BBC representation and participation in the national church is vital for the flourishing of future generations of BBCs and the development of British Chinese spirituality in general.

Figure 3: Landing Card for Revd Mark Nam's grandfather (1920)

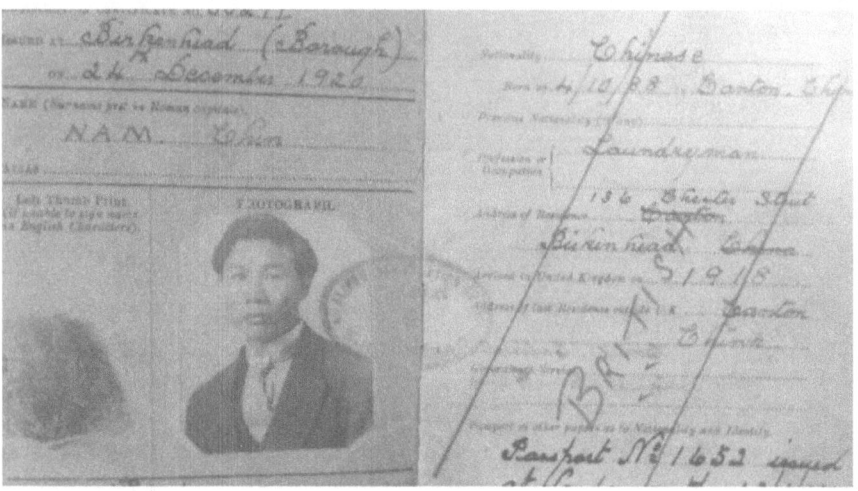

A BBC story: called by name[39]

When my paternal grandfather was a young man, his older brother wrote to him from America saying, 'Little brother, come join me in Chicago. There's money to be made and a new life waiting.' My grandfather made his way to Shanghai, and shone the shoes of sailors to earn enough money to be smuggled on to a boat. After many months at sea, my grandfather was eventually kicked off the ship and when he disembarked, he discovered that he was not in America, as promised. He was, in fact, in a place called Birkenhead, Liverpool. That is how my family ended up in the UK. He never saw his brother again.

When my grandfather was asked by immigration for his name in 1920, he introduced himself in typical Chinese fashion; that is, he introduced himself by his family name first, followed by his given name. The British officials, accustomed to hearing family names last, recorded my grandfather's given name 'Nam' as his surname (see Figure 3), and from that day forward my family have been known as 'Nam' – our original family name was lost.

On the night before I was ordained – exactly 100 years after that fateful day at immigration – my bishop, the Rt Revd Vivienne Faull, asked if she could ordain me using my full Chinese name. Unbeknown to my bishop at the time, she was asking to call me forward by a name that had been lost 100 years ago. And so, on 11 October 2020 at Bristol Cathedral, I was ordained with my full Chinese name – the name of my ancestors – and welcomed into the church.

I share this story because it highlights that for many migrant families, identity is a real challenge from the start. I believe the initial dislocation and loss of identity experienced by my grandfather set the trajectory for the rest of my family. Growing up as a third-generation BBC, I struggled to reconcile my British identity with my Chinese heritage. And yet like Moses, it was by entering into the divine presence of the Lord and being called forward by name – the name of my ancestors – that the fragmented parts of my identity began to come together. As I knelt in the sacred space of the cathedral, God connected the dots of my life, joining me to my Chinese heritage publicly and then directing me forward to embrace my calling as a British Born Chinese priest in the Church of England. It was from that place of wholeness and healing that my vocation became clear.

In contrast to the United States, there is no separation between church and state in the UK. The Church of England is part of the fabric of society, its history intertwined with that of the country. Given the influence it exerts on public life and imagination – and therefore on the lives of BBCs in general – I am convinced that increased BBC representation in the Church of England is vital, particularly given the large influx of Hong Kongers who have moved to the UK over the last few years.

I appreciate this is a big ask for some BBCs, to leave the relative comfort of the Chinese church environment. Moses hesitates to return to Egypt. When God commands him to go to Pharoah, he responds, 'Who am I that I should go to Pharoah and bring the Israelites out of Egypt?' (Exodus 3.11). Moses still struggles with self-doubt about his identity and ability to represent the Israelites before Pharoah. Yet God says to him, 'Say to the Israelites, "The LORD, the God of your fathers – the God of Abraham, the God of Isaac and the God of Jacob – has sent me to you"' (v. 15). God reminds the Hebrew people, as well as Moses, that Moses is one of their own. This is incredibly encouraging for BBCs like myself, who have grown up dislocated from our Chinese heritage and question our eligibility to represent or even speak up for our community.

It also remains daunting for those with Chinese heritage to enter a church that, according to the Archbishop of Canterbury, is 'still deeply institutionally racist'.[40] We read that Moses also doubted his ability to speak truth to power, but God promised to give and teach him the words he would need to be a force for change and a force for good (Exodus 4.11).

For my ordination ceremony, I fundraised to have a special stole commissioned (Figure 4). A stole is a liturgical garment worn around the neck, with two ends hanging down parallel to one another in the front. On each end of the stole respectively, the Chinese characters for East and West were embroidered, representing the coming together of my British and Chinese identities.

Figure 4: Final design of the stole on paper (2020)

It bears repeating that the coming together of my British and Chinese identities was *not* a result of some form of biculturalism or notion of hybridity. Consistent with what I have written above regarding covenant and calling, it was through being unified with Christ that the fragmented parts of myself were reconciled. This is symbolized on the stole by a cross at the nape of the neck, joining the separate ends together. As expressed in Colossians 1.19–20 (NIV):

> For God was pleased to have all his fullness dwell in him, and through him to reconcile to himself all things, whether things on earth or things in heaven, by making peace through his blood, shed on the cross.

As Daniel Lee states: 'Through the gospel, God transforms us deep below the surface of our lives, healing our hurts and affirming our seemingly unpresentable aspects.'⁴¹ Where previously I felt that my Chinese identity was unpresentable, it now forms part of the liturgical garment that accompanies me wherever I serve – literally sown into the fabric of my calling.

Returning to the American context, both Daniel Lee and Joseph Cheah observe that one of the biggest obstacles facing Asian Americans living in the USA is a form of invisibility, brought about by a societal construct that renders them 'perpetual foreigners'. Similarly, no matter how long BBCs have been in the UK, they are seldom recognized as being fully British. Because of this, Daniel Lee argues: 'Thus, true integration must be activist, resisting the marginalizing forces of normativity. For this process to occur, new mental categories that question the status quo and normative assumptions of society must be introduced in a safe environment.'⁴²

Thus, when I walk into places of worship steeped in Western Christian heritage, the wearing of my stole resists marginalizing forces of normativity, or what Renie Chow Choy describes as 'the segregation of Christian (Western) heritage and ethnic (non-Western) heritage into distinct spheres'.⁴³ Similarly, the photograph at the British Library challenges the accepted norms of what a typical English priest might look like, and what BBCs might aspire to be. As Choy observes, things like these:

> have particular significance for ethnic minority Christians who must do the extra – and unnatural – work not required of white Christians, the work of 'self-placement': to somehow insert their story inside a European history in order to make sense of why the latter is personally relevant.⁴⁴

This is why I believe BBC representation in the Church of England is so important for breaking down stereotypes and confronting tropes like the 'perpetual foreigner', which – for as long as they reside in the public imagination – continue to sustain forces that seek to 'other' and marginalize British East and South East Asians ('BESEAs') in the Church of England.

In *Ancestral Feeling*, Choy exposes the Church's tendency to deny minority ethnic Christians the right to lay a claim to Western Christian inheritance – that is, the Church of England – even if they have resided in the UK and worshipped in the Church of England for multiple generations. To quote Choy:

I therefore vehemently argue against a remedy that would propose: 'Christianity is not only Western. So let Western Christians have their Western church history. Now let us find some Chinese church history for the Chinese; let us now find some African church history for the Africans.' Such a position only serves to divide, alienate, marginalize and tribalize, and it is a thin disguise for exclusionary habits.[45]

As a BBC who was baptized, confirmed, married and worships in the Anglican tradition, I resonate with Choy's description of 'ancestral feeling' that minority ethnic Christians have towards Western Christian heritage. Sadly, I am also sensitive to the way this ancestral feeling – or 'elective affinity' – has been denied by those who seek to maintain an imperialistic and nationalistic model of the church, or what Daniel Lee refers to as 'the White hegemony in multiethnic churches'.[46]

Choy's book explores blurring the boundaries between one's ethnic and religious inheritances, to intentionally foster ancestral feeling. She sees this as a possible way to enhance inclusion and reinforce a sense of belonging among ethnic minorities who can now insert their story into European history.[47]

The building up of a new community

The blurring of boundaries explored by Choy brings me on to the final aspect of the photograph in the British Library, and that is the cup of tea I am holding. In 2021, my wife Kayi and I set up a network called The Teahouse.[48] The Teahouse is a national network that seeks to raise the visibility and participation of Chinese heritage clergy in all structures of the Church of England. On the 'About' page of the website it says:

> Tea Houses have been part of Chinese society for thousands of years. Tea is also a quintessential part of British society and therefore represents a beautiful blend of both cultures. Tea is also eminently Anglican. The words, 'More tea, Vicar?' possess an almost liturgical quality, given how often they are uttered in churches up and down the country. It is hoped that *The Tea House* will point people in the direction of clergy with Chinese heritage. As a group we are small in number and are often overlooked in matters that concern us or the communities we represent, particularly on issues of diversity and inclusion. *The Tea House* provides a space where East meets West. We believe we have much to offer and we hope that our unique per-

spectives will be considered and our voices heard within the Church of England, whether related to policy, mission, theological reflection or the life of the Church.[49]

The Church of England occupies a unique and privileged position in British society, and yet Chinese heritage clergy represent less than 0.2 per cent of stipendiary clergy.[50] As I have argued above, I believe it is now time for BBCs to step forward and lay claim to their place in the life of the national church and the history of this nation.

Since its inception three years ago, The Teahouse has enabled Chinese heritage clergy to contribute to discussions on racial justice at General Synod; lead services on BBC Radio; be featured on terrestrial television; meet His Majesty King Charles III; and contribute to national events such as the laying of wreaths at the cenotaph in London on Remembrance Day. It is self-placement and efforts like these that resist what Willie J. Jennings calls 'Christianity's diseased social imagination',[51] an imagination that seeks to prevent those on the margins from truly belonging. This is why I believe the increased representation of BBCs in the Church of England is vital for the acceptance and flourishing of future generations of BBCs in the UK, and the development of British Chinese spirituality as a whole.

My name is Revd Mark Nam 甄英深. I am a British Chinese priest in the Church of England, and I have been called by name.[52]

Notes

1 https://www.britishlibrary.cn/en/events/chinese-and-british/.

2 D. J. Chuang, *Multiasian Church: A Future for Asian Americans in a Multi-Ethnic World* (self-pub, CreateSpace, 2016), pp. 11–13.

3 I recommend reading chapters 1 and 2 of Jonathan Y. Tan's book, *Introducing Asian American Theologies* (Maryknoll, NY: Orbis Books, 2008).

4 The term 'Asian American' refers to American citizens of Asian descent, based on the US census (2013) racial category of 'Asian', defined as, 'a person having origins in any of the original peoples of the Far East, South East Asia, or the Indian subcontinent including, for example, Cambodia, China, India, Japan, Korea, Malaysia, Pakistan, the Philippine Islands, Thailand, and Vietnam'.

5 Joseph Cheah, *Anti-Asian Racism: Myths, Stereotypes, and Catholic Social Teaching* (Maryknoll, NY: Orbis Books, 2023), p. 124.

6 Jung Young Lee, *Marginality: The Key to Multicultural Theology* (Minneapolis, MN: Fortress Press, 1995), pp. 42–70.

7 Lee, *Marginality*, pp. 55–7.

8 Sang Hyun Lee, *From a Liminal Place: An Asian American Theology* (Minneapolis, MN: Fortress Press, 2010), p. x.

9 Renie Chow Choy, *Ancestral Feeling: Postcolonial Thoughts on Western Christian Heritage* (London: SCM Press, 2021), p. 57.

10 Selina Stone, '"If it wasn't for God": A report on the wellbeing of Global Majority Heritage clergy in the Church of England' (Living Ministry – Church of England, 20 October 2022), https://www.churchofengland.org/sites/default/files/2022-10/focussed-study-3-gmh-clergy-wellbeing.pdf.

11 Stone, '"If it wasn't for God"', p. 21; emphasis added.

12 Daniel D. Lee, *Doing Asian American Theology: A Contextual Framework for Faith and Practice* (Downers Grove, IL: IVP Academic, 2022), p. 65.

13 Tan, *Introducing Asian American Theologies*, p. 101.

14 Simon Chan, *Grassroots Asian Theology: Thinking the Faith from the Ground Up* (Downers Grove, IL: InterVarsity Press, 2014).

15 Chan, *Grassroots Asian Theology*, p. 22.

16 Simon Shui-Man Kwan, *Postcolonial Resistance and Asian Theology* (New York: Routledge, 2014), p. 124.

17 Kwan, *Postcolonial Resistance and Asian Theology*, p. 55.

18 Lee, *Doing Asian American Theology*, p. 61.

19 Lee, *Doing Asian American Theology*, p. 61.

20 Hwa Yung, *Mangoes or Bananas? The Quest for an Authentic Asian Christian Theology* (Oxford: Regnum, 1997), pp. 240–1.

21 James Allen, 'Banana, Coconut, and Twinkie', in *American Myths, Legends, and Tall Tales: An Encyclopedia of American Folklore*, ed. Christopher R. Fee and Jeffrey B. Webb (Santa Barbara, CA: Greenwood, an Imprint of ABC-CLIO, 2016), pp. 74–6.

22 Lee, *Doing Asian American Theology*, p. 65.

23 Chan, *Grassroots Asian Theology*, p. 24.

24 https://ecclesialfutures.org.

25 Steve Taylor, email from author, 24 March 2024. Used with permission.

26 Lee, *Doing Asian American Theology*, p. 170.

27 Lee, *Doing Asian American Theology*, pp. 170–71.

28 Lee, *Doing Asian American Theology*, p. 71.

29 Lee, *Doing Asian American Theology*, p. 65.

30 Kwan, *Postcolonial Resistance and Asian Theology*, p. 61.

31 Sadiri Joy Tira and Juliet Lee Uytanlet, eds, *A Hybrid World: Diaspora, Hybridity, and Missio Dei* (Littleton, CO: William Carey Publishing, 2020).

32 https://lausanne.org/gathering/hybridity-diaspora-and-missio-dei-exploring-new-horizons-consultation.

33 Hannah Rasmussen, 'The Role of Bicultural People in the Missio Dei: Creating a Model from Bicultural Bible Characters', *Missiology: An International Review* 50, no. 1 (September 2021), pp. 78–90.

34 James Bennett Pritchard, ed., *Ancient Near Eastern Texts Relating to the Old Testament* (Princeton, NJ: Princeton University Press, 1974), p. 141.

35 Lee, *Doing Asian American Theology*, pp. 173–4.

36 Lee, *Doing Asian American Theology*, p. 20.

37 Lee, *Doing Asian American Theology*, p. 179.

38 Lee, *Doing Asian American Theology*, p. 182.

39 This is the story as it was passed down to me by my father. Among my wider family there is discussion as to the accuracy of some of the details. There is

a theory that the reason my grandfather ended up in the UK and not the USA is because of the Chinese Exclusionary Act that was only repealed in 1943. There are also stories that he first settled in Cuba.

40 'Archbishop Justin Welby's remarks during Windrush debate at General Synod', 11 February 2020, https://www.archbishopofcanterbury.org/speaking-writing/speeches/archbishop-justin-welbys-remarks-during-windrush-debate-general-synod.

41 Lee, *Doing Asian American Theology*, p. 24.

42 Lee, *Doing Asian American Theology*, p. 178.

43 Choy, *Ancestral Feeling*, p. 24.

44 Choy, *Ancestral Feeling*, p. 24.

45 Choy, *Ancestral Feeling*, p. 22.

46 Lee, *Doing Asian American Theology*, p. 199.

47 Choy, *Ancestral Feeling*, p. 24.

48 Madeleine Davies, 'Tea House brings together Chinese-heritage clergy', *The Church Times*, 18 August 2021, https://www.churchtimes.co.uk/articles/2021/20-august/news/uk/tea-house-brings-together-chinese-heritage-clergy.

49 http://www.theteahouse.org.

50 'Ministry Statistics 2020' (The Church of England, July 2021), p. 21, https://www.churchofengland.org/sites/default/files/2021-07/ministry-statistics-2020-report-final.pdf.

51 Willie James Jennings, *The Christian Imagination: Theology and the Origins of Race* (New Haven, CT: Yale University Press, 2010), p. 9.

52 Rather amazingly, the Chinese name 甄英深 that I was christened with when I was 100 days old translates into English to mean 'Deeply British'. This is the name with which I was called forward at my ordination exactly 100 years after my grandfather was naturalized in the UK, which in turn occurred in my 40th year.

6

Beyond the Lion Rock Spirit: A New Expression of British Hong Kongese Christianity

CALIDA CHU

'Lion Rock, Hong Kong, viewed from Lung Cheung Road. In the foreground is the Chuk Yuen Estate, a public housing estate in Kowloon.' Credit: Malcolm Koo, https://commons.wikimedia.org/wiki/File:Lion_Rock,_viewing_from_Lung_Cheung_Road_(Hong_Kong).jpg, under CC BY-SA 4.0 license.

The Lion Rock Spirit implies hard work, resilience and collegiality. This is the migrant mentality inherited from those who moved from mainland China to Hong Kong in the mid-twentieth century.[1] Due to the popularity of the Hong Kong TV show *Below the Lion Rock* (獅子山下 1972), which depicts the life of grassroots migrants living in the Wang Tau Hom Resettlement Area in the 1970s,[2] the Lion Rock mountain, situated between Kowloon and New Territories, symbolizes the Hong Kong spirit of working hard to overcome all adversity.[3]

During the mass migration of Hong Kongese in the 2020s, many carried this mentality again as they settled in their country of destination, such as the United Kingdom, Canada and Australia. Against this backdrop, Hong Kong Christian migrants have attempted to understand their experience through biblical themes, such as the Israelites' exodus from Egypt, and have even labelled themselves as the 'exodus'.[4]

To this end, I propose the phenomenon of 'British Hong Kongese Christianity', which navigates the in-betweenness when moving to new lands because of better opportunities, living environments and, most importantly, belief – the belief that holds them together that God is with them in the midst of any adversity they may face in their new homes. The type of Christianity I propose is distinguished from that of the earlier waves of migrants, who may not identify themselves as Hong Kongese but rather as British Chinese in general. The strong affirmation of Hong Kongese identity is important when discussing this phenomenon.

Throughout the chapter there are three motifs to illustrate my arguments for the emergence of British Hong Kongese Christianity: (1) theology of migration; (2) the book of Numbers; and (3) the Lion Rock Spirit. Theology of migration is employed as the main method to understand the migrants' situation theologically. The book of Numbers, rather than the book of Exodus, is chosen as the biblical text to help comprehend the in-betweenness of the life of Hong Kong migrants. The Lion Rock Spirit is the continuation of the migrant identity as well as the ethos for living in the new land.

The chapter first lays out the framework of theology of migration when considering the Hong Kongese experience in the United Kingdom. Employing Peter Phan's approach, it follows the three steps of theology of migration – namely the socioanalytic mediation, the hermeneutical mediation and the practical mediation, all of which reflect on the *Sitz im Leben* of Hong Kong migrants in the United Kingdom. I argue that a theology of migration for Hong Kong migrants in the United Kingdom in the 2020s must acknowledge the changing sociopolitical situation in contemporary Hong Kong, such as the status of migrants, mental health issues caused by both migration and social events experienced in Hong Kong, and Hong Kongese concerns for justice. These are the major components in British Hong Kongese Christianity and will be ongoing issues that both clergy and laity must focus on in order to serve new Hong Kong migrants.

Theology of migration

A theology of migration is an attempt to understand God's work in the midst of migratory movements – whether temporary or permanent, voluntary or forced – of individuals and groups of people crossing territorial boundaries.[5] Theology of migration as a discipline tends to concern itself with forced migration such as that of refugees and to ponder the events occurring near the US-Mexican border. While the country of destination is usually known as 'wilderness', here we employ Gemma Cruz's interpretation of the term to consider both the negative (a place out of human control) and the positive notes of this term (a place that nurtures the human spirit).[6] This chapter expands the categories of migration through the case study of Hong Kongese migration to the United Kingdom, including both forced migrations (refugees) and voluntary migrations (economic migrants), to highlight the complexity of the movement of people across continents.

The Vietnamese American theologian Peter C. Phan suggests that a theology of migration should be developed in three steps: (1) socio-analytic mediation, which examines the migrants' sociopolitical situations; (2) hermeneutical mediation, which reflects what God and Scripture say about migration experiences; and (3) practical mediation, which offers pragmatic suggestions to and for migrants.[7]

While employing Phan's theological method, I want to highlight two points when applying it to migration scenarios. First, migration experiences vary from person to person, or generation to generation. There can be several factors that legitimate or devalue someone's choice to migrate, such as job satisfaction, children's adaptation to new schools, and marital changes.

Second, although the hermeneutical method may stay the same, individuals' understanding of Scripture can vary based on their different sociopolitical situations. This is not to deny the authority of Scripture; instead, the renewed understanding shows that the Holy Spirit leads God's people to understand God's guidance and presence through God's Word (1 Corinthians 12.7–11). The wisdom and knowledge informed and instructed by the Word of God illustrate God's constant care in different phases of life.

Socioanalytic mediation: the Lion Rock spirit

Hong Kongese are experienced in migration. During the mid-twentieth century, many citizens of South China were forced to migrate to Hong Kong due to the sociopolitical turbulence in mainland China.[8] Many farmers in established villages in New Territories, Hong Kong, could not compete for jobs with this large influx of refugees. They took advantage of the British Nationality Acts between 1948 and 1981 to move to the United Kingdom for better job opportunities and arrived at the same time as the Windrush generation,[9] along with other ethnic-Chinese immigrants from Malaysia and Singapore.[10] Most of them came to the United Kingdom to become chefs in Chinese restaurants, where they were not required to have good English communication skills.[11] In other words, this generation of migrants consisted mostly of economic migrants who filled the Chinese-speaking job market at the time.

Following that, another major wave of Hong Kongese migrated to the Global North in the late 1980s due to two major political events: the confirmation of the 1984 Sino-British Declaration, which approved Hong Kong's return to China as a special administrative region (SAR) in 1997, and the 1989 Tiananmen Square Protests, which led to massive bloodshed in Beijing and intensified Hong Kongese fear of the Communist Party of China.[12] The British government accepted the Hong Kong colonial government's British Nationality Selection Scheme to grant British citizenship to 50,000 households.[13] Originally intended to give people the confidence to remain in Hong Kong, it instead provided a new opportunity for elites to move outside of Hong Kong.

The implementation of National Security Law, following the 2014 Umbrella Movement and the 2019 anti-extradition law protests, triggered yet another wave of migration; however, the migrant identity is more complex than it was in the 1960s and 1980s. The current migrant wave consists of a mixture of refugees and economic migrants. The former have been politically persecuted because of their involvement in the Hong Kong Protests, while the latter, consisting of a mixture of individuals, couples and families with young children, moved to the United Kingdom due to their dissatisfaction with the government and their desire to find a better education system for their next generation. A more sensitive approach to pastoral care is essential depending on the different statuses of migrants.

The brief history of Hong Kongese migration reflects what the Hong Kong sociologist Wong Siu-lun terms 'the refugee mentality'.[14] Not all Hong Kong migrants fall under the UN's (2024) definition of being refugees due to 'feared persecution, conflict, generalized violence' that requires international protection, but one may argue that this kind of mentality is inherited from their previous generations who moved to Hong Kong due to civil war or the cultural revolution in mid-twentieth-century China. For Wong, these Hong Kong migrants take an instrumental approach towards nationality; that is, they perceive nationality as a travel document, rather than having any emotional attachment or loyalty to the nation itself. The Lion Rock Spirit is undoubtedly derived from this kind of refugee mentality: because of the lack of social support and economic capital, migrants have to rely on each other. While the new migrant wave may not experience this lack of economic capital, it is likely that they long for the consolidation of cultural identity, because most feel that Hong Kong is disappearing because of various political events.[15]

In the new phase of life, Hong Kong migrants may have different levels of culture shock that determine the way they interact with the contact culture and their first culture: they may choose to assimilate to the British culture, reject it or integrate Hong Kong culture into it.[16] They may also consider 'deculturating' themselves; that is, denying Hong Kongness while also not accepting the new culture.[17] Yang Fenggang's notion of adhesive identity about Chinese American Christians may facilitate our discussion here.[18] Yang considers there are three major patterns of identity integrations among Chinese American Christians: fragmentary integration, fusive integration and adhesive integration. Fragmentary integration suggests that a person maintains a dominant identity while adopting certain values or lifestyles from the other culture. Fusive integration implies that a person blends different cultures together and brings out distinct characteristics from these cultures. Adhesive integration seems for Yang to be the ideal one,[19] with the person 'adding multiple identities together without necessarily losing any particular one'. Since most Hong Kongese moving to the United Kingdom in the late 2010s era have been first-generation migrants, I perceive that most of them are going through fragmentary integration – while some of them go to churches, it can be that they want to join a Chinese community and not necessarily acknowledge themselves as Christians. Fusive and adhesive integration may come along when these migrants stay longer in the United Kingdom, and should be an observable pattern in their next generation. Whatever stage they and the Christian community are in, it is important to acknowledge these struggles and find an equilibrium that both guests and hosts are comfortable with.

Hermeneutical mediation: God-on-the-move in the book of Numbers

In the Pentateuch, God accompanies the Israelites on their move out of Egypt and guides them as they face different challenges in life. Christian scholars of Hong Kongese migration tend to centre their hermeneutical interpretation on the book of Exodus, where the Israelites begin to leave Egypt. While the book of Exodus pinpoints the reason why the Israelites moved out of Egypt, the shortcoming of focusing on the starting point of migration is that it ignores the fact that migration is not just about the flight arriving at the country of destination; it is more about settling in the new land – finding a new church, learning a new language and acquiring a new set of social skills. As such, I prefer to use the book of Numbers to introduce the concept of God-on-the-move, where God shows God's guidance and continuous presence in various stages of life, in order to ponder migrants' identity both as Christians and as Hong Kongese who will no longer return to their country of origin. The covenantal relationship between God and God's people in the book of Numbers affirms Hong Kongese migrants in the United Kingdom, that their obedience and response to God's calling can be perceived as an active fulfilment of this reciprocal relationship.

The advantage of employing hermeneutical mediation is, as Phan indicates, that:

> the worlds *behind* and *of* the text project a world *in front of* the text, that is, a new way of being and acting in the world which we have to *appropriate* in our lives. Only then are we transformed by the meaning and truth of the text; only then will the interpreting process come to full fruition: from exegesis to criticism to hermeneutics.[20]

Chinese Bible studies tend to emphasize the worlds *behind* and *of* the text but not as much the world *in front of* the text, as if our present life is not as significant as the past. But I should stress that application is as important as learning about the past, and this should be the ethos of all kinds of hermeneutics.

Those familiar with the book of Numbers know that the book itself is beyond numbers, which we get from the Greek name adopted in the Septuagint, because it tells the story of the Israelites *in the wilderness*, the original name of this book in Hebrew. It describes God's guidance for God's people while they are on the move.[21] The rules about rituals and different roles among the tribes are proofs of God's care. The numbers are testimonies to the Israelites implementing God's Word in their migrant life. The Israelites left Egypt to escape economic and political subservience and they sought a better life when they arrived at the land of Canaan. In the midst of all these movements, God of the struggle is with God's people, journeying with them in the new land.[22]

In the first major sections of Numbers (1.1—9.14), God brings order to the constantly changing life of the Israelites and instructs them on how to worship Godself through the setting up of a movable tent and the practice of various rituals. Migrants moving to a new country understandably seek stability. God, who is on the move with God's people, is the source of comfort for migrants, and the church community is their extended family in the new land. Weekly worship in a new country allows them to adapt to an orderly schedule similar to that of their country of origin, while committing to a church community helps them consolidate their sense of identity not only as people of God but also as members of local society.

This sense of belonging cannot be replaced by numbers – in other words, material possessions. Having lived in a capitalistic society, Hong Kong migrants are obsessed with numbers – for example, good postal codes for their new homes, expensive food to show off on social media and new jobs to demonstrate their earning ability. People sometimes try to falsely substitute these numbers for the security provided by God.[23] God does not care about these numbers, nor should clergy and the followers of Jesus.

The Israelites' division of labour in Numbers also illustrates the diversity of God's gifts to God's people (1 Corinthians 12). Those who served in the tent included different groups of people with different duties, such as heavy lifting, handiwork and caring for holy objects (Numbers 3—4). As white-collar workers are the majority in Hong Kong society, some Hong Kongese, including migrants, look down on blue-collar workers because they assume their duties are insignificant.[24] But these seemingly insignificant tasks and unwanted duties keep a society and a church functioning. In the summer of 2022, Edinburgh had a long bin strike, as street cleaners protested their low salaries. The streets were full of rubbish and became quite smelly in the midst of the Fringe Festival.[25] Hong Kongese tend to count numbers too much and look down on people with low incomes but it is exactly these essential workers who keep our lives pleasant – not to mention that many Hong Kong migrants have joined the blue-collar workforce because they cannot get work in their previous industries.[26] We all have different gifts to contribute to the Kingdom of God. It is unhelpful to imply or state that we are better than others, judging and depersonalizing each other based on numbers. We can all serve God in the new land through the diverse gifts God has given us, by serving in church, volunteering in the community and performing our daily jobs.

Practical mediation: imago Dei Migratoris (the image of God the Migrant)

As the children of God, we are all created in the *imago Dei* (the image of God). Both Christians and non-Christians carry God's image. But the difference is that we Christians know that we have a responsibility to be what God calls us to be, through acts such as loving our neighbours (Mark 12.28–34). This act of love can be realized through hospitality, which is heavily emphasized in the literature on theology of migration. When Christians offer gestures of welcome, we do it for Jesus (Matthew 25.40).

The large influx of Hong Kong migrants in the United Kingdom implies that the hosts will welcome both Christians and non-Christians. A recent survey of Hong Kong BN(O) migrants shows that 38.7 per cent of new migrants experienced social isolation, while 15 and 10.9 per cent of those surveyed considered themselves to have social anxiety or depression respectively.[27] Small welcoming gestures can make a big difference as they adjust to their new lives in the United Kingdom.

As the book of Numbers reminds us that we should not judge newcomers by numbers, welcoming gestures should not be directly linked to the state of the faith journey of our guests, which determines the frequency with which they volunteer in church and the amount of their offerings. Likewise, the sort of welcome given to non-Christians should also be given to clergy migrants,[28] who encounter similar difficulties as migrants and do not always receive the support from churches due to their seniority as pastoral leaders before. Among some well-established Chinese diasporic churches there are hidden rules that pastors who migrate to new areas should always seek approval from 'historical' Chinese churches before they establish new churches; otherwise they will be condemned for stealing sheep.[29] Clergy who join Chinese migrant churches will not always steal sheep; instead, they may be traumatized by different sociopolitical events in Hong Kong and choose to stop working as pastoral leaders for healing, or the job supply in Chinese migrant churches may simply be insufficient.[30] This idea of stealing sheep reminds me of my working experience in churches in Southern California in the 2010s. In those days, since migrant numbers were quite stable, clergy focused excessively on where the sheep were stolen from and how they could take them back. God does not judge or reward pastoral leaders based on the number of attendees at their churches. As stated in the parable of the faithful servant (Matthew 25.14–30), we are all given different talents to serve God in various ways.

In the light of political events in Hong Kong and the change in the life cycle of new migrants, the practice of our emotional labour is as important as ever. Emotional labour refers to the regulation of one's personal emotions and the management of others' emotions.[31] As pastoral leaders, we are perceived as attentive to others' emotions as part of our job expectations, regardless of our true feelings.[32] Due to the pandemic and numerous political events, it can be difficult to walk the extra mile for others' needs. However, we are all on this journey together and no one should practise this labour alone. This is why a Christian community is important for the development of our spirituality as well as for those we welcome. Understanding the pain of our sheep and providing places for healing is part of our duty as clergy.[33]

In Chinese Christian culture, especially among clergy, we are taught to serve God 'more', as if the more work we do the more God loves and rewards us. This is a rather Chinese mindset – your performance determines your self-value,[34] and you are only loved when you work hard. Therefore the life of clergy is filled with tasks, evangelistic tasks specifically, to prove you love God enough. Since the care of newcomers cannot be quantified, sometimes we forget that welcoming others is also part of God's ministry, even though these new migrants may not attend your church in the end, and the time you spend welcoming migrants cannot always be recorded as happening on your shift.

Pushing forward Phan's concept of *Deus Migrator* (God the Migrant),[35] I would like to reflect on the responsibilities of being the *imago Dei Migratoris* (the image of God the Migrant). In the book of Numbers, God asks the Israelites to establish a community through rituals, diverse services and various social rules, to illustrate that they are different from the Canaanites and that they are of God. These actions do not happen only after they have settled but rather continuously develop while they are on the move. The service of God does not happen only after a new church plant has functioning Sunday worship with three Sunday Schools; the service of God does not start only after new migrants buy houses or move out of Airbnbs; the service of God does not begin only after migrants become British citizens and have perfect British accents. The service of God starts right after the confirmation of becoming a follower of Christ, whether one is in Hong Kong or the United Kingdom.

Whatever roles we have in church or in British society, our responsibility is to reflect God's image to those around us. Hard work, resilience and collegiality are great, but as the children of God the Migrant, our goal is to point those around us to God, and our actions should be determined by this telos. We are created in the image of God the Migrant. We are of God in this new land.

A new expression of British Hong Kongese Christianity

'Arthur's Seat, Edinburgh, viewed from Pollock Halls, a student housing complex.' Credit: David Monniaux, https://commons.wikimedia.org/wiki/File:Edinburgh_Arthur_Seat_dsco6165.jpg, under CC BY-SA 3.0 license.

Culture is not static because it responds to and evolves with sociopolitical situations. Hence the cultures and experiences of Hong Kong migrants in the 2020s do not mirror those of the 1960s. A new expression of British Hong Kongese Christianity is essential to reflect the challenges and theological developments of the twenty-first century. As such, the Lion Rock Spirit, the migrant mentality that sustained Hong Kongese through adversity, should also be renewed and re-evaluated.

Since the migrant wave in the late 2010s, Hong Kong migrants have tried to give nicknames to different landmarks in the United Kingdom, including the picturesque Arthur's Seat in Edinburgh. Nowadays, new Hong Kong migrants in Edinburgh call it the 'British Lion Rock'.[36] To me, this is nostalgia. The act of naming landmarks in the United Kingdom represents the longing for their homeland, which some of them cannot return to due to persecution.

Those familiar with the history of the Hong Kong Protests have probably heard about the 'Hong Kong Spiderman'. In 2017 this pro-democratic activist hung a banner on the Lion Rock to promote democracy in Hong Kong. He bought a cheap Spiderman outfit from Shum Shui Po, a grassroots neighbourhood in Hong Kong, to represent his distaste for capitalism and his talent for climbing on the hills. He stated: 'The values like hard work and mutual help [in Lion Rock Spirit] are good but we need to build on them, to add a system that protects the disadvantaged and a level playing-ground that ensures fair rewards for that hard work. What we need is a new kind of justice.'[37]

In the past, Hong Kongese were too occupied with numbers – higher salaries, bigger properties and greater numbers of church attendees. In this new wave of migration, a higher calling can be seen. This wave of migrants focuses not only on bread and butter but also on a sense of justice, a calling in their journey of life, and a telos that is motivated by their belief in God and their determination to do what is right in this new land.

While not undermining the contribution of the Hong Kong migrants in the mid-twentieth century, who were instrumental in defining Chinese culture in the United Kingdom and largely represented East Asians before 2020,[38] a lived Christianity should reflect the everyday life and concerns of the believers. In the past, migrants' focus may have been on God's material provision because of the scarcity of economic capital; in 2025 the focus can be on social responsibility, identity construction, and even healing from the social turbulence in their country of origin. This will be the beginning of acknowledging the Hong Kong migrants' sociopolitical experience and reflecting on how they can continue to witness to God in their new lives.

Walking through the wilderness with *Deus Migrator*

The struggle of defining oneself in a foreign country is real. Through encountering other cultures, one may realize who one is or is not. The rise of Hong Kongese identity can be a defence mechanism.[39] Indeed, the consolidation of certain identities sometimes results from the rejection of others, as with Brexit, during which the leave voters maintained a stronger English identity than the remain voters.[40] It is clear that Hong Kong migrants embrace their Hong Kongese identity, but this raises questions about which period of Hong Kong history they connect with, as well as the definition of Hong Kongness. For some Hong Kong migrants, the 2010s era is the real Hong Kong, while the previous generation may consider that the 1980s illustrate the best characteristics of Hong Kong.

Another famous Hong Kong TV show, *The Good, The Bad And The Ugly* (網中人 1979), squarely depicts the dichotomy between new migrants and settlers. Ching Chan (程燦) is a new migrant from mainland China who knows nothing about Hong Kong culture but flees to Hong Kong for upward economic mobility; his brother Ching Wai (程緯) is a Hong Kong-born university graduate who symbolizes a successful Hong Kong citizen of the era. Due to the popularity of the show, 'Ah Ching' (阿燦), Ching Chan's nickname, is used to refer to any plebeian who recently moved to Hong Kong.[41] The different portrayals of migrants in Hong Kong's TV shows illustrate that migrants do not always have a positive image among the Hong Kongese. The migrant identity is continually constructed through the social events of an era. What seems to be a positive move at one time can be interpreted as 'utilizing resources' in another period.[42]

As a Hong Kongese who has lived in the United Kingdom for over a decade, I undoubtedly trust that new Hong Kong migrants can bring the renewed Lion Rock Spirit to work hard in the new land, while also focusing on justice because of recent sociopolitical events in Hong Kong. The type of justice does not have to be limited to Hong Kong political affairs; instead, recent campaigns from Hong Kong migrants show that they can organize fundraising for British citizens and even Ukraine refugees.[43] Establishing a new routine in a new country is hard, but as the ever-caring God was by the Israelites' side in the book of Numbers, so God goes with Hong Kong migrants who are navigating life with *Deus Migrator*.

The point here is not to get rid of the image of 'Ah Ching' as a new migrant but to discern what works best in the new land as Hong

Kongese and children of God. As our beloved Hong Kong Spiderman says: 'We can find Lion Rocks everywhere, each of us can even be a Lion Rock.'[44] In this land full of locally produced milk and honey, may you, as a recent migrant to the United Kingdom, be a Lion Rock who is concerned with matters beyond the material. May you be the image of God the Migrant – when the people in this land see you, may they know that you are of God and with God.

Notes

1 Hong Kong is known as a migrant city with a diverse population. Many of its inhabitants came from South China and South Asian countries after it became a British colony in 1842. For details, see Zhang Shuangqing 張雙慶 and Shi Ruixin 施瑞鑫, 'Yimin chengshi yu Huaqiao wenhua' 移民城市與華僑文化 ['Migrant City and Overseas Chinese Culture'], *Xianggang Wenhua Daolun* 香港文化導論 [*Introduction to Hong Kong Culture*], ed. Wang Guohua 王國華 (Hong Kong: Chung Hwa Book Company, 2014), pp. 232–40.

2 The Resettlement Area symbolizes the living conditions of migrants moving to Hong Kong in the 1960s. For details, see Ko Tim-keung 高添強, 'Zhuixun gong wu de fazhan guiji' 追尋公屋的發展軌跡 ['Tracing the Development of Public Housing'], *Wenhua hulu* 文化葫蘆 [*Hulu Culture*] (2013), https://www.hadplushuluhk.org/y2-f1, accessed 15.08.2023.

3 For a partial translation of the song 'Below the Lion Rock' (1979) associated with the TV show, see Renie Choy, '"獅子山下, Below the Lion Rock": Historian Renie Chow Choy's Response to the Monument to Sir Harry Smith Parkes (1828–1885), by Sir Thomas Brock RA, post 1885', *Pantheons: Sculpture at St Paul's Cathedral (c.1796–1916)*, 2023, https://pantheons-st-pauls.york.ac.uk/voice/renie-chow-choy/, accessed 3.06.2024.

4 'Xianggang ren chu aiji ji' 香港人出埃及記 [Hong Kongese Exodus], *Facebook*, https://www.facebook.com/groups/899777123738890/, accessed 16.09.2023; Au Ka-lun 區家麟, 'Xianggang ren·chu Aiji ji' 香港人·出埃及記 [Hong Kongese: Exodus], *Chao chi* 潮池 [*Tide Pool*] (12 August 2019), https://web.archive.org/web/20220413022432/https://aukalun.blogspot.com/2019/08/blog-post_12.html.

5 Elaine Padilla and Peter C. Phan, 'Introduction', in *Contemporary Issues of Migration and Theology*, ed. Elaine Padilla and Peter C. Phan (New York: Palgrave Macmillan, 2013), p. 2.

6 Gemma Cruz, *An Intercultural Theology of Migration: Pilgrims in the Wilderness* (Leiden: Brill, 2010).

7 Peter C. Phan, '*Deus Migrator*—God the Migrant: Migration of Theology and Theology of Migration,' *Theological Studies* 77, no. 4 (2016), pp. 845–68.

8 Eppie Yuk-ming Wong, 'The Social Participation of the Hong Kong Churches, 1966–1997', PhD diss., Trinity Evangelical Divinity School, 2006.

9 Yip Ching-sze 葉靖斯, 'Xianggang BNO yimin chao: zhan hou Gang ren lici "zou chuqu" de yinyou' 香港BNO移民潮：戰後港人歷次「走出去」的因由 ['The Hong Kong BNO Migration Wave: The Reasons for Why Hong Kongese

Kept "Going Out" after World War II'], *BBC News (Chinese)* (1 February 2021), https://www.bbc.com/zhongwen/trad/world-55874253.

10 Gregor Benton and Edmund Terence Gomez, *The Chinese in Britain, 1800–Present: Economy, Transnationalism, Identity* (Basingstoke: Palgrave Macmillan, 2008), pp. 41–2.

11 Hugh D. R. Baker, 'Branches all Over: The Hong Kong Chinese in the United Kingdom', in *Reluctant Exiles? Migration from Hong Kong and the New Overseas Chinese*, ed. Ronald Skeldon (London: Routledge, 1995), pp. 293–303.

12 For detailed figures on Hong Kongese migrating to the global North in the late 1980s, see Ronald Skeldon, 'Hong Kong in an International Migration System', in *Reluctant Exiles? Migration from Hong Kong and the New Overseas Chinese*, ed. Ronald Skeldon (London: Routledge, 1995), pp. 21–51.

13 The National Archives, 'The British Nationality (Hong Kong) (Selection Scheme) Order 1990', SI1990/2292, *UK Legislation* (20 November 1990), https://www.legislation.gov.uk/uksi/1990/2292/made.

14 Wong Siu-lun, 'Emigration and Stability in Hong Kong', *Asian Survey* 32, no. 10 (Oct. 1992), pp. 930–1.

15 Ackbar Abbas, *Hong Kong: Culture and the Politics of Disappearance* (Minneapolis, MN: University of Minnesota Press, 1997); The Initium 端傳媒, 'Xiaoshi de Xianggang' 消失的香港 ['Disappearing Hong Kong'] (1 July 2021), https://theinitium.com/project/20210701-hongkong-culture-city-disappearance/.

16 Catherine Collier, Alejandro E. Brice and Geraldine V. Oades-Sese, 'Assessment of Acculturation', in *Multicultural Handbook of School Psychology: An Interdisciplinary Perspective*, ed. Giselle B. Esquivel, Emilia C. Lopez and Sara G. Nahari (Abingdon: Routledge, 2017), pp. 354–66.

17 Dinesh Bhugra and Matthew A. Becker, 'Migration, Cultural Bereavement and Cultural Identity', *World Psychiatry* 4, no. 1 (February 2005), p. 21.

18 Yang Fenggang, *Chinese Christians in America: Conversion, Assimilation, and Adhesive Identities* (University Park, PA: Pennsylvania State University Press, 1999).

19 Yang, *Chinese Christians in America*, p. 185.

20 Peter C. Phan, 'Betwixt and Between: Doing Theology with Memory and Imagination', in *Journeys at the Margin: Toward an Autobiographical Theology in American-Asian Perspective*, ed. Peter C. Phan and Jung Young Lee (Collegeville, MN: The Liturgical Press, 1999), p. 130; emphasis original.

21 Philip J. Budd, *Numbers*, Word Biblical Commentary 5 (Edinburgh: Thomas Nelson, 1984), pp. xvii–xxxii.

22 Cruz, *An Intercultural Theology of Migration*, pp. 272–9.

23 According to *The Telegraph*, Hong Kongese have become the highest percentage of overseas property buyers in August 2023, both for buy-to-let and self-ownership. See Ruby Hinchliffe, 'Surge in Hong Kongers buying up British homes', *The Telegraph* (17 August 2023), https://www.telegraph.co.uk/money/property/buying-selling/influx-hong-kongers-buy-up-british-homes/.

24 According to the Hong Kong government's statistics, 71.1 per cent of Hong Kong citizens were white collar in 2022. Census and Statistics Department, 'Quarterly Report on General Household Survey: October to December 2022', *Hong Kong Special Administrative Region* (February 2023), https://www.censtatd.

gov.hk/en/data/stat_report/product/B1050001/att/B10500012022QQ04B0100.pdf.

25 Paul Hutcheon and Kris Gourlay, 'Edinburgh bin worker strikes may be over as union suspends industrial action', *Edinburgh Live* (2 September 2022), https://www.edinburghlive.co.uk/news/edinburgh-news/edinburgh-bin-worker-strikes-over-24916558.

26 'Yi Ying Gang ren cong diceng zuo qi: bailing zhuan lanling, chu jingyan zuo tiaoban' 移英港人從低層做起 白領轉藍領 儲經驗作跳板 ['Hong Kong Migrants in the UK Work from the Bottom Level: White Collar Turns to Blue Collar, Gaining Experience to Jump to Other Jobs'], *Xingdao ribao* 星島日報 [*Sing Tao Daily*] (25 October 2022), https://bit.ly/3OAAgbG.

27 'Diaocha: jin si cheng yi Ying Gang ren xian shejiao guli, buzu 3% xiang huiliu Xianggang' 調查：近4成移英港人陷社交孤立 不足3%想回流香港 ['Survey: Around Forty Per Cent Hong Kong Migrants Experienced Social Isolation, Less Than Three Per Cent Want to Move Back to Hong Kong'], *Guang chuanmei* 光傳媒 [*Photon Media*] (23 August 2023), https://bit.ly/3tos1ih.

28 Ko See-man 高思憫, 'Wei you mu zhi ruhe jianshou zhaoming? Yi Ying mu zhe de zhengzha' 未有牧職如何堅守召命？移英牧者的掙扎 ['How to Sustain One's Calling When Not Working as Pastoral Staff? The Struggle of Pastor Migrants in the United Kingdom'], *Shidai luntan* 時代論壇 [*Christian Times*] (12 November 2021), https://bit.ly/3KR6fUf.

29 Ng Woon-sing 吳煥星 and Tin Tsz-fung 田子豐, 'Qiang yang shenxue' 搶羊神學 ['The Theology of Stealing Sheep'], interviewed by Au Chun-li 歐春麗 and Michael Chee-man Tang 鄧智文, *Shenxue yima gen* 神學姨媽根 [*Theological Period*] (1 June 2023), https://bit.ly/3OPdoWg.

30 Lai Tsz-wing 黎祉穎, 'Gang ren yimin chao xia Yingguo jiaohui de wei yu ji' 港人移民潮下英國教會的危與機 ['The Challenges and Opportunities of British Churches under the Waves of Hong Kongese Migration'], *Shidai luntan* 時代論壇 [*Christian Times*] (12 November 2021), https://bit.ly/44Bhlnr.

31 Arlie Russell Hochschild, *The Managed Heart: Commercialization of Human Feeling* (Berkeley, CA: University of California Press, 1983).

32 Gail Kinman, Obrene McFall and Joanna Rodriguez, 'The Cost of Caring? Emotional Labour, Wellbeing and the Clergy', *Pastoral Psychology* 60 (March 2011), pp.: 672–673, https://doi.org/10.1007/s11089-011-0340-0.

33 Steven L. Porter, 'Mentally Healthy and Healing Church: Spiritual Formation and Soul Care as Ecclesiology', *Journal of Spiritual Formation and Soul Care* 15, no. 1 (May 2022), pp. 3–5.

34 Chen Wei-Wen and Wong Yi-Lee, 'Chinese Mindset: Theories of Intelligence, Goal Orientation and Academic Achievement in Hong Kong Students', *Educational Psychology* 35, no. 6 (2015), pp. 714–25, https://doi.org/10.1080/01443410.2014.893559.

35 Peter C. Phan, 'God, the Beginning and the End of Migration: A Theology of God from the Experience and Perspective of Migrants', in *Christian Theology in the Age of Migration: Implications for world Christianity*, ed. Peter C. Phan (Lanham, MD: Lexington, 2020), pp. 123–4.

36 DJ Diary, 'Di yi ci zai Aidingbao xing shan, Aidingbao you ge Shizi Shan' 第一次在愛丁堡行山， 愛丁堡有個獅子山 ['First Time Hiking in Edinburgh,

Edinburgh has a Lion Rock'], *YouTube* (12 January 2022), https://youtu.be/mSpdddSAWOY?si=EHIBG_9ss3F4NvTf.

37 Chan Yuen, 'The new Lion Rock Spirit – how a banner on a hillside redefined the Hong Kong Dream', *Huffpost* (6 December 2017), https://www.huffpost.com/entry/the-new-lion-rock-spirit_b_6345212.

38 Note that Hong Kong-born residents were the second-largest East Asian group in England and Wales (32.5 per cent), while mainland Chinese were the largest (48.9 per cent). Census 2021, 'Country of Birth (Detailed)', *Office for National Statistics* (13 December 2022), https://www.ons.gov.uk/datasets/TS012/editions/2021/versions/1/filter-outputs/465d4ae7-f53e-4c59-a6dc-bd1491977c6d.

39 Lui Tai-lok 呂大樂, *Wu gai, maidan: yige shehui xue jia de Xianggang biji* 唔該，埋單：一個社會學家的香港筆記 ['Please, Pay the Bill: A Sociologist's Note About Hong Kong'] (Hong Kong: Oxford University Press, 2007), pp. 102–3.

40 Richard Ashcroft and Mark Bevir, 'Pluralism, National Identity and Citizenship: Britain after Brexit', *The Political Quarterly* 87, no. 3 (2016), pp. 355–9, https://doi.org/10.1111/1467-923X.12293.

41 Ma Kit-wai 馬傑偉 and Tsang Chung-kin 曾仲堅, *Yingshi Xianggang: shenfen rentong de shidai bianzou* 影視香港：身份認同的時代變奏 [*Hong Kong Films: The Changing Era of Identity*] (Hong Kong: Chinese University of Hong Kong, 2010), pp. 27–49.

42 See the label of grasshopper for mainland Chinese in the 2010s: He Guifen 賀桂芬, 'Xianggang shehui si lie: "huangchong" yu "zougou" de tanpai shike' 香港社會撕裂：「蝗蟲」與「走狗」的攤牌時刻 ['The Split of Hong Kong Society: The Breaking Point of "Grasshoppers" and "Running Dogs"'], *Tianxia zazhi* 天下雜誌 [*Commonwealth Magazine*] (30 September 2014), https://www.cw.com.tw/article/5061529.

43 The Chaser News 追新聞, 'Pujing qin Wu 1 nian zhuanti: canyu she yun bei Bu hou li Gang, BNO Gang ren zhu Wukelan nanmin andun Yingguo' 普京侵烏1年·專題：參與社運被捕後離港 BNO港人助烏克蘭難民安頓英國 [Special Issue of the Anniversary of Putin Invading Ukraine: BNO Hong Kongese Participated in the Social Movements, Arrested, and Left Hong Kong. Now They Helped Ukrainians Settle in the United Kingdom], *Zhui xinwen* 追新聞 [*The Chaser News*] (23 February 2023), https://bit.ly/49JpVTW.

44 Chan, 'The new Lion Rock Spirit'.

PART III

Re-imagining Community and Church

7

Beyond the Balance Sheet: A Ministry Reflection on Mainland Chinese Student Ministry in the UK

CANDY ZHANG

Introduction

A substantial influx of international students from mainland China arrives in the UK for higher education each year, and this number has been consistently growing for almost two decades.[1] As a result, Christian work focused on this demographic has become an important ministry in the UK among Chinese churches and Chinese Christian organizations, as well as other local churches and Christian organizations.

Currently there are three main types of student ministry groups: 1) church-affiliated student fellowships, which are often led by church pastoral staff or church-designated lay leaders; 2) independent campus fellowships, which are usually started by mission organizations and led by full-time student workers; and 3) student churches, which are missional communities consisting mainly of students. The size of each group can range from 10 to 50 students. Alongside these local student ministry groups, which may meet on a weekly basis, another aspect of mainland Chinese student ministry is national student conferences organized by Christian mission organizations such as the Chinese Overseas Christian Mission (COCM), which generally serve over 100 students at each event.[2]

The goals of most mainland Chinese student ministries are, first, to share the gospel, viewing this demographic as a vast mission field and an unreached people group and, second, to disciple and prepare them to return as missionaries to mainland China. Therefore this ministry holds strategic importance for mission to the Chinese diaspora in the UK as well as for mission to China through the returnees. This is one of the unique aspects of this ministry, especially when compared to

Chinese student ministry in the USA, which has had a significant impact on church development – many American Chinese churches started as campus fellowships or Bible study groups.[3] However, most mainland Chinese students in the UK do not settle in the UK after their studies; they do not follow the same trajectory as their American counterparts in evolving from campus fellowships to churches, nor do they continue to serve in British churches. Therefore the emphasis in the UK lies more on broader missiological endeavours.

In fact in the wider context of student ministry, overseas student ministry is considered crucial for global mission. Ideally, international students from a less-reached country would become Christians during their time abroad and return to their homeland, to make a positive contribution to their society as well as serving as an influential mission force. One example of this is Yiqi Mei, who converted to Christianity during his studies in the USA and later became an influential politician, physicist and educator in China in the early twentieth century. As president of Southwest United University during the Anti-Japanese War, his 'honesty, frugality, and generosity were highly respect'.[4] Duplicating such success and seizing the opportunity in the UK has been one of the key underlying motivations for many student workers.[5] However, in recent years, particularly after the Covid-19 pandemic, the landscape of the Chinese diaspora in the UK has been shifting, with a possible decline in the mainland Chinese student population and new waves of British National (Overseas) (BN(O)) immigrants from Hong Kong.[6] Consequently, the dynamics of Chinese diaspora ministry have been changing, especially in regards to strategic focus, mission priority and resource allocation.

This chapter grows out of my ministry reflection as someone who has been involved in mainland Chinese student ministry in the UK both in a local setting and in national level conferences and consultations since 2013 with COCM. It will suggest that churches and organizations in the UK engaging mainland Chinese students need to transcend the utilitarian mindset that now evaluates this ministry as having a low return on investment. Rather, a divine calling needs to be responded to: churches in the UK need to be a home for the students God brings into our midst.

A ministry with a low return on investment

Compared with other ministries, mainland Chinese student ministry is both costly and demanding. Due to the sheer number of students, a significant number of workers are required to meet their practical, emotional and spiritual needs. Since most students come to the UK for undergraduate or taught postgraduate studies, typically lasting a few years, the turnover rate for the ministry is exceptionally high. For example, in a typical mainland Chinese student fellowship, student workers would start welcoming new students at the beginning of the academic year and bid them farewell at the end of the following summer.

Within this short timeframe, student workers need to build and deepen relationships with students so that they can share the gospel, address each student's specific needs, solidify new converts' faith and prepare graduates for the transition from student to working life and from the UK to China. Building meaningful bonds within such a brief period requires an enormous investment of time and energy. Moreover, the programme content needs to cover evangelism, basic discipleship and transition preparation, which adds to the demanding nature of the ministry preparation for workers.[7] Furthermore, the high turnover rate means starting afresh each year, which drains the workers emotionally, with frequent farewells and relationship-building.

While having a team to share the workload is ideal, it remains a luxury for most mainland Chinese student fellowships due to the rarity of individuals capable of staying and committing to help the ministry. In the USA, where undergraduate studies span four years and master's programmes last two to three years, students of upper years can serve as assistants to student workers and help at the student fellowship by taking care of their juniors and contributing to the running of the fellowship. Unlike the situation in the USA, most taught postgraduate students in the UK graduate after one year, leaving almost no one available to assist the fellowship.

Moreover, student workers must keep up with the rapidly changing student culture, otherwise they may struggle to relate to the students. Not only do they need to understand the culture but they must also be quick to adapt to new communication methods, ideas and pop culture trends to effectively connect with and minister to students. This demands continuous curiosity to learn, creativity to respond and flexibility to adapt from student workers.

Financially, this ministry is both costly and demanding. Apart from regular gatherings such as evangelistic talks and Bible studies, other activities, such as meals, social activities and outings, are seen as a must to engage students, and this requires financial input. Additionally, it might be challenging for those with full-time jobs or family commitments to accommodate the rhythm of university student life, such as meeting up during the daytime, weekends and late nights. Therefore, employing full-time student workers may be essential for churches and Christian organizations, which means a significant cost. However, while non-Christian students will not contribute financially, Christian students may have limited means to tithe, easily resulting in a deficit for the ministry.

All the aforementioned factors – high turnover rate, rapid cultural changes and significant financial investment – contribute to the costly and demanding nature of this ministry. However, the return on investment seems to be rather low, as the perceived 'fruits' are few. First of all, the conversion rate is lower than the expectations of student workers. Although student ministry groups function well as social hubs, providing practical, emotional and social support, many students join the gatherings for reasons other than a genuine interest in Christianity. For example, events with fun activities and meals tend to draw larger crowds than more serious talks on Christianity and Bible studies, showing a preference for socializing over engaging with faith matters. Moreover, students who are interested in Christianity often grapple with various kinds of concerns, including traditional doubts about religion and science as well as postmodern thoughts like pluralism and relativism. Practical issues, such as the aspiration to find jobs in the Chinese government or state-owned companies and objections from family members, also deter students from coming to faith.

Even if students become Christians during their stay in the UK, it is difficult for many to keep their faith on returning home. Since Christianity is perceived by many Chinese students as intrinsically linked to Western culture and the English language,[8] adapting to a foreign environment for faith after converting to Christianity in the UK is challenging. Students who are used to a certain kind of worship in the UK may find, on returning to mainland China, that both state-sanctioned churches with the Three-Self Patriotic Movement and unregistered house churches are alien, which may result in a disconcerted feeling – some may feel that 'Songs were more old-fashioned or the language and behaviour more formal. In other cases prayers and preaching were *less* formal and more ad-hoc.'[9] While the mainland Chinese church environment acts as a push factor for these new converts to drift away from faith, the familiarity of their old lifestyle and environment acts as a pull factor for reverting to their previous ways. Also, as students transition to new life stages, such as pursuing career ambitions and starting a family, their motivation to continue pursuing the faith may diminish. Consequently, the retention rate is not ideal.[10]

For students who hold on to their faith after returning to China, they often struggle with the clash of competitive values and government restriction on religion, making it challenging to live out and share their faith with the wider community. At the societal level, there is limited freedom to explicitly share faith. Returnee Christians may participate in philanthropic activities such as volunteering at orphanages or contributing to non-profit organizations like the Red Cross but there will be very few opportunities to be involved in direct mission work and evangelistic outreach. Consequently, the impact on mission work in China, as hoped for in the strategic positioning of mainland Chinese student ministry in the UK, is small. The gospel may be shared within the confined interaction with family and close friends, rather than making broader social impact. In some cases, rather than having an evangelistic influence on family and friends, Chinese returnees may encounter pressure 'from parents who did not approve of church involvement and from parents or peers who regarded time spent in church as a distraction from the more important job of increasing earnings'.[11]

As shown above, while mainland Chinese student ministry in the UK may succeed in providing social support to and building friendships with students, it may not be as effective in direct forms of mission work such as evangelism and discipleship. If evaluated based on effectiveness, particularly the goal of evangelizing students during their time in the UK so that they might evangelize mainland China, the ministry may not meet expectations. Given the costly and demanding nature of the ministry and its undesirable outcomes, it may be considered a low return on investment ministry.

Mainland Chinese Student ministry at the crossroads

Despite the challenges and perceived low return on investment, for the past decade mainland Chinese student ministry has been considered an important ministry area, especially within Chinese churches and Chinese Christian organizations in the UK. However, in recent years, after the Covid-19 pandemic, various factors, including shifting political climates and evolving demographic trends, have prompted the need for a reassessment regarding resource allocation and strategic focus within the realm of Chinese Christian ministries: is mainland Chinese student ministry in the UK worth continuing?

The widely accepted view of mainland Chinese student ministry stresses its key strategic position in mission, especially in mission to China. Although the ministry may not yield immediate and tangible benefits for churches in the UK, these students could serve as key players in future mission works in China. Facing the vast number of students coming to the UK every year, it would be a wasted mission opportunity not to evangelize them. Moreover, Chinese Christian returnees could serve as a missionary force to evangelize the hard-to-reach areas in China. Therefore, mainland Chinese student ministry should definitely continue and also keep improving its effectiveness in response to solving the low return to investment issue.

For the past decade, the increasing number of students from mainland China has been one of the main drives behind the allocation of significant attention and ministry resources to this area, especially within Chinese churches and Chinese Christian organizations in the UK. However, the growing trend might come to a stop or even go in another direction. Before the Covid-19 pandemic there was a continual growth in numbers, but the landscape may change due to incidents of discrimination against Chinese and heightened political tensions between China and the West, which may hinder Chinese students from coming to the UK. Additionally, stricter immigration rules and dependant visa regulations in the UK may cause the UK to be a less popular destination for Chinese students planning to pursue overseas education.

With limited resources, it would be reasonable to consider adjusting the ministry focus if the numbers of mainland Chinese students drop, especially in the light of the influx of BN(O) immigrants from Hong Kong over the past few years, whose needs appear to be more urgent. Moreover, compared to transient students, the majority of whom will eventually leave permanently, BN(O) immigrants are more likely to have a substantial and long-term influence on local church development in the UK. Additionally, within Chinese churches, different views on politics and the Chinese government's Covid-19 policies have caused conflicts between Mandarin-speaking mainland Chinese and Cantonese-speaking Hong Kong Christians,[12] which call for necessary separate-language ministries and hence add more burdens on limited ministry resources. Given these factors, churches and Christian organizations may prefer to invest in this new emerging demographic over mainland Chinese students.

Valid concerns indeed arise when faced with a low return on investment, limited church resources and a new influx of needs that require support. Some may suggest exploring better ways to increase the effectiveness of existing ministry, thereby increasing the return on investment. However, what if, despite employing newer strategies, there is no perceived increase in fruits and the number of incoming students keeps dropping? Others might favour lowering the importance of mainland Chinese student ministry to reallocate resources for substantial long-term and more promising ministries, such as BN(O) ministry. Both approaches demonstrate an underlying pragmatic emphasis aimed at making the balance sheet of a certain ministry appear to be more fruitful regarding the investment in ministry effort. But is this the only criterion by which one decides to start, continue or stop a ministry?

Reasons for Mainland Chinese Student ministry in the UK

Not for the project but for the calling

Universities in the UK have welcomed a significant number of students from mainland China, a primary contributing factor here being the profitable return on investment. In comparison to local students, international students, including those from mainland China, generally need to pay double or triple the tuition fees of home students,[13] as well as paying for housing costs. Consequently, they are considered lucrative assets to the universities.[14] In addition, international students emerge as a strong consumption force during their stay in the UK, which brings economic benefits for the national economy.[15] Therefore it is not surprising that universities in the UK actively seek to attract students from mainland China for such promising economic benefits.

By contrast, as shown above, Christian ministries focusing on students from mainland China present a distinctly different picture, with very limited return on investment. From a utilitarian perspective, one might argue that the significance of Mandarin student ministry in the UK should be re-evaluated. However, unlike the profit-driven ethos prevalent in universities and secular society, the church should demonstrate its countercultural value system by making ministry decisions that extend beyond the utilitarian principle.

The determination of whether any ministry is worth the effort and investment should not be based on effectiveness or the quantity of fruits it bears. Instead, it needs to be assessed by how faithfully it responds to God's calling to serve a specific demographic – in this case, mainland Chinese students in the UK. Therefore, if a church or organization plans to continue Mandarin student ministry, they need to resist the temptation to measure the worth of their endeavours through the lens of utilitarian principles. While secular institutions like universities prioritize tangible returns on investment when dealing with mainland Chinese students, Christian ministries must be guided by their commitment to the divine calling entrusted to them by God.

Not as means to an end but as ends themselves

As presented in the previous section, strategic emphasis has been placed on student ministries targeting overseas populations, especially those from traditionally unreached or challenging-to-access regions such as mainland China. Instead of sending missionaries directly to these countries from the UK, churches and organizations aspire to evangelize and disciple mainland Chinese students during their time in the UK, with the aim of subsequently sending them back as missionaries to their home country. However, given the low retention rate and the limited observed influence of Christian returnees within their environments, this mission strategy appears to be ineffective, which makes some people question the validity of student ministry targeting mainland Chinese students.

Setting aside the discussion on the effectiveness of such a mission strategy, which regards the time mainland Chinese students are in the UK as a training period and mission mobilization opportunity, it also raises a serious ethical concern: the danger of instrumentalizing students as mere means to an end – namely, as instruments for missionizing mainland China – rather than recognizing them as ends in themselves. Karl Marx critiques the capitalist ideology that people are objectified and alienated as mere human resources for production, a sentiment that contributed to the Communist revolution in China. Ironically, regarding mainland Chinese students as potential missionaries to China could easily lead to a form of spiritual capitalism, objectifying and alienating individuals as tools for mission.

At the core of Christianity lies a relational understanding of the triune God. In Martin Buber's terms, Christianity should emphasize and encourage an I–Thou relationship instead of an I–It relationship. When a human being is reduced to a tool, the sacredness of his or her life as created uniquely in God's image is seriously violated. Therefore churches and organizations engaged in student ministry should always prioritize relational authenticity over utilitarian calculations, even for a notable cause such as world mission. Mainland Chinese students should not be treated as a faceless labour force that could be useful for potential missionary work in mainland China. It is essential for churches and Christian organizations to affirm each student's uniqueness and individuality and to build authenticity and loving relationships with each individual, ministering to their unique needs, irrespective of the perceived utility in a broader mission to China.

Being a home for the 'homeless'

Welcoming strangers and foreigners is deeply rooted in biblical mandates of hospitality. As a result, many churches and organizations actively engage in welcoming refugees, exemplified by initiatives such as Welcome Churches. Currently there are nearly 1,400 UK churches signed up to be part of the network committed to the mandate of hospitality to strangers and foreigners.[16] In comparison to refugees, the 'homelessness' experienced by mainland Chinese students is less visible yet equally poignant, because home does not merely refer to physical shelter but, more importantly, to a space marked by belonging and acceptance where individuals are welcomed unconditionally for who they are. In this context, mainland Chinese students can be defined as homeless on two levels.

First, living in a perpetual unsettled state makes Chinese students feel no sense of belonging. Within the Chinese culture and tradition, the notion of home holds profound significance as the centre of one's belonging and the ground for one's identity. Therefore, leaving their home for a foreign land doubtlessly shakes their sense of security and their understanding of identity. As shown in a case study involving 11 Chinese students who came to study as a group, despite having familiar fellow students in the same programme they still expressed feelings of isolation.[17] This sense of isolation was probably worsened in recent years by the impacts of the Covid-19 pandemic, including anti-Asian racism and xenophobia. According to research on Chinese students' experiences of racism during the Covid-19 pandemic in the UK, the phrase 'We are invisible' was used to describe their unwelcome and neglected condition.[18] This heightened sense of disorientation, fear and isolation might explain the mental health challenges faced by mainland Chinese students.[19]

Most immigrants experience an initial phase of feeling homeless before adapting to the new environment and eventually feeling settled, and this process normally requires a significant period of time.[20] Many mainland Chinese students come to the UK for postgraduate studies that typically last little longer than a year. Despite adapting to a new culture, the feeling of confusion, isolation and disconnection may be a natural stage for any immigrant. But the short duration of mainland Chinese students often leaves them in a perpetually unsettled state – in other words, in a perpetual homeless state, with hardly enough time to progress to the next stage in cultural adaptation.

Second, studying abroad transforms the concept of home into a conditional space where acceptance is granted based on academic success and parental approval, and this contributes to the homelessness experienced by mainland Chinese students. Raised in a culture that places high value on academic achievement and success, these students often bear the weight of family expectations. The previous one-child policy in China, which only came to an end in 2015, further adds pressure on individuals to succeed, not only for themselves but also for the honour of their families.

Despite living in a foreign land, physically distant from their families, many students live in the shadow of familiar expectations and pressures. Consequently, the home they left behind may no longer feel like home – their home no longer gives them a sense of belonging and unconditional acceptance and their re-entry into their home is contingent on their performance during their time studying abroad. In this sense, mainland Chinese students find themselves in a state of homelessness.

In response to these 'homeless' mainland Chinese students, churches and Christian organizations should serve as a home for them with unconditional love and acceptance, where these students need not conform to a certain cultural norm that is often expected in secular host cultural environments, or perform well with academic achievements as expected by their families in their home country. Rather, these should be places where students can authentically be themselves and find a sense of belonging, comfort and home. It is crucial that the warm embrace of home should never be contingent on the students' conversion to Christianity. Otherwise the church would no longer feel like home because religious conditions are imposed as the entry requirement for such a 'home'. Therefore a key motivation for mainland Chinese student ministries in the UK is to provide a home for the 'homeless' with unconditional love and hospitality, which should extend beyond evangelism and conversion.

Being a spiritual home

Besides offering unconditional acceptance and hospitality to mainland Chinese students, churches and Christian organizations in the UK serve as spiritual homes for those who find Christ during their time in the UK, as well as for existing Christian students. Although the number of converts may seem insignificant compared to the total mainland Chinese student population each year, the value of each new life born in Christ is beyond numerical measure. For those who encounter Christ and embrace Christianity during their time in the UK, churches and Christian organizations become their spiritual homes where these new Christians receive their initial exposure to Christian faith, Christian practices and Christian community. Despite the transient nature of these students' stay, the impact and importance of this Christian initiation period cannot be neglected, because it lays the foundation for their future faith journey in mainland China.

Given the fact that most students will return to China on graduation, the need to prepare them for their return holds a prominent position in mainland Chinese student ministry. On returning to China, these new Christians may face a sense of spiritual alienation, leaving behind their spiritual home where they were born in the UK. In this context, China, their home country, becomes a foreign land spiritually. Thus, in addition to helping new Christians walk the initial faith journey with essential discipleship, churches and Christian organizations need to go the extra mile – providing ongoing support and connections with former returnees to help new Christians adjust smoothly to their onwards faith journey in China until they find churches in China to be their spiritual home that gives them a sense of belonging. Nevertheless, churches in the UK still feel like home, because some returnees will call their current church in China their home church and the church in the UK where they became Christians their *niang jia* church (a Chinese concept referring to a married woman's parents' home).

For mainland Chinese students who are already Christians before coming to study in the UK, churches here play a pivotal role in welcoming them home into the global Christian community. Due to the unique societal circumstances and religious regulations in mainland China, Chinese Christians rarely have opportunities to connect with Christians from other churches. Therefore, for Christian students brought up in such environments, most of them lack exposure to other expressions of faith, resulting in a limited understanding of God, the Bible and Christianity. Studying in the UK provides mainland Chinese Christian students with a gateway to connecting with the wider Christian community, enriching their understanding of the faith.

Churches and Christian organizations in the UK should welcome these Chinese Christian students not as guests or visitors but as fellow family members within the same body of Christ. This means including them in the running of church ministries and being open to hearing their insights and experiences brought from their home churches in mainland China. The openness to reciprocal exchange and service is a key demonstration of fellowship and unity, reflecting the reality of the global church as one family.

To summarize, the significance of mainland Chinese student ministry extends beyond evangelism and discipleship programmes. It functions as a spiritual home for those who convert to Christianity during their time in the UK by supporting their initial growth in faith and their subsequent transition to the next step in mainland China. Additionally, it serves as a spiritual home for existing Chinese Christian students coming to the UK by embracing and including them in the global church family. Through this ministry, churches and Christian organizations in the UK not only nurture the spiritual growth of individual new Christians but also contribute to the unity and enrichment of the global Christian community.

Final thoughts

When talking about the Chinese diaspora in the UK, the focus often falls on immigrants, whether from mainland China, Hong Kong or South East Asia, and on children of these Chinese heritage immigrants. However, students from China are rarely mentioned due to the transient nature of their short stay in the country. Therefore, they are often seen and treated as guests or visitors because their final destination is China, not the UK.

This reflection aims to draw attention to this demographic, which constitutes a vast population that is sometimes neglected or presented as a faceless group. Each student's story and journey, not just their destination, is important. Their time in the UK, though short, is nevertheless a privilege for churches and Christian organizations in the UK to be part of. This chapter is not a thorough research study but merely represents a perspective from someone working in the front line of this ministry. It is hoped that this reflection could inspire future research to delve deeper into the stories and voices of these students, enriching the tapestry of Chinese Christianity in the UK.

Notes

1 According to the Higher Education Statistics Agency, the total number of students in higher education from mainland China for academic year 2021/2022 is 151,690. 'Where do HE students come from?', *Higher Education Statistics Agency*, 31 January 2023, available at https://www.hesa.ac.uk/data-and-analysis/students/where-from.

2 The information regarding fellowship type and size is mainly gathered from the annual Mandarin Student Ministry Consultation held by COCM. Examples of student conferences include COCM's annual Year-end Student Gospel Camp (https://www.cocm.org.uk/ministries-year-end-camps) and Easter Discipleship Student Camp (https://www.cocm.org.uk/ministries-easter-camp).

3 Su Wenfeng 蘇文峰, 'Beimei huaren jiaohui de jinxi he weilai' 北美华人教会的今昔和未来 ['The past, present, and future of Chinese churches in North America'], *Behold*, 26 January 2024, available at https://behold.oc.org/?p=61910. For more examples of the evolution of American Chinese churches, see Su Wenfeng 蘇文峰, ed., *Dayang bi'an de change: Meiguo huaren cha jing ban huigu yu zhanwang* 大洋彼岸的长河——美国华人查经班回顾与展望 [*The History of Chinese Bible Study Groups in America: Its Review and Outlook*] (Torrance, CA: Overseas Campus Ministries, 2015).

4 Stacey Bieler, 'Mei Yiqi', *Biographical Dictionary of Chinese Christianity*, available at https://bdcconline.net/en/stories/mei-yiqi, accessed 16.05.2024. For more examples, see Carol Lee Hamrin with Stacey Bieler, eds, *Salt and Light*, 3 vols (Eugene, OR: Pickwick Books, 2009–11).

5 In this chapter, I use 'student worker' as the common term to describe lay and ordained pastoral workers with focused ministry to mainland Chinese students.

6 The number of Chinese students fell to 11,630 for the first time in 2023 since 2014. John Morgan and Patrick Jack, 'UK's Chinese student decline could be "sign of diversification"', *Times Higher Education*, 29 August 2023, available at https://www.timeshighereducation.com/news/uks-chinese-student-decline-could-be-sign-diversification.

About 140,300 people arrived in the UK from Hong Kong under the BN(O) visa route between 2021 and 2023. National Statistics, 'Safe and legal (humanitarian) routes to the UK', *Gov.uk* (29 February 2024), https://www.gov.uk/government/statistics/immigration-system-statistics-year-ending-december-2023/safe-and-legal-humanitarian-routes-to-the-uk.

7 For information on yearly student fellowship planning, see publications from the 2017 and 2018 UK Mandarin Student Ministry Forums hosted by COCM.

8 Lin Ma, 'Religious Pursuits? Chinese International Students Encountering Christianity in Britain', *Journal of Contemporary Religion* 36, no. 33 (Nov. 2021), p. 410.

9 Deborah Dickson, 'Coming Home: A Study of Values Change among Chinese Postgraduates and Visiting Scholars who Encountered Christianity in the UK' (PhD thesis, University of Nottingham, 2013), p. 253; emphasis original.

10 Due to the difficulty of conducting surveys among the returnees in China, there is no concrete number available. Some estimate the retention rate is below 25 per cent.

11 Dickson, 'Coming Home', p. 255.

12 Yinxuan Huang, Kristin Aune and Mathew Guest, 'COVID-19 and the Chinese Christian Community in Britain: Changing Patterns of Belonging and Division', *Studies in World Christianity* 27, no. 1 (March 2021), p. 22, https://doi.org/10.3366/swc.2021.0323.

13 Take University College London, which had most Chinese students in the 2022/23 academic year, as an example. For 2024/25 academic year, a home student enrolled in the Computer Science MSc programme would need to pay £19,300 while the overseas tuition fee is £37,500. See https://www.ucl.ac.uk/prospective-students/graduate/taught-degrees/computer-science-msc, accessed 17.05.2024.

14 'Chinese money is pouring into British universities', *The Economist*, 12 March 2022, available at https://www.economist.com/britain/2022/03/12/chinese-money-is-pouring-into-british-universities.

15 Take Chinese students in London as an example. London & Partners' Strategy and Insight team, London's official promotional organization, has published a report showing that in 2013–14, students from China were the biggest contributors with an estimated spend of £407 million. London & Partners, *The Economic Impact of London's International Students* (London: London & Partners, n.d.), available at https://files.londonandpartners.com/l-and-p/assets/media/students_impact_report.pdf.

16 See their website, https://welcomechurches.org.

17 Daguo Li, 'Out of the Ivory Tower: The Impact of Wider Social Contact on the Values, Religious Beliefs and Identities of Chinese Postgraduate Students in the UK', *Race, Ethnicity and Education* 15, no. 2 (Oct. 2010), pp. 246–7, https://doi.org/10.1080/13613324.2011.585339.

18 Jingran Yu, Rohini Rai, Miguel Antonio Lim and Hanwei Li, 'The post-racial myth: rethinking Chinese university students' experiences and perceptions of racialised microaggressions in the UK', *Higher Education* (Nov. 2023), https://doi.org/10.1007/s10734-023-01126-5.

19 Guangxiang Liu, Wentao Li and Yueshan Zhang, 'Tracing Chinese International Students' Psychological and Academic Adjustments in Uncertain Times: An Exploratory Case Study in the United Kingdom', *Frontiers in Psychology* 13 (Sept. 2022), https://doi.org/10.3389/fpsyg.2022.942227.

20 A popular concept is the four stages of cultural shock: the honeymoon stage, the negotiation stage, the adjustment stage and the adaptation stage. While the length of each stage depends on the individual, it is suggested that the whole process might take 12 months. 'The stages of culture shock – how it occurs and how to overcome it', *University of West of Scotland, London*, 12 September 2023, available at https://www.uwslondon.ac.uk/student-life/the-stages-of-culture-shock/.

8

Be Not Conformed To This Land: A Pastoral Theology for Migrants

KAN YU

Introduction

The Apostle Paul's teaching in the Letter to the Romans reveals the truth of Christianity that has engendered incalculable impact on Jesus Christ's followers ever since. In particular, a well-loved Bible verse from Romans 12.2 (NRSVA) reads:

> Do not be conformed to this world, but be transformed by the renewing of your minds, so that you may discern what is the will of God – what is good and acceptable and perfect.

Paul begins by emphasizing: do not be conformed to this world, so that the followers of Jesus Christ can discern God's will by the renewing of their minds through an unexpected transformation. But what does it mean for Hong Kong Christians who recently migrated to the UK in fear of, or in anticipation of danger from, the rapidly changing political situations brought about by the People's Republic of China? How does the experience and trauma of being uprooted from home affect Christian relationships in the UK?

This chapter uses pastoral theology to examine the complexity of Hong Kong Christians (i.e. Chinese Christians with the tradition and culture from Hong Kong) who are learning to adapt their discipleship in this new land. It is a worthwhile theological study to discover how and why British Chinese Christianity could behave and develop, influenced by an influx of Hong Kong Christians in the past few years. Since pastoral theology is contextual and correlative to its praxis of the church in its local setting, 'the land' in the title refers particularly to the Hong Kong Christian community in south-west London, where the writer is serving in ordained ministry.

Mapping the landscape

Invaluable research conducted by the British and Foreign Bible Society and the London School of Theology in 2023 stated that 'the British Chinese community is at a unique moment in its history [due to] a huge influx of immigration from Hong Kong'.[1]

This phenomenon is unprecedented. Many push factors have facilitated this mass migration, which can be called a 'Hong Kong Exodus'. On the one hand, the driving force was triggered by the radical social and political movement in Hong Kong in 2014, and later in 2019 and 2020. On the other hand, the UK government issued a new immigration policy by opening a British National (Overseas) visa route in the hope of honouring the historical responsibility to its former colonial residents in Hong Kong.

Under the BN(O) visa scheme, all Hong Kong residents who have British National (Overseas) status and their dependants are eligible to apply for a safer, simpler, direct and relatively cheaper migration route to Britain, starting from 31 January 2021.

The radical immigration policy has attracted many Hong Kong people to leave Hong Kong and migrate to Britain to pursue a safer and better life with democratic freedom. At the end of 2023, the UK government swung open its doors to welcome Hong Kong people by granting over 320,000 BN(O) visas.[2] Among all these Hong Kong migrants, the Christian population cannot be ignored.

According to the aforementioned research project, entitled *Chinese Christianity in Britain*, between 2021 and 2023 there has been nearly a 29 per cent increase in the Chinese Christian community in Britain, with 27 new congregations established.[3] This has been an epic growth of the British Chinese church, fuelled by newly migrated Christians as well as yet-to-be Christians from Hong Kong, creating a significant movement of church growth across the UK.

The study shows that the majority of Chinese Christians in Britain, including Hong Kong Christians, value good, grounded Bible teaching and hold a high view of Scripture. Their pursuit of discipleship and spiritual growth reveals their Christian maturity in experiences, Scripture, tradition and reason within a church setting, as well as a socially inflected understanding of God and the church in society.[4]

This unprecedented growth in numbers has not only shocked the Chinese churches in Britain but has also revealed a desire on the part of Hong Kong Christians to join local English-speaking churches in order to express Jesus' witness and presence in the community that they are part of. This desire highlights numerous opportunities for church growth as well as underlying challenges in forming a new relationship between the existing, and yet dwindling, historic British churches and the enthusiastic Hong Kong Christians when they begin to live out their discipleship in this new land.

Methodology

Being uprooted from their home, willingly or unwillingly, Hong Kong migrants have shown a great tendency to rediscover their identity in order to establish their lives in the new land. Hong Kong Christians also try to comprehend their Christian identity by engaging and contrasting themselves with their surrounding cultural contexts, with the familiarity of the Christian faith and with a sense of meaning from back home. This is a natural and historical way of expressing Christ's presence among the people of God and the wider community.

It demonstrates that the search for identity is inextricably tied to the land where people reside. To better examine the praxis of the churches in Britain in reaction to these changes, opportunities and challenges, as it relates to Hong Kong migrants, this chapter focuses on a local cultural context in south-west London to represent the 'new land' into which nearly more than 300 Hong Kong Christians have entered. This is a first-hand account of the writer's experience, which will guide the discussion.[5]

Studying a specific group of Hong Kong Christians in south-west London will not reflect the entire British Christian landscape across the UK. Nevertheless, this enables the writer to search for an authentic and precise description of a phenomenon leading to profound new ways of being followers of Jesus Christ – for both the Hong Kong Chinese guests and the pre-existing Christian hosts in this land. The writer hopes to discover a wider pattern of God's good, acceptable and perfect will through this unprecedented phenomenon of Hong Kong migrants that may contribute to the making of British Chinese Christianity in this time and space.

Experientially, the common image of migrants has often been portrayed as a group of strangers residing in a strange land with its existing hosts. But in reality, migrants are also transitioning from temporary status to permanent citizen. So often, the relationship between guests and hosts has more layers and complexities because it involves Chinese culture and expectations among Hong Kong Christians attempting to practise their Christian faith in a contemporary Western context. To address the issues, this study will draw on theological dialogue in three main areas:

Hospitality between host and guest;
Life together in God's household;
Resistance to forging a genuine and godly relationship.

Where does the story begin?

The story begins in a market town with a few renowned grammar schools for boys and girls and a number of outstanding primary schools as feeder schools. At the centre of the town, an iconic Grade II-listed building has been the home of an English-speaking Wesleyan Methodist Church since the early twentieth century. A local ecumenical partnership between the Methodist Church and the United Reformed Church was formed in the early 1970s in response to the increasingly diverse needs of migrants in the town, whose children longed to secure a place in a local grammar school. It is a convincing factor too for many Hong Kong parents, who heavily focus on and are involved in their children's education.

With its denominational traditions and ecumenical mission, the English-speaking church has been blessed with diverse ethnicities representing the demographic depth of the town. That said, for the past decades the church has been led by a group of predominantly White British Christians, and a strong White British Christian culture prevails.

The engagement between the English-speaking church and Hong Kong Christians started during the Covid-19 lockdown in January 2021, when a small group of Hong Kong Christians who had recently migrated to south-west London wanted support for their Christian faith. To respond to this demand, the writer set up a bi-weekly Zoom meeting to facilitate and provide a safe space for them to be listened to and to find support in prayer.

Later, when the lockdown policy was gradually lifted, some participants were yearning to convert the online gathering into an in-person gathering for prayer and worship. Eventually, the writer, a Methodist, represented the group of Hong Kong migrants to engage with the local English-speaking church connected with her Methodist denomination. 'Do you have room to host us for a new fellowship on Sunday afternoon?' 'Come, you are welcome!' the minister of the church replied with positive warmth.

With gladness, a group of around 60 new Hong Kong Christians, including children and youth, enjoyed the very first Cantonese-speaking worship on a Sunday afternoon. Thanks to YouTubers and the outstanding grammar schools in south-west London, the town the writer worked in became a 'little Hong Kong', with over 400 families residing there in the first year. Though the church gathering only happened on the second and the fourth Sundays, the attendance grew phenomenally to 250 people in a year.

The remarkable growth has resonated with what Christine Pohl, a renowned professor of Christian social ethics, has argued about hospitality: it happens where the deep human longing yearns to belong, to find a place to share one's gift and be valued by the hosts,[6] especially for new migrants.

To meet with the huge demand from Hong Kong Christians, the English-speaking host church offered generous hospitality by permitting the use of church premises for Sunday gatherings and organizing English classes and coffee mornings to engage with Hong Kong Christians. They demonstrated their willingness to embrace them into their hospitable welcome and the community the new Hong Kong Christians were learning to call home.

Immersion in dialogue

Christian hospitality is not new to Christian communities. In fact, hospitality is at the heart of God's nature and in the people of God. At the turn of the millennium, Christine Pohl reclaimed this valuable ancient and biblical gem among Christian communities (Genesis 18; Exodus 12; Leviticus 19; John 13) as a marker of Christianity.[7]

In hospitality, a common meal is shared. From the time of God's salvation of his people Israel, the Passover has been shared. This common meal marked the beginning of the meal-sharing tradition, signifying hospitality to each other in God's household, which was then renewed and remade by Jesus on the night before he was betrayed.

His dying on the cross and his rising from the dead were summarized and symbolized in this meal, a meal Christians call the Lord's Supper, where Jesus is the host. This is a sacrament that manifests God's hospitality in and through people's daily living and in the community where they belong, not just trying to fit in. Indeed, every meal, regardless of any tradition or faith, has a host to offer the hospitable welcome that may satisfy the invited or, sometimes, unexpected guests who knock on their door.

This generous hospitality was experienced by the disciples in Jesus' time. Their eyewitness accounts prove that the risen Christ was and is made known in the breaking of the bread (Luke 24.35). Their proclamation affirms the covenantal and genuine relationship that God has with his people. The practice of the Lord's Supper has therefore become a Christian tradition of all God's household as a shared meal. It has become a shared symbol and a communal narrative that enacts God's salvation in Christ Jesus and his resurrection power, which has restored life to his beloved creation.

The understanding and action make clear that at the heart of Christian faith, hospitality and welcome are God's nature and foster his genuine relationship with his people. With that in mind, the relationship is not static. In actual fact, no relationship between two parties is static but mutually dynamic. This is true of the relationship between host and guest in Christian communities. Hospitality should not be restricted by or limited to the hospitality industry; it is also a Christian virtue.

In addition, Pohl's insight helpfully reveals the truth that the practice of hospitality is vital for Christian communities when reaching out to others. That being so, they are working, whether or not they know it, to strengthen their internal relationships with rest and renewal, gifted by the guests.[8]

In Jesus' teaching, reaching out to the 'other' is what he does when he proclaims that the Kingdom of God is at hand. As the followers of Jesus Christ, Christians are called to be like Christ and to do what he does. So who is the 'other'? It must be understood in its biblical reference. That is, the poor, widows, orphans, strangers, foreigners and migrants alike – all who are different from the host, who can provide for them or share without diminishing their existing power.

Hospitality, host and guests in south-west London

What does hospitality look like for the Hong Kong migrants who fuel the epic church growth in south-west London?

The writer speaks out of her lived experiences when leading a newly formed fellowship that was called into being for Hong Kong Christians and others who looked for a Cantonese-speaking church community in south-west London.

The English-speaking church with its iconic landmark building in the town was compelled to open its doors and arms to welcome the Hong Kong Christians. The host offered a kind and hospitable act to this brand-new Christian group. Any welcome in a Christian context serves as a sign of Jesus' welcome. It is a sign showing that the host is not afraid to share their treasures of truth and peace[9] with the 'other', engendering liveliness within the existing context. Indeed, the church premises came alive even in the post-pandemic period, with many Hong Kong Christians, who were yearning to rediscover their identity by making friends, adjusting their new lives and re-establishing church life in a new country they learnt to call 'home'. The host church practised a great degree of Christian hospitality. For them, it was a pleasant calling to live out being the hands and the feet of Jesus in the world for those who were in need.

But Pohl debunks this as simplistic naivety. She explains: 'Recognition involves respecting the dignity and equal worth of every person and valuing their contributions to the larger community.'[10] When the host recognizes that the guests are equals before God, a subversive and countercultural dimension of Christian hospitality becomes apparent to the host and their existing community.

In fact our host church was challenged to recognize that these guests were migrants, but they were not economic migrants who were desperately in need of a hot meal, a place to stay, financial aid or English classes.[11] In reality, they were political migrants whose needs were intrinsic, caused by a complex political agenda that often burdened them with hurt, frustration, fear, separation, loss and anger. They yearned for a safe place where they would be welcomed and accepted. They looked for a community where they could share frustrations and find support to face adjustment issues. They also longed to contribute and integrate with their new community as a proof of their self-worth and to affirm their identity and existence.

It was not surprising to witness the attendance increase as the fellowship continued. With over 250 attending regularly after a year, it was no longer feasible to regard it as a fellowship: it was a local congregation.

Praise God for a growing church! It was super good news to the writer's denomination because Methodists were trying hard to counter the trend of decline in membership and the closure of local churches. Seeing the buzzing lives on Sunday afternoons when the Hong Kong fellowship met in the host church's premises was promising. It generated a hope among the Hong Kong migrants that they could show their inclination to share their lives more fully with the host church, as part of God's household in this place. The tendency to form a closer relationship in a church setting was a very Christian way of life.

Christian communities have served as a basis for social, political and religious identity and cohesion throughout Christian history.[12] It was true and important for the early church. It remains true for Christian communities in Britain in the twenty-first century. That said, no one should naively believe that Christian communities only pursue unity and holiness, without acknowledging the diversity and the differentiated functions that exist within them.

Life together in God's household

All Christian churches are historically and theologically seen as the household of God, regardless of culture, language or race. It has been a powerful theological and social reality[13] to live out the life of Christ on earth through faithful Christians who want to follow him together in daily life, not just on Sundays. In God's household, existing members, new migrants, strangers, foreigners and new believers become family members for one another and form a relationship in the same household.

And relationship it is, when living together in Christ and for Christ!

All relationships in God's household should be dynamic because our relationship with God is dynamic. Therefore developing or deepening a relationship is a process of relational dynamic. And part of the relationship development process requires both guest and host to go through it together in order to form a genuine and godly relationship in God's household.

The togetherness of God's covenanted and godly people is always at the heart of God's will and his desire for created humanity. God has already fulfilled it in and through Christ Jesus (Ephesians 1.10; Colossians 1.15–20), and continues through his redeemed people to restore the broken creation under one Lord, one faith, one baptism, one God and Father of all (Ephesians 4.1–6), till Christ comes again. The writing of the late renowned scholar and priest John Stott reminds us that it is only good and pleasant *if* the people of God live together in unity.[14]

That is a big 'if'.

The ambivalence in this hope brings us to reflect on the real situation in south-west London. Is it possible for Hong Kong Christians and an English-speaking host to experience God's blessedness through hospitality and welcome in the UK, when the number of guests becomes greater than the host? Does this upset the hospitable welcome?

Sadly, it does. The unprecedented increase in numbers of Hong Kong Christians brought joy and opportunities as well as challenges to this part of God's household. For instance, the use of space, creating regular opportunities for small group fellowships, relationship building, the demand for peer support, emotional support, volunteering opportunities – all of these factors were becoming increasingly heavy and could no longer be ignored. As a result, the guest–host relationship became more strained.

When the need of the guests is greater than what the host can offer, does it change the guest–host relationship? Unfortunately, it does.

The writer's experience with the host church that shared her Methodist roots did not go well when discussing a closer partnership in God's household. In the end, the growing fellowship with 95 per cent new Hong Kong Christians was asked to set up as an independent entity and to start weekly worship in order to carry on renting the same venue. In June 2023 the fellowship was called into being as a local church and named itself Sutton HongKongers' Church.

This is not new in Christian communities.

When the initial equilibrium of the guest–host relationship is tipped, or when the host is urged to permit the novelty of others to shake its once habitual perceptions through the consciousness of Christ, the kind and hospitable welcome is likely to become overstayed. At the same time, the motivation of the hospitable welcome from the host and the inner thoughts of the migrants who are often perceived as victims will come to the surface. It is a reality about which Jesus has warned his hearers in Matthew 10.34 (NRSVA), 'Do not think that I have come to bring peace to the earth; I have not come to bring peace, but a sword.' This is a stark remark from Jesus experienced by Christians over the centuries through suffering when trying to live together in God's household.

A vivid example can be found in Dietrich Bonhoeffer's classic exploration of Christian community, *Life Together*. In this work he calls for self-reflection about living together – with what and with whom?

For true discipleship and life together, it is essential to recognize and banish the human dreams and ideology of Christian community that are based on human love. That done, when we talk about establishing and seeking sustainability in God's household, a genuine spiritual love that comes from Jesus Christ is the only thing that will make it achievable. The spiritual love described by Bonhoeffer 'does not desire for control but serves'.[15] This originates in Christ alone, who mediates our relationships with one another in God's household.

In short, Bonhoeffer warns us that the quicker we can debunk and let go of the human illusion that life together is fabricated by human love, the quicker God can act on us to uphold our distinct uniqueness as well as bind us together by faith, not by experience. For Jesus is our peace who gives us access to one another in and through his love.[16]

Bonhoeffer's exhortation simply commands all Christians not to be conformed to this world. All shapes, sizes and colours of Christians, whether taking on a role as host or guest in English-speaking churches in Britain or among Hong Kong Christians in south-west London – all are called to live out the true human identity in Christ rather than conform to the land. That being so, Christian migrants and Christian hosts can truly live in a divine reality in which Christ binds them together.

Facing resistance

The powerful exposition in Bonhoeffer's *Life Together* will hardly be achieved without rejection and resistance.

Many theologians, pastors and church leaders across the centuries, including Bonhoeffer himself, have struggled and suffered from this. They have tried to comprehend their lived experience of the reality of a Christian community that is called by God. Many have spoken plainly by acknowledging that overcoming the resistance to pursuing life together in God's household can become dangerous,[17] painful[18] and even costly.[19]

William Barry and William Connolly offer a remarkable insight that all genuine relationships do not develop smoothly.[20] Human beings have a paradoxical tendency by which, on the one hand, we resist change and development and, on the other hand, yearn to have new things by knowing more about the 'other'.[21]

To develop a genuine relationship with God and with others in God's household as described by Bonhoeffer, the presence of resistance is inevitable.[22] All resistance goes against humanity's tendency to inertia. In so doing, it easily brings forth anxiety due to encountering another's otherness, negative emotions or behaviour when facing disorganization of experience (i.e. chaos) caused by change. This can be fear of changing one's self-image, which is dependent on acceptance from others, and fear of losing the pattern of one's personality when change and exposure to human vulnerability occur.

Barry and Connolly stress that resistance is not a crime but a necessary concomitant to any effort at growth that involves change.[23] It is what Jesus did when he died on the cross. The determination of Jesus to stay in God's love exposed the deepest vulnerability of human beings in broad daylight under the cruel violence of the Roman Empire. We can see that resistance and vulnerability go hand in hand in developing and deepening a genuine relationship. There are no easy solutions. It is disheartening to see and be. It does not feel Christlike at all.

The writer experienced this when trying to bring a newly formed and growing Hong Kong Christian community together with their English-speaking Christian host over the course of two years. Towards the end, the hospitable welcome turned into a list of terms and conditions, the warm welcoming smiles turned into stern-faced reproach, English lessons and coffee mornings turned into thin air and discussions of further partnership opportunities turned into stagnated conversation. These were a few things that the writer and the leaders of the Hong Kong congregation experienced.

Illumination and theological reflection

Through this first-hand account of the writer's ministry in south-west London, we can begin to understand the phenomenon of the 'distorted' hospitality from the local Christian hosts in the UK towards the emerging Hong Kong Christian communities. In response, should Hong Kong Christians in the UK conform to the pattern that 'this land' offers through the local hosts?

Conversing in dialogue with theologians and pastors from past centuries in previous sections of this chapter, we have discovered that resistance is a pathway to a genuine hospitality and relationship in God's household. It is an essential expression of a daring faith going through resistance and vulnerability in a community in order to be true to Christ and thus to others.

Therefore non-conformity is the key. It is the foundation of true discipleship for all Jesus' followers. It is what Jesus prays for in his final discourse in the Gospel according to John – oneness in God's self-giving love (John 17). In turn, he urges his followers to do likewise. Therefore one's openness to the Holy Spirit will let Christ come in, so that Hong Kong Christians should not be afraid to stand alone in this land rather than forging a distorted relationship with the host when the door that enables both parties to meet as equals has closed.

However, the praxis of non-conformity may betray the desire of Hong Kong Christians to belong and be accepted, valued and loved in a new community after going through a journey of migration caused by the situation of turmoil in Hong Kong political unrest.

Moreover, church is often seen as a safe space to begin experiencing what the migrants have lost when coming to Britain, especially friendship and affirmation of identity and self-worth in a new community. Christians throughout the centuries have upheld the belief that all of them share: one Lord, one faith, one baptism in one God's household; that is, the church where Jesus is the head of his visible body on earth in different contexts. It is a place of unity to embrace, welcome, accept and love, not to 'rock the boat' of integration.

With these prerequisites, not conforming becomes radical. The choice for the Hong Kong Christians to create a separate entity instead of integrating with the dwindling host was deemed to be disrespectful and perhaps unchristian. Yet this revolutionary practice also exposed the vulnerability and hurt of a newly formed Hong Kong Christian community in a strange land without the support of the hosts.

In light of these dilemmas, there are new ways for Hong Kong Christians to avoid getting bogged down in relation to their host church and have the courage to pursue a genuine relationship in Christ, even though the non-conforming journey is hard and long.

New possibilities of not being conformed

The truth is that confronting and thus accepting resistance that is not projected by others but seen from within is part of the growing process that fosters a genuine relationship. It generates a true sense of belonging, friendship, company and a community called by God. Throughout the centuries it has been a way of life that enables Christians such as Julian of Norwich, Dietrich Bonhoeffer, Thomas Merton, the Methodist movement, the Taizé community and the Anglican communion to arrive at the divine reality of love. The Christian baseline is that everyone is loved by God. Love is a choice without any coercion. Therefore when engaging with others for the greater glory of God, everyone should be given the space and freedom to express God's love through the unique gifts and ethnic backgrounds that God has created.

With that illuminating understanding, Christians should expect to meet with others who are different. In so doing, no Christian should be too surprised to bump into resistance when it surfaces in a relationship, whether between people, groups or communities. There will be times when different Christian communities work separately to reach out to more people in their own contexts.

Similar lived experiences among Chinese Christians in Britain happened 70 years ago. The late Reverend Stephen Wang, who was a Methodist minister, founded the Chinese Overseas Christian Mission

(COCM)[24] and the Chinese Church in London (CCiL)[25] in the 1950s to reach out to Chinese people in the UK without the support of his own Methodist mother church where he had been ordained into ministry. With the recent epic growth of Hong Kong Christians, both organizations have received exponential growth in size and number of faithful Christians to spread the good news of Christ.

All these successes are without merit, except that they point towards the divine reality for all Christians – all are one with Christ in God's one household for eternity. This implies that all followers of Christ have a greater calling to conform to the divine reality of God's household. For this reason, the Apostle Paul explicitly exhorts believers to 'Let the same mind be in you that was in Christ Jesus' (Philippians 2.5, NRSVA). No Christian can or should work and stay in their own comfortable Christian community without working out how to forge friendships with 'other' Christians with religious differences.

In practice, it is important to understand what it does *not* mean for Hong Kong Christians not to conform to this land.

'Do not conform' does not mean that Hong Kong Christians cannot collaborate with other local Christians to live out the unity that Jesus prays for his disciples in his final discourse before dying on the cross (John 17). It does not mean ignoring Christians of this land with differences that are too 'alien', with whom it is impossible to stay in any connection.

'Do not conform' does not mean that Hong Kong Christians see English-speaking congregations as an oppositional 'them versus us' but as brothers and sisters in Christ with diversity in the same Christian faith, the same Christian love. It does not mean that we cannot love mutually or help each other even when both parties cannot work together in a human-made and limited system in the current time and space.

We need to be mindful that Christian faith is to fulfil God's purpose for all his creation. We should not miss an excellent opportunity for British Chinese Christianity, which is currently dominated by Hong Kong Christians, to turn the tide from being inward looking and insular, to being outward looking towards society and other Christian communities in Britain.

When we look back to Methodist tradition and learn from it, we discover the founder, John Wesley, who ministered in the eighteenth century, warning of the danger of human conformity in his troubled era. Resonating with Bonhoeffer's view on human love, Wesley argued that human conformity was likely to suppress basic human rights and civil justice in the name of human hospitality.

John Wesley even went further when preaching a sermon called 'The Catholic Spirit' in a century wearied by religious wars. He exhorted his fellow Christians to 'follow their own conscience and walk by the best light they had'[26] in their turbulent religious context, because that would enable them to live out the Christian faith in their era. He championed the significant right of all Christian communities to maintain their distinctive emphases and practices that best served their respective contexts. That being so, no Christian should react to inhuman behaviour by translating religious difference 'into liabilities in terms of basic rights, entitlements, and protections'[27] that coerce strangers into conformity. Following this path would only harness a false sense of belonging, friendship and fellowship that was fabricated by human ideals (i.e. a culture of fitting-in). Wesley then asked some rhetorical questions:

> Though we cannot think alike, may we not love alike? May we not be of one heart, though we are not of one opinion? Without all doubt, we may. Herein all the children of God may unite, notwithstanding these smaller differences.

It certainly was a groundbreaking insight in the eighteenth century for Christian communities to be established and grounded in God's holy catholic love. It is still a groundbreaking insight for Christians in Britain, including Hong Kong Christians, in this very stagnant twenty-first century context.

The fact is that the Christian population in the UK is dwindling and its spiritual crisis is looming. In order to restore the true belonging and unity of the diverse Christian communities, it is vital to be Christ's witnesses by holding on to the core Christian belief: God has already gathered all things in Christ, things in heaven and things on earth (Ephesians 1.10). It is the divine reality revealed in Christ that all his human creatures are inextricably connected, valued and loved.

The Pillars of Grace

Learning from Methodist core values, this divine reality may gradually become real for Hong Kong Christians and all Christians as followers of Christ, if we begin to offer what can be considered the Pillars of Grace: *mutual respect, space, humility* and *dialogue*. We need to work on the common ground that is Christlike, rather than maintaining a status quo of Christian unity that is ill-protected by distorted human love.

These Christlike Pillars of Grace surely form the pathway of hope that engenders the greater calling – one God, one love, one household in and through Christ and by the power of the Holy Spirit. This is the Trinitarian love. This is God who is love eternal and love dynamic, Father, Son and Holy Spirit carrying out his project of reconciliation, flowing in and through all Christian communities.

In practice, it is healthy to realize the current situation and not to be sucked into the vicious cycle caused by rejection and separation. Rejected people see rejection everywhere. Hong Kong Christians are at an advantage, because they have already harvested the spirit of non-conformity when they encountered the social movement in 2019 and decided to emigrate to the UK. With courage and daring faith, it is vital to ask and unpack the fundamental questions under each of the Pillars of Grace from above.

Mutual respect

Each life is preciously created by God, whose Spirit flows between us and all lives in the world. The power of connection between people or Christian communities is greater than that of any human being because it is rooted in love and grounded in the compassion of Christ. It is beneficial to ponder:

> What motives do we have in the relationship?
> Are they from human disillusion or from the divine reality of unity?
> What image of the other person do we see?
> What image of the Christian community do we see?
> Do we see others through the eyes of Christ, filled with love and full of compassion?

Space

Without space, hardly anyone breathes. For self-giving love is a choice, not a 'must'. Giving people space invites all communities to step back and make space to reflect on:

> Who are we reaching?
> With what and with whom, and for what purpose?
> What do we live together with and with whom in faith?

Humility

The development process of a genuine relationship will include experiencing moderate anxiety or even resistance when we encounter people who are different from us.[28] Humility is an essential pathway to opening ourselves to 'the novelty and mystery of the other by shaking the patterning of the relationship that has developed from the prior experiences'.[29] It resonates with the Apostle Paul telling Christians in his time not to look to one's own interests but to the interests of others, just like Christ (Philippians 2.4). It is wise to reflect on:

> What is resistance?
> Are there healthy signs to living out the divine reality?
> What are the distorted perceptions, culture, language and theological understanding that are blocking the way?
> Are they mainly human disillusionment, a desire to control others or a wish to submit to others?

Dialogue

Dialogue in the Spirit of truth brings communities to engage on an equal footing, letting their guard down, setting fears aside and dropping preconceptions. It creates a time to hold hands with strangers by listening to other voices and values. A genuine dialogue requires elements of interactivity, sincerity, openness and patience that allow a stream of meaning to flow among, through and between all the participants.[30]

Tensions and paradoxes will undoubtedly surface in a genuine dialogue due to the differences and doubts coming from the various communities. In this way dialogue becomes a healthy pathway to seeking authentic and collective wisdom. New possibilities may organically emerge in spaces between the communities that can move everyone involved on to an entirely new territory of humility, justice and forgiveness in and through Christ. It is necessary to contemplate:

> Is it a dialogue or a shouting match?
> What do we hear?
> Is the Spirit who gives unity dwelling in people's hearts?
> How do we handle tensions and paradoxes?
> Do we appreciate other voices and the values they represent?

Conclusion

In this chapter, the phenomenon of the epic growth of Hong Kong Christians in south-west London has called forth an examination of Christian hospitality between guest and host. All hospitality in God's household that is rooted in human love or human ideals has inevitably resulted in limitations and boundaries when the needs of the guests become greater than the host expected.

Recognizing and debunking these signs of human love, ideals or disillusionment is crucial. Consequently, facing resistance becomes the pathway to a healthy development of all relationships in God's household by rediscovering faithful identity as Jesus' disciples in the UK in this time and space. Therefore not being conformed to the host in this land is essential if we are to follow Jesus' commands to foster genuine and godly relationships. The entire process resonates with the Apostle Paul's exhortation in Romans 12.2, as quoted at the beginning of the chapter, which seeks to bring Christ alive in our midst to serve the present age.

Though non-conformity is foundational to living out a true discipleship in Christ, it poses a paradoxical dilemma for Hong Kong Christians who want to be part of an existing host as well as being faced by resistance. This chapter has opened up new possibilities for Hong Kong Christians to stand firm and take courage. It is an important mission for them to take the opportunity, because they are called to carry out Jesus' commands, bringing the divine reality of oneness with the host by offering Pillars of Grace – mutual respect, space, humility and dialogue – in the years to come.

In truth, going through these non-conforming Pillars of Grace is life-giving in all genuine relationship. They empower people to review, reflect and uncover the motives of resistance so that by faith, new possibilities in Christ will compel the followers of Christ, whether Hong Kong Christians or local British Christians, to return to the Lord who is the mediator of all relationships. For Jesus is our peace. It is he we conform to through loving one another as he loves us.

Notes

1 Yinxuan Huang, *Chinese Christianity in Britain: A Booklet of Ten Vignettes* (Swindon: British and Foreign Bible Society, 2023), p. 3.

2 National Statistics, 'Safe and legal (humanitarian) routes to the UK', *Gov. uk* (29 February 2024), https://www.gov.uk/government/statistics/immigration-

system-statistics-year-ending-december-2023/safe-and-legal-humanitarian-routes-to-the-uk, accessed 20.03.2024.

3 Huang, *Chinese Christianity in Britain*, p. 3.

4 Alexander Chow and Stephanie Wong, 'Chinese Christian Theology', in *St Andrews Encyclopaedia of Theology*, ed. Brendan N. Wolfe et al. (St Andrews: University of St Andrews, 2023), https://www.saet.ac.uk/Christianity/Chinese ChristianTheology, accessed 20.03.2024.

5 Using a framework of heuristic inquiry, the next section will recount the writer's own experience of welcoming new Hong Kong Christians. This first-hand account explores the writer's interaction with a church within her own denomination in south-west London. The process, including immersion, illumination, explication and creative synthesis, was all undergirded by a pastoral theology approach. See Bruce Douglass and Clark Moustakas, 'Heuristic Inquiry: The Internal Search to Know', *Journal of Phenomenological Psychology* 25, no. 3 (Summer 1985), pp. 39–54, https://doi.org/10.1177/0022167885253004.

6 Christine Pohl, *Living into Community: Cultivating Practices that Sustain Us* (Grand Rapids, MI: Eerdmans, 2012), p. 159.

7 Christine Pohl, *Making Room: Recovering Hospitality as a Christian Tradition* (Grand Rapids, MI: Eerdmans, 1999).

8 Pohl, *Living into Community*, pp. 159–60.

9 Jean Vanier, *Community and Growth*, rev. edn (New York: Paulist Press, 1989), p. 266.

10 Pohl, *Making Room*, p. 61.

11 Tom Calver, 'What the UK's 184,000 new Hongkongers really think about life here', *The Sunday Times* (18 January 2024), https://www.thetimes.co.uk/article/what-the-uks-184000-new-hong-kongers-really-think-about-life-here-pm95lhjtt, accessed 20.03.2024.

12 Pohl, *Making Room*, p. 41.

13 John Elliot, *A Home for the Homeless* (Philadelphia, PA: Fortress, 1981), pp. 182, 188 and 221.

14 John Stott, *John Stott's Favourite Psalms: Growing Closer to God* (London: Monarch Books, 2003), p. 102.

15 Dietrich Bonhoeffer, *Life Together*, trans. John Doberstein (London: SCM Press, 2005), p. 12.

16 Bonhoeffer, *Life Together*, pp. 7–26.

17 Charles E. Moore, ed., *Called to Community: The Life Jesus wants for his People* (New York: Plough Publishing House, 2016), p. xiii.

18 Moore, *Called to Community*, p. 139.

19 Pohl, *Living into Community*, p. 161.

20 William A. Barry and William J. Connolly, *The Practice of Spiritual Direction* (New York: HarperCollins, 2009), p. 80.

21 Barry and Connolly, *The Practice of Spiritual Direction*, pp. 80–81.

22 Barry and Connolly, *The Practice of Spiritual Direction*, pp. 80–100.

23 Barry and Connolly, *The Practice of Spiritual Direction*, p. 92.

24 'History of Chinese Overseas Christian Mission (COCM)', *Chinese Overseas Christian Mission*, https://www.cocm.org.uk/who-we-are-our-history, accessed 20.03.2024.

25 'History of Chinese Church in London (CCiL)', *Chinese Church in London*, https://ccil.org.uk/en/about-us/our-history, accessed 20.03.2024.

26 John Wesley, *Sermons on Several Occasions*, trans. James Holway (Ilkeston: Moorley, 2007), p. 394.

27 Pohl, *Making Room*, pp. 82–3.

28 Barry and Connolly, *The Practice of Spiritual Direction*, pp. 82–5.

29 Barry and Connolly, *The Practice of Spiritual Direction*, p. 85.

30 David Bohm, *On Dialogue* (Abingdon: Routledge, 2004), pp. 6–7.

9

Beyond the Immigrant Church vs Local Church Dichotomy: Towards an Internetworked Church

ALEXANDER CHOW

Introduction

'He and his wife no longer go to the Chinese church. They go to the local church.' This was the reply of a mother when I enquired about her son's well-being. It didn't have an implied assessment of which was better – the 'local church' or the 'Chinese church'. He and his wife were simply doing well. Indeed, they were flourishing. It just so happened that the young couple now found the 'local church' to be their spiritual home.

I begin with this story to illustrate a simple point: in the British context, there are some who make a distinction between a 'local church' and an 'immigrant church'. Theologically, this is a bit of an anomaly, given that surely an immigrant church is also a local church that represents a particular expression of the universal church. But perhaps the descriptor of 'local church' also comes about in the British context because of the historical precedence of local *parish* churches. As an American, I'm not used to a parish mentality; that is, seeing a local church include and care for people in a delineated geographical area beyond the church building, whether or not they attend church at all. Indeed, historically, churches in the United States were often established to serve their local communities. This is true of many White-majority churches, as well as Black and Asian American churches in ethnic ghettos formed through the complex history of slavery, racism and migration. The demographics of these American neighbourhoods have evolved over time. Hence, since the latter part of the twentieth century, many American churches are considered 'commuter churches' with churchgoers travelling quite a distance to attend church services. Critics have charged these commuter churches with being *consumer* churches because they gather congregants due to practical or theological preferences. Many detractors have instead promoted a refocus on the local community and, in an interesting turn in history, advocated for the need to establish 'new parishes'.[1]

In the United Kingdom, the idea that a church is to serve its local community or to exist as part of a parish is not something new or novel. Rather, the local parish church has been a theological and administrative ideal in British ecclesiology since at least the medieval era.[2] It continues to loom large today as a part of the ecclesial identity of historic national churches, such as the Church of England, the Church of Scotland and the Roman Catholic Church. Historically, nonconformists have often contested the geographical claims of parish churches. More recently, the parish system has been challenged due to the sobering decline in British Christianity, especially as seen in the 2021 census in the United Kingdom. Hence there are many from within these churches who are debating the future of the local parish systems.[3] In contrast to the decline in these long-standing denominations, some of Britain's fastest-growing churches today are newer 'immigrant churches' or 'diaspora churches'.[4] While they are still addressing a particular locale, to some extent these are commuter churches in that churchgoers may come from a wider region to congregate together. Conversely, these churches do not necessarily see themselves as integrally connected to individuals in the wider neighbourhood of their church buildings if they do not regularly attend their worship services. So these are not local parish churches in the sense that they don't address the 'parish' – which, by definition, includes those residing beside or by the church.[5] But the language of 'immigrant church' or 'diaspora church' also doesn't consider the make-up of these churches, which includes many who were either born in the United Kingdom or those who were migrants at one point but have made this country their 'home'. Therefore they are not so much a 'diaspora' with a 'home' elsewhere. Furthermore, seeing these churches as anything other than a local church implicitly dismisses them as not being truly part of British Christianity.

Mindful of the complexity of these terms and the ways they are loaded with meaning, this chapter will begin with a brief exploration of the missiological theories that underpinned the rise of British Chinese churches and the difficulties this introduces to the British ecclesial landscape. It will also discuss some of the biblical and theological language employed around migration. Ultimately, it argues that the future of British Christianity requires a revised ecclesiology – what I call an 'inter-networked church'.

British missiological methods in Britain

The Britishness of a historic British church is rarely contested. But this is not necessarily the same for churches started by immigrants or with a large percentage of Global Majority congregants. What I hope to show in this section is that part of the reason for the foreignness of so-called 'immigrant churches' is due in part to the missiological practices of Western churches – indeed, historic *British* missiological theories that were once applied to 'non-Christian' lands and are now being re-applied to Britain.

While this chapter and this volume is largely focused on British Chinese Christianity, it is worth briefly considering the case of another expression of Global Majority Christianity in the United Kingdom: the Redeemed Christian Church of God (RCCG), a Nigerian-originated neo-Pentecostal denomination. According to the last *UK Church Statistics*, the RCCG is one of the fastest-growing denominations in Britain – up 22 per cent in five years from 59,000 members in 2015 to 72,000 in 2020.[6] The rapid growth of the church is due to the leadership of Enoch Adejare Adeboye, RCCG's General Overseer since 1981, who has promoted a vision to 'plant churches within five minutes walking distance in every city and town of developing countries and within five minutes driving distance in every city and town of developed countries'.[7] In RCCG's terminology, these churches are envisioned as 'parishes' – a term that predates Adeboye, as the language was used earlier by the founding General Overseer, Josiah Olufemi Akindayomi. It is through a strategy of establishing and multiplying parishes that the RCCG has spread across the globe.[8] Given that both Akindayomi and Adeboye were formerly associated with Anglican mission churches in present-day Nigeria, as were many other early leaders of Nigerian neo-Pentecostalism,[9] it should come as little surprise that the RCCG has adapted Anglican ecclesiology and practices into its unique expression of Christianity.[10] These Nigerian missiological theories include an adaptation of earlier British missiological theories, albeit first deployed a hundred years earlier going in the other direction. Hence it is not only part of the evolution of Christianity in Nigeria but now creates a complicated situation when new RCCG parishes are established in the United Kingdom where parishes of other churches have existed for centuries. For some, this raises the question: Why should immigrants create *their own* churches in Britain, rather than simply join (shrinking) *British* churches?

The case of the RCCG provides a helpful comparison to the history of British Chinese Christianity. While the first British Chinese church was established in 1910, the most significant growth of British Chinese Christianity has occurred through the pioneering work of Stephen Wang, who in the 1950s established the Chinese Church in London and the Chinese Overseas Christian Mission (COCM).[11] In a short article entitled 'The Chinese on our Doorstep', Wang lamented the small number of Christians found among the Chinese in the United Kingdom. He challenged his readers about the lack of Christian work among them and, even more, the lack of prayer: 'China itself is often prayed for, but if you want to save the souls of the Chinese on your doorstep you must pray for them, and pray earnestly and constantly.'[12] It was for this reason that he created COCM. He explained:

> The chief aim of the society is to carry a positive evangelism to the Chinese outside China ... In the second place it is desired to help the Chinese Christians to establish their own Church in accordance with the principle of self-support, self-management, and self-government.[13]

Why such a focus on the Chinese outside of China? First, this article was published in 1952 following the establishment of the People's Republic of China in 1949 and the subsequent ousting of foreign missionaries from the country. While many British Christians grieved the end of the missionary era in China, the Chinese in the United Kingdom were overlooked. But Wang recognized that it was not only the average Brit who overlooked these Chinese – he too hadn't been all that concerned for them. But now he saw the urgency in the work of sharing the gospel with the Chinese 'on our doorstep'.

Second, Wang not only wanted to evangelize the Chinese in the United Kingdom, he wanted Chinese Christians to establish their own church. In the quote above, he invokes the three-self principle (albeit with a slight error); that is, the missiological theory formulated by Henry Venn and Rufus Anderson in the 1800s to establish indigenous churches that were self-governing, self-supporting and self-propagating. The theory was becoming influential in China in the 1900s because it was promoted in the China Centenary Missionary Conference in Shanghai in 1907 and was an underlying principle for establishing the largest church union in China in 1927, the Church of Christ in China.[14] It is no coincidence, then, that Wang's article was published in the periodical *World Dominion*, which was a prominent journal among missionaries advocating for the indigenous church.[15] Wang was adamant that:

The vision of the mission is that its work will be of a temporary character. As soon as God brings an indigenous Church into existence in a particular locality, the object in that place will have been fulfilled, and the work handed over to the Church. This means that eventually the mission, its aims being achieved, under the blessing of God, will cease to exist.[16]

Here we see reverberations of Henry Venn, who held that the purpose of a mission was to work towards the establishment of an indigenous, three-self church, followed by 'the euthanasia of the mission'.[17] Likewise, Wang saw the work of COCM as temporary, the goal being to establish the Chinese Church – but rather than in China, now in Britain. This was likewise apparent in the Chinese name of the main church he started, the Chinese Church in London: Lundun Zhonghua Jidu Jiaohui. While 'Lundun' is simply the Chinese transliteration of 'London', the latter phrase 'Zhonghua Jidu Jiaohui' is the Chinese name of the Church of Christ in China. Wang saw his church as part of the most significant indigenous church formed in China – but now with a branch in London.

Seventy years on from Wang's endeavours, the recent influx of Hong Kongese has been accompanied with newer missiological initiatives. For instance, in May 2021 a new Hong Kong Christian Church in United Kingdom was established, now with four churches in Edinburgh, Glasgow, Sheffield and Birmingham 'for and by Hong Kong immigrants'.[18] Although the denomination is in fact part of the Cumberland Presbyterian Church, it has chosen to brand itself around its Hong Kongese identity. How does this new British Hong Kongese church relate not only to historic British churches but also to historic British Chinese churches?

RCCG, COCM and these new British Hong Kongese churches have had different implicit and explicit missiological outlooks. Many have adapted previous Western or British missiological theories that were focused on establishing churches in 'non-Christian lands' – and Britain is now another 'non-Christian land'. These missiological theories are farsighted in offering missiological frameworks to start new churches, but they are shortsighted in hindering the ecumenical flexibility needed to engage with preexisting churches. How do these new forms of church relate to the latent parish mentality prevalent within British Christianity? How does twenty-first-century British Christianity re-imagine itself to support the growing proliferation of 'immigrant churches' alongside the decline of 'local churches'? Does it actually need to be such a dichotomy or is there a more generous perspective that can be engendered?

Sojourner church

When considering the Christian theological and ethical discourse around migration, it is informative that the most prevalent theme has been 'hospitality'. While I don't see this as wrong per se, we often forget that hospitality is extended to 'guests' – and guests eventually go home. What happens if guests (or migrants) overstay their welcome?

The English word 'hospitality' is often used in the New Testament as a translation of the Greek word *philoxenia* (Romans 12.13; Hebrews 13.2; 1 Peter 4.9). The Greek etymology points to a much stronger idea of loving (*phileō*) the foreigner or migrant (*xenos*), the latter of whom would otherwise be vulnerable because they had little protection in this new land. In part, some of the New Testament teachings are echoing a Greco-Roman cultural-religious virtue of hospitality.[19] But we also see Jesus' teachings about feeding and caring for 'the least of these' as anticipating the Kingdom of God (Luke 14.12–24; Matthew 25.31–46). Taken together, these ideas become formative in the early church's development of a distinctive Christian understanding and practice of hospitality.[20]

Of course, the New Testament texts also carry the weight of Old Testament theological ideals. For instance, God explains in Leviticus 19.33–34 (NRSVA):

> When an alien resides with you in your land, you shall not oppress the alien. The alien who resides with you shall be to you as the citizen among you; you shall love the alien as yourself, for you were aliens in the land of Egypt: I am the LORD your God.

We see God instructing Israel to care for the alien or sojourner in their land because they too were once vulnerable foreigners in the land of Egypt.[21] The command is communicated in both the negative (to 'not oppress the alien') as well as in the positive (to 'love the alien as yourself'). The latter echoes the command a few verses earlier to 'love your neighbour as yourself' (Leviticus 19.18, NRSVA), which is of course later used by Jesus as part of his Greatest Commandment. The meat of this passage is found sandwiched between these negative and positive proclamations, whereby YHWH instructs Israel to treat the sojourner in their midst as a 'citizen' or 'native'. As one commentator suggests, the foreigner is to be treated as 'one whose lineage has "roots" in the land, one who belongs to the group that possesses the land'.[22] What a powerful image! Nobody wants to be treated as a foreigner for ever. Migrants want to be treated as equals – as citizens and indeed as natives, rooted in the land.

We see echoes of Leviticus 19.33–34 in the New Testament, when Paul writes to the Gentile Christians in Ephesus to tell them that, in Christ, 'you are no longer strangers and aliens, but you are citizens with the saints and also members of the household of God' (Ephesians 2.19, NRSVA). As we can see in Ephesus, the Leviticus teaching is now offered new meaning among Christians, between those who have had a privileged position (Jewish Christians or, now shall I say, White British Christians) and those who are newcomers (Gentile Christians or Global Majority Christians). The latter are more vulnerable because they have less historical and spiritual heritage and currency. They are less established within the community and can easily be perceived as outsiders. But now they are to be re-rooted and made citizens or natives.[23] This is a *Christian* understanding of hospitality.

If we extend this idea to think about the church, we can consider what Peter Phan has argued: that, historically, as far back as the first few centuries of Christianity, the church has always been made up of migrants. As such, 'migrantness is a note of the true church, because only a church that is conscious of being an institutional migrant and caring for all the migrants of the world can truly practice faith, hope, and love'.[24] So new and old migrants should be re-imagined as natives in historic British churches. But it is not only people who are sojourners but churches too. British Chinese churches and British Hong Kongese churches are sojourner churches. These sojourner churches are to be considered *natives* in the United Kingdom – as native British churches.

Sojourner churches are unique expressions within British Christianity. When compared with many historic British churches, they tend to have three interconnected characteristics: fewer human and financial resources, a weaker sense of British Christian heritage and identity, and a more restricted civic reach. The 200 British Chinese churches were mainly started by immigrants in the past few decades, and they tend to be autonomous rather than part of any denomination. Hence this limits their institutional resources and history, as well as their connectedness to the wider expressions of British Christianity and British society. Sojourner churches of this sort tend to be perceived as homogeneous, if not monocultural.[25] In part this is why British Chinese churches have grown with the recent influx of Hong Kongese migrants.[26] But most of these churches were established through earlier waves of migration and are made up of different heterogeneous ministries that cross linguistic, cultural and socioeconomic boundaries.[27] Being formed by earlier waves of migration, these churches have added cultural-linguistic differences from recent migrants and relate differently to the sociopolitical unrest in Hong Kong.[28] Yet at the same time, British Chinese churches have rich experiences in navigating the challenges for new immigrants adapting to British society. They also have much more experience with the bicultural negotiations of second and later generations and the experience of racism and rejection, although arguably more work can be done in these areas. Hence while sojourner churches do not have as much civic reach as historic British churches, their main civic contributions are in supporting recent immigrants and longer-standing Global Majority populations.

It should be instructive that the passage in Leviticus 19 about treating the sojourner as a native is part of a larger chapter that gave Jesus the words of the second greatest commandment: 'love your neighbour as yourself' (Leviticus 19.18, NRSVA). Love the sojourner church as your church.

Between the local and the universal

Apart from rethinking the relationship between sojourner churches and historic British churches, we also need to rethink the traditional vocabulary we use to discuss the church. Theologians differentiate between two aspects of the church – the local church and the universal or catholic church. Protestants have tended to focus on the local church at the expense of the universal church because during the time of the Reformation, the Roman Catholic magisterium saw itself as the main representative of the universal church.[29]

Many Chinese churches in Asia are influenced by a Confucian conception of community. This Confucian ideal is often conceived as a series of concentric circles whereby the individual relates to and impacts their family, their family relates to and impacts their local society and this ultimately relates to and impacts the state and the world. Chinese Christians in Asia often gravitate towards this concentric model as a pattern for the church, whereby the pastor and church leadership are at the centre, influencing the church and ultimately influencing the broader society, the state and the world.[30]

In the United Kingdom, this concentric model of a church very much parallels the local parish church, whereby the local parish minister and, by extension, the local church have spiritual and civic responsibilities for the local parish community, whether or not those individuals are

Christians or attend the church. Furthermore, as indicated in Figure 1 by the dotted circles, in practice both these models are more aspirational than actual in their impact beyond the congregation and within their wider communities.[31] Apart from the conventional models of the local parish church or churches in Chinese societies, we also see the rise of British commuter churches – which, as already suggested, include British Chinese churches. The main limitation of the commuter church is in its influence in the local region. Some commuter churches are mindful of this and have life groups or house groups throughout the city, with hopes of somehow having greater influence in the wider community; but they too have limited impact on their local communities.

Figure 1: Three conventional church models

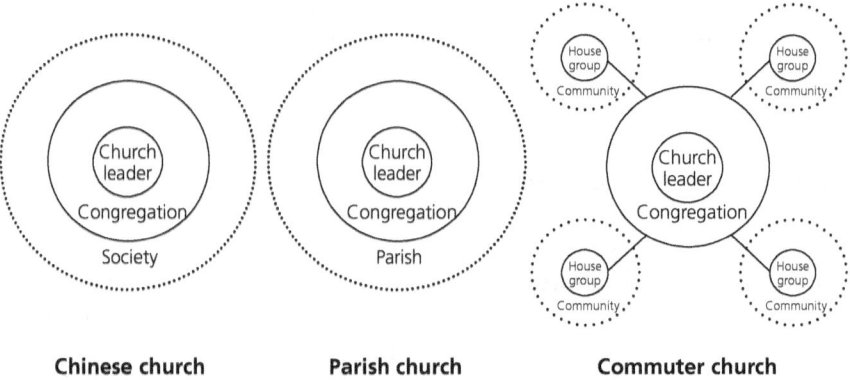

Chinese church   **Parish church**   **Commuter church**

In contrast to these more conventional models, in recent decades we have been shifting towards a more amorphous understanding of church. What counts as 'church' and 'Christian community' is much bigger than a single local church. There are those who may mainly attend a British Chinese church for Sunday worship but because of limited resources or language skills send their children to the children's programmes and youth ministries of a local parish church. There are those who are active in the congregational life of a historic British church but yearn for connections with those of shared heritage and so they join monthly networks or fellowships or annual conferences that cater for those of similar Hong Kongese or British Chinese backgrounds. This may be criticized as a consumerist approach to Christianity. But in practice they are attempts by Global Majority Christian to navigate the faith for themselves and their families while recognizing different aspects of spiritual, interpersonal and cultural-linguistic need.

Such negotiations are, of course, not unique to British Chinese. In a study of Korean Christian migrants in Scotland, similar decisions were being made as to whether to attend a British Korean church or a historic British church. Those who chose the latter did so in the hope of better 'integrating' into British culture. But many came to realize the difficulty in 'fully integrating' due to 'the feeling of in-between-ness without entirely belonging to anywhere' and, after living in British society for some time, subsequently switched to a British Korean church.[32] In another study, a Local Ecumenical Partnership church[33] in England included roughly 85 per cent White British and 15 per cent first-generation migrants. Despite the ecumenical and multiethnic nature of the church, more than half the migrants were part of informal networks developed with those of similar backgrounds. One of these was explicitly formed 'to maintain the culture, language and all intact and pass it on to our children' but most were perceived 'as distinct from participation in a local church'.[34] These studies highlight the desire of Christians to be rooted in a local church. But they also demonstrate the complex yearnings for something their congregations could not fully address.

The sociological changes occasioned by migration are becoming even more complicated due to advancements in telecommunications technologies that offer more digitally available resources today than ever before.[35] While the past models of church are focused on specific locations, during the Covid-19 pandemic in the United Kingdom and in digitally progressive contexts of Asia like Hong Kong and Singapore, Christian solidarity was widely experienced without being limited by space.[36] How many Christians have prayed for another person on a video chat, shared an encouraging word or verse through instant messaging or social media or listened to a podcast for inspiration? Migratory Hong Kongese in the United Kingdom can attend British churches but remain connected to worshipping communities back in Hong Kong, attending hybrid church services or connecting with former small groups through instant messaging. Likewise, British Born Chinese may be actively serving in their local British Chinese church but choosing to supplement its teachings with podcasts and online pulpits from elsewhere in the United Kingdom or, indeed, the world. With the rise in digital technology, the missional role of the 'local' church is no longer limited to the physical location but can span large distances within the United Kingdom or in places like Hong Kong. One major example has been Flow Church in Hong Kong, which started in 2019 during the social unrest and has garnered a significant global engagement through its online platforms, especially among the Hong Kongese diaspora.[37] These are all aspects of the wider universal church that are not restricted by the physical location of the local church.

Towards an internetworked church

These social and technological changes have been constrained by our ecclesiology. We tend to see local churches as self-sufficient and with rigid boundaries, whereby all the ministries are self-contained within the church. In a Britain that is increasingly hostile to Christianity, local churches *need* each other. It isn't healthy for church leaders or for churchgoers to remain siloed from one another, especially if they are mindful of the risks of emotional, spiritual and psychological illness. This does little to respond to Jesus's prayer in John 17 that, among God's people, unity could be experienced across diverse denominations, traditions, demographics and so forth.

Instead of a rigid model of the local church based on relatively self-contained concentric circles, I suggest that local churches and church leaders should embrace a more internetworked ecclesiology, recognizing that the universal church is made up of a network of networked communities. Underscoring the universal church as internetworked is to recognize more porous or permeable boundaries for the local church, whereby local churches have a looser grip over who is counted as 'their' members, as illustrated in Figure 2 by the dotted circles around each

Figure 2: An internetworked church afforded by migration and digital technologies

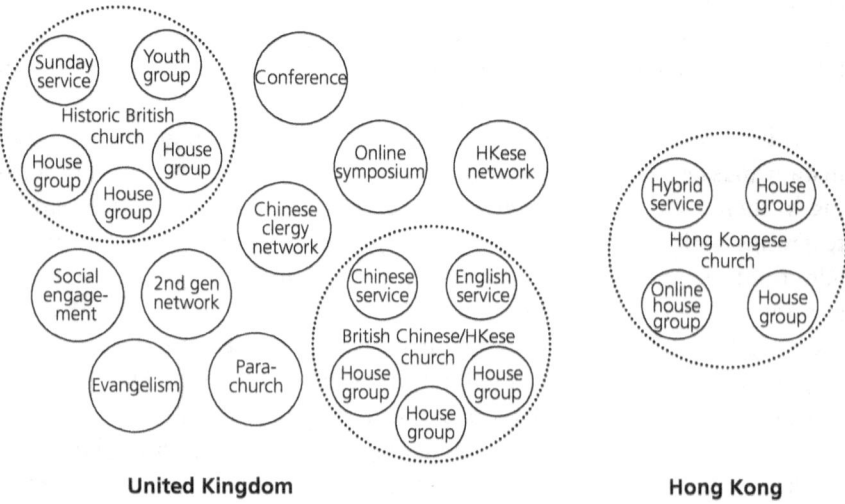

local church. After all, each local church is ultimately part of God's universal church. And given the increased use of digital technologies and provision of online or hybrid church services or meetings, individuals can engage across the United Kingdom as well as across to local churches in Hong Kong. Practically speaking, this is for church leaders to be humble enough to recognize their limits and to bless their congregants to participate in other ministries that facilitate their spiritual nourishment. It is also for church leaders to extend participation in their youth groups or children's ministries to other local churches that may be struggling because of the lack of resources.[38] This, of course, requires collaboration between churches and loving the sojourner church as your church.

Church leaders should allow, indeed should encourage, Christians to nurture the faith through committing to a local church but supplementing that with alternative means. This may include some of the ministries of other local churches but also cross-regional networks and conferences, in person or online, in Britain or elsewhere in the world.[39] There are also other cross-denominational mechanisms that support a local church's mission, whether through various parachurches or other outlets for evangelism and social engagement. It should not primarily be about whether this church is better than that church or whether one church is stealing sheep from another. The reality is that Christians are already engaging church beyond a single church in order to address the limitations of their local church, and they should be free to do so – all of this is part of the universal church. Furthermore, we need even *more* fora and resources like this, to offer solidarity, to highlight role models and clouds of witnesses and to equip those of Chinese heritage to live and witness in British society. This is all for the betterment of the church – local, national and universal.

An internetworked church upholds what theologians call 'catholicity'; that is, a recognition, a celebration and an embrace of the beauty that comes from each local church as it enriches and enlivens and emboldens the universal church of God. This only comes through communicating with one another, learning from one another, being challenged by one another, serving one another and loving one another. We do not have to wait until the end times to see the Revelation 7 vision of all nations before the Lamb of God. We have the world church, in miniature, here today in British society.

In this historic moment, we need to be mindful not only of the new Hong Kongese migrants or historic Chinese migrants but also African migrants, South Asian migrants, continental European migrants and so forth. We cannot forget or ignore the ways migration shapes and reshapes British Christianity. Sojourner churches need historic British churches as much as historic British churches need sojourner churches. Both should be seen as part of the native British church. Indeed, without both we will have no British Christianity to speak of in the foreseeable future. With both, British Christianity is far more enriched, and we are offered a foretaste of the eschatological church in the here and now.

Notes

1 For instance, see Paul Sparks, Tim Soerens and Dwight J. Friesen, *The New Parish: How Neighborhood Churches are Transforming Mission, Discipleship and Community* (Downers Grove, IL: IVP Books, 2014).

2 For a helpful historical overview, see Andrew Rumsey, *Parish: An Anglican Theology of Place* (London: SCM Press, 2017), pp. 121–54.

3 For some of this debate, see Steven Croft, ed., *The Future of the Parish System: Shaping the Church of England for the Twenty-First Century* (London: Church House Publishing, 2006); Doug Gay, *Reforming the Kirk: The Future of the Church of Scotland* (Edinburgh: St Andrews Press, 2017); Michael Moynagh, *Church in Life: Innovation, Mission and Ecclesiology* (London: SCM Press, 2017).

4 We see this explicitly in the two last publications of the UK Church Statistics, where the 2018 edition refers to 'immigrant churches', to a large extent with respect to Brexit, whereas the 2021 edition talks about 'diaspora churches'. Oddly, neither volume pays much attention to Global Majority Christians in historic British churches, nor do they discuss those born in the United Kingdom. Peter Brierley, *UK Church Statistics No 3: 2018 Edition* (Kent: ADBC, 2017), § 16.5; Peter Brierley, *UK Church Statistics No 4: 2021 Edition* (Kent: ADBC, 2020), § 0.2, pp. 5–6.

5 The word 'parish' comes from the Greek word *paroikia*, which is a compound word that brings together *para* (beside or by) and *oikos* (house or dwelling). Before it was used theologically, it was a civic term in Greco-Roman society to speak of a neighbour or a non-citizen who lives in a foreign land without the same rights and protection of the community.

6 Brierley, *UK Church Statistics No 4*, § 0.2, p. 6.

7 'Mission and Vision', *The Redeemed Christian Church of God*, https://www.rccg.org/mission-and-vision/, accessed 9.05.2024.

8 For a helpful discussion of Adeboye's method of RCCG's expansion through parishes, see Asonzeh Ukah, 'Reverse Mission or Asylum Christianity? A Nigerian Church in Europe', in *Africans and the Politics of Popular Culture*, ed. Toyin Falola and Augustine Agwuele (Rochester, NY: University of Rochester Press, 2009), pp. 117–18; Asonzeh Ukah, *A New Paradigm of Pentecostal Power: A Study of the Redeemed Christian Church of God in Nigeria* (Trenton, NJ: Africa World Press, 2008), pp. 110–18.

9 See Richard Burgess, 'Crisis and Renewal: Civil War Revival and the New Pentecostal Churches in Nigeria's Igboland', *Pneuma* 24, no. 2 (Fall 2002),

pp. 213–14, esp. fn 39, https://doi.org/10.1163/15700740260388045; A. O. Nkwoka, 'Interrogating the Form and the Spirit: Pentecostalism and the Anglican Communion in Nigeria', in *Creativity and Change in Nigerian Christianity*, ed. David O. Ogungbile and Akintunde E. Akinade (Oxford: African Book Collective, 2010), pp. 87–9.

10 Much of their ecclesiological polity is fundamentally episcopal and much of their liturgical practice (communion, baptismal and marriage ceremonies etc.) are adaptations from the Anglican Book of Common Prayer. Ukah, *A New Paradigm of Pentecostal Power*, pp. 59, 89–110, 177, 212 n. 59, and 272 n. 34. For an analysis of how Adeboye perceives and engages with other churches, including Anglicans, see Ukah, *A New Paradigm of Pentecostal Power*, pp. 285–7.

11 For this history, see Chapter 1 of this volume.

12 Stephen Wang, 'The Chinese on our Doorstep', *World Dominion* (September–October 1952), p. 267.

13 Wang, 'The Chinese on our Doorstep', p. 268.

14 John C. Gibson, 'The Chinese Church', *China Centenary Missionary Conference Records* (New York: American Tract Society, 1907), pp. 1–33; *Let Us Unite! The Church of Christ in China and Church Unity in China* (Peiping: Church of Christ in China, 1938), p. 59. Due to the prominence of the three-self principle in missiological circles, the term was later employed in the formation of the Three-Self Patriotic Movement in the 1950s, the main state-sanctioned Protestant entity under the People's Republic of China.

15 Significant in this was the press's reprint of Sidney J. W. Clark, *The Indigenous Church* (London: World Dominion Press, 1928). Another influential missionary theorist associated with the *World Dominion* journal and World Dominion Press, and who likewise was a major proponent of indigenous church-planting, was Roland Allen. See Steven Richard Rutt, *Roland Allen: A Missionary Life* (Cambridge: Lutterworth Press, 2018), pp. 83–104.

16 Wang, 'The Chinese on our Doorstep', p. 268.

17 Wilbert R. Shenk, *Henry Venn: Missionary Statesman* (Maryknoll, NY: Orbis, 1983), pp. 44–6.

18 'Hong Kong Christian Church in United Kingdom', available at https://www.hkcc.uk, accessed 10.05.2024.

19 For instance, we may consider the Hebrews 13.2 discussion of hospitality and the possibly of entertaining angels. This is probably connected to Old Testament narratives of hospitality as in Genesis 18 and 19. But it also has an interesting parallel in Greco-Roman writings. We see this in Ovid's poem *Metamorphoses*, which speaks about hospitality to the disguised gods Zeus and Hermes – alluded to in Acts 11.11–13 when Barnabas is called Zeus and Paul is called Hermes. See Luther H. Martin, 'Gods or Ambassadors of God? Barnabas and Paul in Lystra', *New Testament Studies* 41, no. 1 (January 1995), pp. 152–6.

20 Chistine D. Pohl, *Making Room: Recovering Hospitality as a Christian Tradition* (Grand Rapids, MI: Eerdmans, 1999), pp. 16–23.

21 The NRSVA translates the Hebrew word *gēr* as 'alien'. My own preference is to use the more archaic term 'sojourner', as it best conveys the precarity and migratory nature of such persons. See Frank Anthony Spina, 'Israelites as gērîm, "sojourners", in Social and Historical Context', in *The Word of the Lord Shall Go Forth: Essays in Honor of David Noel Freedman in Celebration of his Sixtieth*

Birthday, ed. Carol L. Meyers and M. O'Connor (Winona Lake, IN: Eisenbrauns, 1983), pp. 323–5.

22 Baruch A. Levine, *Leviticus*, JPS Torah Commentary 3 (Philadelphia: Jewish Publication Society, 1989), p. 134.

23 In Ephesians, the Greek word *sympolitēs* is rendered 'citizen' (NRSVA) or 'fellow citizen' (NIV or ESV), derived from the preposition *syn* ('with') and the noun *politēs* ('citizen'). Given the precious status offered to Roman citizenship of the day, Paul's emphasis is clear: Christ radically transforms the alien or sojourner into an insider and a fellow citizen. See Benjamin H. Dunning, 'Strangers and Aliens No Longer: Negotiating Identity and Difference in Ephesians 2', *Harvard Theological Review* 99, no. 1 (January 2006), pp. 1–16, https://doi.org/10.1017/S001781600600109X.

24 Phan makes this point through an examination of the second-century *Letter to Diognetus*. Peter C. Phan, 'Doing Ecclesiology in World Christianity? A Church of Migrants and a Migrant Church', in *Asian Christianities: History, Theology, Practice* (Maryknoll, NY: Orbis Books, 2018), p. 184.

25 Harvey Kwiyani, *Multicultural Kingdom: Ethnic Diversity, Mission and the Church* (London: SCM Press, 2020), pp. 121–34.

26 See Chapter 3 of this volume, by Yinxuan Huang.

27 Alexander Chow, 'British Immigration Policies and British Chinese Christianity', in *Ecclesial Diversity in Chinese Christianity*, ed. Alexander Chow and Easten Law (New York: Palgrave Macmillan, 2021), p. 116, https://doi.org/10.1007/978-3-030-73069-7_5.

28 For a discussion of these differences, see Chapter 6 of this volume, by Calida Chu.

29 Robert Schreiter argues that, leading up to the Reformation, Roman Catholicism moved towards a juridical sense of catholicity, whereas Protestants emphasized a mystical sense, mirroring the Eastern Church. Robert J. Schreiter, *The New Catholicity: Theology Between the Global and the Local* (Maryknoll, NY: Orbis, 1997), p. 121.

30 See Alexander Chow, *Chinese Public Theology: Generational Shifts and Confucian Imagination in Chinese Christianity* (Oxford: Oxford University Press, 2018), pp. 146–59; David Ng, 'A Path of Concentric Circles: Toward an Autobiographical Theology of Community', in *Journeys at the Margin: Toward an Autobiographical Theology in American-Asian Perspective*, ed. Peter C. Phan and Jung Young Lee (Collegeville, MN: Liturgical Press, 1999), p. 85.

31 Andrew Rumsey offers a historical explanation for this decline in Anglican parishes as due to the shift in social services from the church to the state. See Rumsey, *Parish*, pp. 131–42.

32 I Sil Yoon, 'Korean Christian Students' Adaptation and Integration in British Society: Their Identity Formation and Negotiation Processes', *Studies in World Christianity* 26, no. 2 (July 2020), p. 142, https://doi.org/10.3366/swc.2020.0293.

33 In the United Kingdom, Local Ecumenical Partnerships bring together several denominations under a single congregation. This example brought together the Baptist Union of Great Britain, the Church of England, the Methodist Church and the United Reformed Church, with Roman Catholics and Quakers as associate members.

34 See Emma Wild-Wood, 'The Experience of Migrants in a Native British Church: Towards Mission Together', in *Global Diasporas and Mission*, ed. Chandler H. Im and Amos Yong (Oxford: Regnum, 2014), p. 185.

35 The communications dimension was anticipated by Robert Schreiter as early as 1997, just as the Internet was beginning to become a worldwide phenomenon. Schreiter believes this pushes us towards a new kind of catholicity due to the connections made across cultures. While I agree with this, I am effectively arguing that this is further magnified through migration and a catholicity that can be witnessed in our globalized cities. See Schreiter, *The New Catholicity*, pp. 127–8.

36 See Alexander Chow and Jonas Kurlberg, 'Two or Three Gathered Online: Asian and European Responses to COVID-19 and the Digital Church', *Studies in World Christianity* 26, no. 3 (November 2020), pp. 298–318, https://doi.org/10.3366/swc.2020.0311. For other discussions of the intersection of migration, Christianity and digital technology, see Agnes M. Brazal and Randy Odchigue, 'Cyberchurch and Filipin@ migrants in the Middle East', in *Church in an Age of Global Migration: A Moving Body*, ed. Susanna Snyder, Joshua Ralston and Agnes M. Brazal (New York: Palgrave Macmillan, 2016), pp. 187–99, https://doi.org/10.1057/9781137518125_13; Yoon, 'Korean Christian students', p. 148; Briana Wong, 'Longing for Home: The Impact of COVID-19 on Cambodian Evangelical life', *Studies in World Christianity* 26, no. 3 (Nov. 2020), pp. 281–97, https://doi.org/10.3366/swc.2020.0310.

37 Chow and Kurlberg, 'Two or Three Gathered Online', pp. 311–13.

38 The top three concerns of British Chinese church leaders are the lack of Christian workers, the demand in youth ministry and the need for space to host the rapid growth in Chinese churchgoers. Yinxuan Huang, *Chinese Christianity in Britain: A Booklet of Ten Vignettes* (Swindon: British and Foreign Bible Society, 2023), p. 39.

39 Some Christian traditions have developed ecclesiological practices like this, such as Methodist 'connexionalism' and Roman Catholic 'synodality'.

10

A New Family: Pauline Adoption and its Contribution Towards a British Chinese Christian Identity

JOSH SHEK

British Chinese Christian identity – an emerging theological context

The Christian's identity is grounded in one's understanding of salvation. Scripture provides many concepts and metaphors through which these understandings can be explained, but with each new context into which the gospel is brought comes the task of determining how any given community's cultural and religious background shapes their particular perception of the meaning of the life and death of Christ. As Timothy Tennent argues: 'Every culture has universal questions we all share in as members of Adam's fallen race. Every culture also has questions and challenges peculiar to their particular context.'[1] Thus the task of theology includes understanding a given community's cultural values in order to help determine what images, concepts and metaphors will most persuasively and attractively convey the work of Jesus to a given context.

How does this task of exploring one's spiritual heritage play out when a community emerges from the coming together of two existing cultures, such as the British Chinese?[2] As many Chinese heritage immigrants in the 1960s and 1970s were not Christians prior to coming to the United Kingdom,[3] how do they negotiate their Chinese upbringing with the Western context where they first encountered Christianity? The tension is probably even more stark for their British Born Chinese (BBC) children, who may find themselves at a theological fork in the road when it comes to identifying their spiritual heritage. Is their identity to be explored primarily under the influence of the evangelical tradition they find themselves among, or from the lens of their Chinese background, especially as imparted within the home? While Western individualism may run against the Chinese emphasis on prioritizing one's family, perhaps the gospel can speak equally to one's need for personal salvation while also transforming our familial relationships with each other.

British Chinese like myself are indebted to evangelical soteriology, which has helpfully explained salvation and spiritual identity from a more judicial understanding of penal substitution. However, legal framings often overlook communal aspects of sin and salvation. When it comes to considering how the life, death and resurrection of Jesus can bring about their salvation, British Chinese Christians, given their unique experience of existing within two cultural environments, may wonder what models of atonement most persuasively engage their view of the world and most relevantly explain how Jesus can transform both the individual and collective aspects of their identities through faith in his atoning death and resurrection. What I propose in this chapter is the need to hold on to a judicial framework of atonement, while also being mindful of ways of thinking relationally about salvation. Thus it will explore the soteriological doctrine of adoption (*huiothesia*) as Paul deploys it in his Epistles as one of his many metaphors of salvation,[4] and how, as a more familial concept in contrast to other models of atonement, it might provide a valuable and contextually enriching understanding of spiritual identity for British Chinese believers. In so doing, I hope to contribute towards a British Chinese perspective of salvation as a foundational aspect of their emerging spiritual context.

The need for a familial metaphor of salvation

For many in the evangelical tradition, their understanding of salvation could be described as primarily dealing with their relationship with God with regard to their individual standing before the law of God. As Norman Kraus argues, evangelical approaches have dealt 'almost exclusively with the relation of the Cross to *guilt*'.[5] Tennent provides a more empirical critique, observing that, despite the term 'shame' and its derivatives occurring more than twice as often as 'guilt' in both Testaments, the overwhelming majority of systematic theology textbooks do not even account for shame.[6] As Thomas Schreiner asserts: '*penal* substitution is the heart and soul of an evangelical view of the atonement'.[7] Such a perspective on salvation is necessary and helpfully articulates how Christ's work on the cross deals with our legal guilt before the law of God. Recent debates around the subject of what Paul really intended in his use of justification and righteousness – the so-called New Perspective on Paul – has begun to address this penal focus on salvation by arguing that it actually possesses familial and collectively restorative consequences for spiritual identity. However, the thematic language of justification as an explanatory metaphor of salvation still relies on legal terminology rather than familial concepts to explain one's transformed spiritual identity.[8]

Thus, as critical as these concepts and models are for establishing their understanding of their spiritual identity in Christ, for some British Chinese believers they perhaps only address part of their bicultural sensitivities. As people who find themselves in a cultural environment where there has been a long tradition of the rule of law, soteriological concepts such as penal substitution may only help their understanding of how Christ transforms their legal status before God through his substitutionary atonement. However, where concerns around familial acceptance, public honour and right relationships may be specific issues for British Chinese Christians who retain stronger cultural ties to their Chinese heritage,[9] presently dominant evangelical soteriological themes may not provide sufficiently satisfying articulations of salvation that address the perceived needs of the more social aspects of spiritual identity and belonging. To be sure, Scripture contains a multifaceted perspective on the doctrine of salvation, drawing on various spheres of human experience to explain our salvation holistically. The task of theology is, then, to ascertain a fuller picture of salvation as Scripture reveals, and for the church to embrace a multifaceted understanding of salvation in a mixed-economy of soteriological concepts. As British Chinese Christians are most prevalently found in evangelical churches, the dominant presentations of atonement leaves a gap in their culturally informed awareness of identity. How can this insufficiency be addressed?

I propose that the penal focus on the evangelical understandings of salvation would benefit from a complementary focus on a social and relational dimension of soteriology, in order to become more sufficient. The thesis of this chapter is that the notion of adoption could fill that gap and contribute towards the development of a British Chinese spiritual identity.

Adoption – exploring a familial metaphor of salvation

Adoption – a Pauline salvation metaphor

Among Paul's various metaphors and concepts of salvation, one less discussed idea is that of the believer's adoption (*huiothesia*) by the Father.[10] In curating this metaphor, Paul synthesized the differing understandings of adoption as it was, on the one hand, practised by his Roman compatriots as a process of familial transfer[11] and, on the other, understood by those from Paul's Jewish community as God having adopted the Hebrew people as his 'son' during the events of the Exodus.[12]

As a biblical concept, Paul's five uses of the term in three of his letters can be categorized in a way that highlights adoption's function as an organizing concept of salvation. Chronologically, humanity was predestined for the status of sonship[13] to God even before the world was created (Ephesians 1.4–5). Hence adoption is covenantally promised as a blessing to the Israelites (Romans 9.4). Furthermore, adoption grounds an understanding of the present spiritual and familial identity of Christians as sons and heirs of God (Galatians 4.4–5), and is effective for all who have received the Holy Spirit – the 'Spirit of adoption' (Romans 8.15–16, ESV). Ultimately, adoption will also have a future, eschatological fulfilment to it by the bodily resurrection of the revealed sons and daughters of God (Romans 8.22–23).[14]

James Scott notes that, as a familial concept, *huiothesia* means 'the process or the state of being adopted as son(s)'.[15] Trevor Burke adds: 'Adoption is a family term that in the ancient social world of Paul's day denoted many things, but above everything else it signified the transfer of a son (usually an adult) as he is taken out of one family and placed in another.'[16] In this way, adoption provides us with a concept distinct from Paul's other metaphors of salvation. Justification draws from the realm of the law court, propitiation from the sacrificial system and redemption from the slave market. Adoption provides an alternative perspective because it 'complements these other expressions because it draws on a completely different conceptual field, that of the ancient family'.[17]

As we consider adoption as a complementary understanding of salvation for the British Chinese in their bicultural setting, we are reminded that, in Christ, believers can have their familial identities transformed and come into possession of filial acceptance before God as a divine Father. This forms two important aspects of adoption's value as a contextually relevant concept. For immigrants and children of immigrants who may find themselves caught between two cultures, the question of one's true familial and social belonging may potentially be answered by adoption. It relationally locates the believer neither in the social context of being raised entirely culturally British, nor in the ethnic and familial heritage of being culturally Chinese. Rather, they are ultimately within the spiritual identity and culture of being sons and daughters brought and placed into God's family.

In further assessing this potential, we now turn to explore some of adoption's covenantal, soteriological and eschatological features, and consider how these aspects might provide even more insight into a spiritually transformed identity.

The promise of adoption – exile, enslavement and covenant

As a diasporic group, the British Chinese may experience a sense of separation from their heritage communities. For many British Born Chinese, this sense of isolation may be exacerbated by having to work in their parents' restaurants and takeaways in the evenings and weekends and by not having many other BBC friends in their schools and localities. The parental demand to help out with the family business may sometimes result in tensions between the first-generation parents and the second-generation BBCs, who may resent such demands on their time and denial of opportunities to socialize with friends.[18] Further, many British Chinese children continue to experience racism in their schools and workplaces.[19] How might a covenantal history of adoption resonate with people who experience this sense of familial and social dissonance?

One important aspect of Israelite heritage that provides perspective on how Paul's Jewish audience may have understood his adoption metaphor, and that probably underpinned part of Paul's *huiothesia* background, is the notion of Israel's adoption as a nation. Scholars source the root of this idea principally in the Exodus event when God, in Exodus 4.22, commands Moses to say to Pharaoh, 'Thus says the LORD, Israel is my firstborn son' (ESV).[20] Further, James Scott notes of 2 Samuel 7.14 that 'God would redeem his people from Exile in a Second Exodus; he would restore them to a covenantal relationship; and he would adopt them, with the Messiah, as his sons.'[21] Scott helpfully locates a Jewish concept of adoption that is not orientated around the custom of adopting individuals but the adoption of an entire nation by God in order to provide salvation to them through a Messiah. In this manner, adoption is grounded in the covenantal plan of God to bring salvation to his people.

What kind of relationship are God's people adopted from? When theologians consider the state of the relationship that humanity has to God in the light of this covenantal history, two distinct descriptors of the pre-adoptive state can be discovered: those of 'sonship to Satan' and 'enslavement to sin'. Several scholars describe the filial identity of sinful humanity as one of sonship to Satan (John 8.44; 1 John 3.10).[22] John Girardeau indicatively puts it as such: 'adoption supposes the previous existence of the adopted in the family of the devil.'[23] Martyn Lloyd-Jones agrees when he states: 'There is no meaning in the doctrine of adoption unless it is our basic and fundamental postulate that every man by nature is a "child of wrath", as Paul puts it in Ephesians 2:3.'[24] As such, the notion of filiation to the devil provides one thematically integral way of understanding the pre-adoptive state, given that it corresponds to the concept of *patria potestas*, or the 'power of a father', within the Roman background (cf. Ephesians 1.3–5; Romans 8.15–16). That is, prior to their adoption Christians find themselves under the authority of the devil as their *patria potestas*[25] and are influenced to obey his will rather than that of their creative Father.

Second, the concept of enslavement to sin or being under the power of the law provides a Jewish perspective on the pre-adoptive state (Galatians 4.4–7). As Tom Smail asserts: 'We used to be slaves who were under the condemnation of the law and outside the realm of the Holy Spirit.'[26] The sons by constitution, denied any claim to heirship by their familial heritage in disobedient Adam and their own disobedience, now find themselves enslaved to the demands of the Father in the law due to the corruption of their filial image, and in need of a saviour who not only can restore their image of sonship but can also confirm it as one of perfected obedience and worthiness of inheritance.[27] Enslavement, as Israel found itself in under Egyptian oppression, becomes the metaphorical spiritual state in which all humanity finds itself – and in need of rescue from.

As children born into a 'foreign' land, some BBCs may experience a sense of exile as members of an ethnic minority and may feel safer among others who come from their own ethnic background. Conversely, other BBCs may instead feel a sense of wanting to escape their Chinese identity in order to better integrate and settle into British society. Both of these postures point towards an experience of identity dissonance as BBCs grapple with their ultimate sense of social and familial identity. However, as God promises his covenant people that he will one day adopt them back into his family and out of a state of exile, BBCs may well find hope in knowing that the promised Messiah was not only for

Israel but would also, by his work, bring all who find themselves in a foreign place or in a foreign family, back 'home'.

The fulfilment of adoption – transformed relationships with God, other and self

Within Paul's adoptive framework, the Father, out of his ongoing love, protologically wills the adoption of the elect before time. Burke notes of Ephesians 1.3–5 that 'Paul here qualifies "predestine" with the prepositional phrase "in love" (*en agapē*) to underscore the Father's deep affection in "marking us out" as his adopted sons.'[28] Burke's identification of adoption here as motivated by the Father's love helps us see how, in distinction from a purely forensic schema of salvation, a paterology of adoption emphasizes God's paternally affectionate heart for the salvation of his lost children – re-establishing himself as a compassionate paterfamilias of his household.[29] When we understand this, we also realize that the Father's love towards believers is not in *response* to their being adopted into his family but rather a *prerequisite* of their adoption.[30]

Jesus, by his Incarnation, lives a life of an obedient son in accordance with the Father's will. In doing so, he fulfils the expectations of humanity's original constitutional sonship and makes believers' sonship possible again by the mechanism of adoption. As David Garner explains: 'The primary soteriological point is *that* Christ obeyed as the suffering Son, and that by his obedience in life and death, he *became* qualified in his resurrection as the ever-interceding Savior of sinners.'[31] Indeed, it is the very notion that Christ *suffered* in his obedience that marks his filial relationality as perfectly obedient – his meritorious works are not merely confined to the duties of filial compliance but are enhanced by his submission to the paternal demand to even suffer undeserved death for the sake of the adoptive mission (Philippians 2.8) and, further, by his suffering the consequences of filial disobedience even though he himself never rebelled as a son.[32] This is precisely what makes salvific adoption possible since, on the cross, 'God offers to God the obedience that is appropriate to us, out of the midst of the human situation into which he has entered wholly.'[33] When a believer then places faith in Christ's atoning death, it is Christ's achievement of obedience that is ascribed to them in exchange for the consequences of their disobedience. And this is what qualifies believers for adoption by the Father[34] – Christ's *qualified* character of sonship (though not his particular and unique relationship of Son to Father in the Trinitarian sense)[35] is what is graciously given as a substitute to believers.[36] Their now obedient status then renders them worthy of adoption as sons, saved from exile and enslavement to sin. This adoption is *both* juridically founded *and* relationally constitutive; actualized by the sonship of Christ as the obedient son of God.[37] Thus adoption provides salvation not only through filial restoration but by filial approval through union with the perfected, *obedient sonship* of Christ.

Furthermore, in the Pauline context, such a transfer into a new family had social consequences for the adoptee. In the Roman practice of adoption, the newly adopted son would have acquired the honour that came from his association with his new family. Similarly, by having God as their new pater familias, the believer is also ascribed the honour that is due to Christ by his obedient achievements. That is, the honour that Christ ascribes to us does not originate from himself but from the Father whom he glorifies.[38] Therefore, and most critically, 'The exaltation of Jesus to the place of highest honor in the cosmos (Eph 1:20–22) is thus an honor in which all faithful believers now share (Eph 2:6).'[39] Because of their possession of the supreme honour of Christ, the 'Elder Brother' of the new family of God, believers are no longer judged as shameful.[40] This may be paralleled with the notion that, through justification, God also now judges humanity to bear Christ's supreme righteousness. That is, what imputed righteousness is to justification, ascribed honour is to adoption.

In the framework of adoption, the honourable obedience of Christ is important for one's understanding of one's own transformed spiritual identity. For people of any culture that may be sensitive to the familial demands of filial compliance, alongside the social demands of public honour, the notion that Christ's perfectly obedient sonship is attainable will displace any sentiment that their own efforts may never be enough to satisfy the demands of either their earthly family or God. Instead, through adoption, believers may have assurance that, in Christ, their status as sons and daughters is regarded with approval and affirmation by their heavenly Father, and that they are further welcomed into a family in which they possess the position of honour both before their brothers and sisters, as well as within the public realm of the cosmos.

For some BBCs, that may particularly apply where performance is demanded by both their familial context with its culturally Chinese expectations, as well as the public context of their schools and workplaces, which may present entirely different cultural pressures. By adoption, they may recontextualize their relational identity ultimately as sons and daughters of God the Father, belonging to the most honourable of families because of the achievements of Jesus. Such an adoptively realized identity can have the effect of freeing the British Chinese from feeling bound to the demands of honour of both their Chinese culture and the performative pressures in society. Christ's perfected sonship satisfies and overcomes the demands of performance that we fail to achieve by our own effort, and frees us from the social shame that we encounter in that failure.

What is the Holy Spirit's role in this adoptive mission of God, and how might an adoptive pneumatology further contribute towards a BBC spiritual identity? Through faith, believers are brought into union with Christ by the work of the Holy Spirit,[41] and that union is what allows the meritorious character of Christ's obedience to be effectively imparted to believers for their salvation through adoption. The Spirit's role is to particularize the paternally orientated obedience of Christ into each believer by his own indwelling and, by doing so, to enable the Father to re-establish his paternal relationality of acceptance and affirmation towards his adopted children. In Romans 8.15–16, the reception of the Spirit is not meant as a *condition* of sonship but, as James Scott argues, 'as an indication that the Spirit is *inseparable* from sonship',[42] such that he may be identified as the very 'Spirit of adoption'. This pneumatologically consummated sonship of believers is, then, what also grounds their future hope of resurrection – as the Holy Spirit raised Jesus from the dead, so the same Spirit of adoption will provide the means by which believers will participate in the same resurrection.[43] The adopted sons and daughters of God will one day, like Jesus, be resurrected in their bodies as the final consummation of their adoption.

This pneumatological adoption not only soteriologically transforms our relationship to the Father but also transforms the believers' relationship with one another, uniting them through their adoptive fraternity with Christ. One particularly important aspect of this understanding is that it counteracts an individualist approach to soteriology. Colin Gunton notes that traditional understandings of Christ's death, metaphorically understood as sacrifice, tend to 'create an individualistic apprehension of the work of the Spirit: the work of Christ is mediated to the believer, rather than to believers.'[44] That is, while a penal reading of justification only explicitly rationalizes the reconciliation of believers to God, and implicitly their relationship to other believers, a doctrine of pneumatological adoption explicitly redefines the relationship of believers to each other as familially transformative into one of brotherhood. Erin Heim agrees that Paul's use of *huiothesia* is 'a performative utterance, [whereby] the metaphor enacts a mental simulation in the minds of the audience where *other community members are understood as brothers and sisters of the same family*.⁴⁵ Soteriological adoption is not an individualistic investment of sonship, but believers are collectively included into the family of God by pneumatological union. Thus human fraternity is no longer grounded on their source of creative paternity but on the commonality of their renewed spiritual relationship to the same Father in Christ.

As a diasporic group, it is possible that some British Chinese may import some of their Chinese cultural values into their theological understandings of identity and pastoral formation of community. Instead, as explored here, a pneumatology of adoption may helpfully ground believers' relationship with one another not on a sense of shared ethnicity or cultural practice but instead on the greater unifying power of the Spirit who unites believers from our multiple clans and into one family. Similarly, while the Christian practice of identifying one another as 'brothers and sisters' within the church may come across as mere sentimentality, an adoptive pneumatology compels us to realize that our familial relationships and obligations towards one another are, indeed, real. Such a soteriology has the potential to inform British Chinese Christian practice as no longer about showing outward respect towards members of our own cultural or ethnic community but serving one another out of an authentic desire to love those in our transformed spiritual family, aided by the power of the very Spirit that enabled Jesus himself to obediently serve his Father and his brothers and sisters.

The future of adoption – heirs of God, welcomed home

The eschatological consequences of adoption are not limited to the reconstitution of believers' physical bodies. It will also result in their receiving the inheritance that was available to Adam in his probation – had he proved himself a worthy son – but subsequently conferred on Christ in his successful achievement of obedient sonship. By their spiritual, familial and personal union with Christ, believers, through their own hope of glorification, may hope to share in Christ's inheritance, and trust in their status as co-heirs with Christ (Romans 8.17).⁴⁶

What is the content and nature of this inheritance? Two connected ideas come to light. In fulfilment of the covenantal promises made to Abraham and Israel, the revealed sons of God will one day inherit a new creation for their inhabiting and, further, they will inherit God himself by his living among them in the new creation.⁴⁷ The believer's present status as co-heirs with Christ will one day be made perfect when they finally come into possession of what we may particularly understand, within a schema of adoption, as the realized experience of perfected relational context. They will be children who will live in a familial dwelling among true brothers and sisters, with their Father in loving presence, Christ as their glorious and eternal Elder Brother, and the Spirit of sonship in their hearts for ever – both the possession of a perfected home and the enjoyment of a perfected family.

These combined ideas of a future perfected family in a welcoming home as the adopted believers' future inheritance may also contribute towards a spiritual outlook for British Chinese Christians. As they wrestle with a potential sense of loss of any ancestral inheritance, the notion of one's ultimate inheritance, in the form of a place of eternal belonging and rest, is a hope in Christ that can be spiritually assuring. The additional idea that one's salvation not only pertains to one's individual future but, through adoption, also unites all believers into one secure family provides greater conviction to love others in the present outworking of eternal relationships, regardless of how we may presently find commonality towards them in either ethnic or cultural ways. As such, an adoptive eschatology may help retrieve an eternal perspective into the formation of a British Chinese spiritual identity.

A new family – towards a British Chinese spiritual identity

As British Chinese Christians continue to explore the theological questions that arise out of their complex bicultural heritage, we have briefly explored how adoption could provide a complementary soteriological perspective towards the formation of their spiritual identity. While penal atonement models should remain an important facet of their self-understanding of redeemed identity, the familial concept of adoption can provide a more thematically relational framework to the individualistically orientated models that remain popular among teachings in their evangelical environment. In the light of being persons of Chinese heritage, adoption may provide more relevant answers to questions about familial belonging, public honour and future inheritance.

Of course, we must also be careful to not overstate the value of adoption over other soteriological perspectives that can provide the British Chinese – or evangelical Christians of any other cultural heritage – with a more comprehensive understanding of their spiritual identity. Our aim should be to embrace the full picture of salvation that Christ affords us in his atoning work, not necessarily allowing one model to dominate our understanding of spiritual identity over others. Paul himself uses multiple concepts to speak to his often multicultural audience of Jews, Romans and Greeks. The concepts of justification, propitiation, redemption, reconciliation and adoption all appear in the Epistle to the Roman church and provide multiple perspectives on how they might better understand their holistic spiritual identity. As the British Chinese start to discover how the gospel meets them where they are in their bicultural particularity, the British Chinese church would also do well not to settle for just the fundamentals that work for them. They also need to aim to explore an expanded and more holistic appreciation of spiritual identity formation through, for example, engaging with other biblically grounded, soteriological concepts from both inside and outside the evangelical tradition.

In that way this present chapter has helped us see how British Chinese Christians might also contribute towards a widening of the evangelical perspective on salvation by helping cultivate a mixed economy of soteriological appreciation. As they bring their multicultural perspectives to bear on Scripture and theological reflection, they, and other multiculturals, may be adept at curating a wider set of theological perspectives that are both multiculturally balanced yet culturally accessible. As a bi-cultural himself, Paul seems to be aware of the need to choose metaphors and concepts that will be suitable for his diverse audience. Without his distinct knowledge of Roman legal adoption and Jewish emphasis on divine filiation by adoption, Paul would not have found it as easy to present a metaphor of salvation that could speak to both cultures. Similarly, as British Chinese Christians continue to explore their spiritual identity from the lenses of both their Western and Chinese values, they too may be able to discover greater soteriological and theological riches and present them in accessible ways back into the evangelical tradition.

Notes

1 Timothy Tennent, *Theology in the Context of World Christianity* (Grand Rapids, MI: Zondervan, 2007), p. 12.

2 Alexander Chow locates the emergence of the term 'British Chinese' in the 1990s as an alternative way to point to the 'complex hybrid identity which draws from both British and Chinese cultures'. Alexander Chow, 'British Immigration Policies and British Chinese Christianity', in Alexander Chow and Easten Law (eds), *Ecclesial Diversity in Chinese Christianity* (New York: Palgrave Macmillan, 2021), p. 115.

3 Chow, 'British Immigration Policies', p. 110.

4 In this chapter, by describing soteriological concepts as 'metaphors', I am not claiming that they are somehow 'fake' or not 'real'. Rather, I am speaking about these ideas as metaphorical in the sense that they draw on a human idea to convey a transcendent reality. That is, while the effects are real, the biblical usage draws from human experience to explain a divine action. For instance, Colin Gunton explains the idea of transcendent metaphor, while N. T. Wright argues that justification is an important and necessary legal or law-court metaphor. Colin E. Gunton, *Father, Son and Holy Spirit: Toward a fully Trinitarian Theology* (London: T&T Clark, 2003), pp. 181–200; N. T. Wright, *What St Paul Really Said* (Oxford: Lion Hudson, 1997), p. 117.

5 C. Norman Kraus, 'The Cross of Christ: Dealing with Shame and Guilt', *Japan Christian Quarterly* 53, no. 4 (1986), p. 223; emphasis added.

6 Tennent, *Theology in the Context of World Christianity*, p. 92.

7 Thomas R. Schreiner, 'Penal Substitution View', in James Bielby and Paul R. Eddy (eds), *The Nature of the Atonement: Four Views* (Downers Grove, IL: IVP, 2006), p. 67; emphasis added.

8 N. T. Wright, in his defence of the New Perspective, notes how the result of justification is a united familial relationship between believers regardless of their ethnic or social background. Wright, *What St Paul Really Said*, p. 146.

9 Te-Li Lau briefly explores the dynamic of shame in Chinese familial life. Te-Li Lau, *Defending Shame: Its Formative Power in Paul's Letters* (Grand Rapids, MI: Baker Academic, 2020), pp. 188–9. Daniel Eng also notes that the shame–honour dynamics of an honour-based world view remain prevalent in contemporary Asian American consciousness. Daniel Eng, 'Finally Belonging: The Reception of the Parable of the Prodigal Son among Asian Americans', *The Journal of Asian American Theological Forum* 6, no. 2 (2019), p. 1.

10 Paul is the only New Testament author to use the concept of believers' adoption. Note that Paul's understanding and employment of the adoption concept differs substantially from the contemporary practice of adopting children as we know it today. For contemporary explorations of the Christian doctrine of adoption, see Trevor J. Burke, *Adopted into God's Family: Exploring a Pauline Metaphor* (Downers Grove, IL: InterVarsity Press, 2006); David B. Garner, *Sons in the Son: The Riches and Reach of Adoption in Christ* (Phillipsburg, NJ: P&R Publishing, 2016).

11 Burke, *Adopted into God's Family*, p. 40.

12 Edward W. Watson, *Paul, his Roman Audience, and the Adopted People of God: Understanding the Pauline Metaphor of Adoption in Romans as Authorial Audience* (Lewiston, NY: Edwin Mellen, 2008), p. 174.

13 When I use the terms 'son' or 'sonship', I am referring to both male and female believers in their filial relationship to God and in no way mean to exclude females from the doctrinal applicability. In principle, I use adoption in agreement with Caroline Johnson Hodge's position when she says: 'Paul assumed that all the baptized gentiles, whether slaves, free, male, or female, would have appropriated the status of heir for themselves … Paul sees God as extending the patriarchal privilege of sons to all gentiles-in-Christ, including women and slaves of both genders.' Caroline Johnson Hodge, *If Sons, Then Heirs: A Study of Kinship and Ethnicity in the Letters of Paul* (New York: Oxford University Press, 2007), p. 69.

14 This narrative organization is suggested by Tim J. R. Trumper, 'An His-

torical Study of the Doctrine of Adoption in the Calvinist Tradition' (PhD thesis, University of Edinburgh, 2001), p. 3.

15 James M. Scott, 'Adoption, Sonship', in Gerald F. Hawthorne, Ralph P. Martin and Daniel G. Reid (eds), *Dictionary of Paul and his Letters* (Downers Grove, IL: InterVarsity Press, 1993), p. 16.

16 Burke, *Adopted into God's Family*, p. 40.

17 Trevor J. Burke, *The Message of Sonship* (Nottingham: IVP, 2011), p. 141.

18 For anecdotal testimony of BBCs regarding their having to work in the family business, and stories of the racial prejudices they experienced, see Angela Hui, *Takeaway: Stories from a Childhood Behind the Counter* (London: Trapeze, 2023); Elaine Chong, 'Meet the kids who grew up in Chinese takeaways', *BBC Stories YouTube channel*, https://www.youtube.com/watch?v=Ii9o8B_9sXo, accessed 3.07.2023.

19 One survey reports that in the view of British Chinese schoolchildren, 'racism was a relatively everyday occurrence'. Louise Archer and Becky Francis, 'Constructions of Racism by British Chinese Pupils and Parents,' *Race Ethnicity and Education* 8, no. 4 (2005), p. 391.

20 Several scholars categorize this event as the first thematic instance of Israel's adoption by God. Michael Peppard, *Son of God in the Roman World: Divine Sonship in its Social and Political Context* (Oxford: Oxford University Press, 2011), p. 139; Salaam Corniche, 'Adoption in Christ: The Best Gift Ever', *St Francis Magazine* 9, no. 2 (2013), p. 74; James I. Cook, 'The Concept of Adoption in the Theology of Paul', in James I. Cook (ed.), *Saved by Hope: Essays in Honor of Richard C. Oudersluys* (Grand Rapids, MI: Eerdmans, 1978), p. 136.

21 Scott, 'Adoption, Sonship', p. 17.

22 Mark Stibbe, *From Orphans to Heirs: Celebrating our Spiritual Adoption* (Oxford: Bible Reading Fellowship, 1999), p. 31; Thomas Houston, *The Adoption of Sons: Its Nature, Spirit, Privileges and Effects: A Practical and Experimental Treatise*, 2nd edn (Brighton: Ettrick Press, 2021), p. 45. John Owen, *The Works of John Owen*, vol. 2 (Edinburgh: Banner of Truth, 1965), p. 207.

23 John L. Girardeau, *Discussions of Theological Questions*, ed. George A. Blackburn (Richmond, VA: Presbyterian Committee of Publication, 1905), p. 469.

24 D. Martyn Lloyd-Jones, *Romans: An Exposition of Chapters 8.5–17: The Sons of God* (Edinburgh: Banner of Truth, 1974), p. 154.

25 Stibbe, *From Orphans to Heirs*, p. 31.

26 Tom Smail, *The Forgotten Father: Rediscovering the Heart of the Christian Gospel* (London: Hodder & Stoughton, 1996), p. 145.

27 Daniel J. Theron, '"Adoption" in the Pauline Corpus', *Evangelical Quarterly* 28, no. 1 (1956), p. 10.

28 Burke, *Adopted into God's Family*, p. 77.

29 Burke, *Adopted into God's Family*, p. 83.

30 Smail, *The Forgotten Father*, p. 130.

31 Garner, *Sons in the Son*, p. 218; emphasis original.

32 Houston, *The Adoption of Sons*, p. 59.

33 Smail, *The Forgotten Father*, p. 125.

34 Trevor J. Burke, 'The Characteristics of Paul's Adoptive-sonship (HUIOTHESIA) Motif', *Irish Biblical Studies* 17, no. 2 (1995), p. 70; Tim J. R. Trumper, 'The Metaphorical Import of Adoption: A Plea for Realisation. II: The Adoption

Metaphor in Theological Usage', *Scottish Bulletin of Evangelical Theology* 15, no. 2 (1997), p. 104; Houston, *The Adoption of Sons*, p. 49; Thornton Whaling, 'Adoption', *Princeton Theological Review* 21, no. 2 (1923), p. 230.

35 David Garner clarifies: 'union with Christ creates no absorption into or ontological participation in the hypostatic union; union involves no appropriation of divine attributes by the redeemed.' Garner, *Sons in the Son*, p. 252.

36 Girardeau notes: 'What was conditional in Christ's case is unconditional in that of his people. His perfect obedience as a Son is by the Father transferred to their account.' Girardeau, *Discussions of Theological Questions*, p. 491.

37 Tom Smail, *Once and For All: A Confession of the Cross* (London: Darton, Longman & Todd, 1998), p. 100.

38 Burke, *Adopted into God's Family*, p. 153.

39 David A. deSilva, *Honor, Patronage, Kinship and Purity: Unlocking New Testament Culture* (Downers Grove, IL: InterVarsity Press, 2000), p. 73.

40 Trevor J. Burke, 'Adoption and the Spirit in Romans 8', *Evangelical Quarterly* 70, no. 4 (1998), p. 323. There are an increasing number of Christologies that discuss the concept of Christ as Elder Brother, especially from an Asian American perspective. See Peter C. Phan, *Christianity with an Asian Face: Asian American Theology in the Making* (Maryknoll, NY: Orbis Books, 2003), pp. 125–45.

41 Trumper qualifies the nature of this adoptive union: 'As real as is this union, it is neither symbiotic (deifying the sons of God and humanising the Son) nor ontological (admitting us entrance to the Godhead) … While they share with Christ an identity of relation to the Father, he remains forever the firstborn Son (*primus inter pares*).' Tim J. R. Trumper, 'A Fresh Exposition of Adoption: I. An Outline', *Scottish Bulletin of Evangelical Theology* 23, no. 1 (2005), pp. 72–3.

42 James M. Scott, *Adoption as Sons of God: An Exegetical Investigation into the Background of Huiothesia in the Pauline Corpus* (Tübingen: Mohr, 1992), pp. 260–1; emphasis added.

43 Scott, *Adoption as Sons of God*, p. 266.

44 Gunton, *Father, Son and Holy Spirit*, p. 196.

45 Erin Heim, *Adoption in Galatians and Romans: Contemporary Metaphor Theories and the Pauline Huiothesia Metaphors* (Leiden: Brill, 2017), p. 230; emphasis added.

46 Joel R. Beeke, *Heirs with Christ: The Puritans on Adoption* (Grand Rapids, MI: Reformation Heritage Books, 2008), loc. 1078, Kindle.

47 Thomas R. Schreiner, *Romans*, Baker Exegetical Commentary on the New Testament 6 (Grand Rapids, MI: Baker, 1998), p. 427.

Conclusion: The Journey Continues

BERT HAN

There's this ancient Chinese proverb attributed to Laozi, *Qian li zhi xing, Shi yu zu xia* (千里之行，始於足下) which is often translated, 'The journey of a thousand miles begins with a single step.' It's an expression that reminds us that the journey forward is taken one step at a time, and perhaps it's that first step that is hardest. The thing about starting a new path is that we often forget about the adventure that it took to get here. For every Chinese immigrant who arrived in Britain, for every Chinese Christian, there is a story for how they arrived on these shores and into the Christian faith. It's what makes an anthology like this so valuable. It is also in the journey where much of the shaping happens. We are often so consumed with the destinations that we forget that it is in the journey that both the traveller and the ones the traveller encounters are shaped. In the long history between the Chinese and the British we see that cross-cultural influence has happened to both sides along the way. But this anthology reminds us that cross-cultural influence has also shaped the Christian faith. The Christian faith experienced and expressed by those of Chinese heritage has influenced and continues to influence believing Christians here in Britain today.

Perhaps the first step in this journey of understanding Chinese Christianity's influence on British Christianity is recognizing the past and people. In Chapter 1 of this volume, Alexander Chow begins by providing a historical backdrop to Sino-British relations. It provides a glimpse of some of those first steps in this journey: from the first migrants, to locally born generations, up to the latest wave of new migrants. And it's from this first chapter that we begin to see a theme arising – the Chinese in Britain are diverse. Chow writes: 'in contrast with what is seen from the outside, there is a tremendous amount of diversity within British Chinese churches. It is hardly as homogeneous as some missiologists may claim. And with this variety have come, at times, intra-Chinese tensions.' In Chapter 3, Yinxuan Huang reinforces this idea with his sociological and empirical study on the current state of Chinese in Great Britain. In his conclusion he points out that: 'Statistics on both individual and church levels suggest that "the Chinese church" is not a singular, static concept. It is filled with diversity, change and even conflict, although it also possesses unique aspects compared to other British churches.' Just because they look the same on the outside doesn't mean they think the same on the inside. To better unpack this, it's helpful to begin by defining culture and ethnicity more adequately. Far too often we simply equate ethnicity with race. However, ethnicity is more distinct and specific. In her work *Beyond Colorblind*, Sarah Shin says: 'Ethnicity refers to common ancestry, tribe, nationality and background, often with shared customs, language, culture, values traditions, and history.'[1] Race, on the other hand, exists as a human-made historical construct classifying people according to supposed physical traits and attributes. For the most part, the term 'Chinese' has acted as a racial, ethnic, national and cultural delineation. However, as seen through this anthology, political backgrounds, cultural preferences and nationality often differ among the Chinese. They may come from Taiwan, Hong Kong, different parts of mainland China, Malaysia or Singapore, or be Chinese born in Britain. Each of these 'types' of Chinese is similar yet distinct. It's Huang's deep statistical research[2] that brings to light the composition of the Chinese here, and their places in churches. Recognizing the diversity among the Chinese then gives space for further exploration into the Chinese influence in Britain. Allowing us to delve deeper, we begin to see that this diversity of Chinese extends into how Christianity itself is expressed and how those different expressions then impact Christianity in Britain.

The cultural diversity among the authors helps to bring these aspects to light. Mark Nam writes as a third-generation British Born Chinese, serving in the Church of England; his opinions and perspectives differ from second-generation British Born Chinese James So and Josh Shek. Calida Chu and Kan Yu both hail from Hong Kong and understand the context of the latest wave of Hong Kong Chinese immigrants, with the former considering the reasons for migration and the latter the challenge of finding a place in Britain. Candy Zhang, a former student from mainland China, discusses the temporary migration of international students from China but, like Yu, she addresses the importance of place and belonging. And Renie Chow Choy, whose ethnicity is tied to Hong Kong and Canada before receiving her doctorate from the University of Oxford and now residing in England, draws together how the tragedies of British colonialism and British cultural Christianity affect those Chinese Christians finding a place and a home here. This diversity of authors unintentionally points to one of the biggest challenges going forward for the Chinese Christians: What does it look like to make a home here?

With every group of migrants the question is always the same. Much has been said about how Britain has treated previous waves of immigrants. And even now, the Westminster government wrestles with the challenges of refugees and how open their borders should be to immigration. For Christians, the question also needs to be asked: 'What does a Christian home look like for the Chinese, for the migrant, for the ethnic minority?' The response has, up until now, focused on hospitality, welcome and integration into society. In Chapter 9, Alexander Chow excellently points out that *hospitality*, as used within the British English context, focuses on welcoming; but the original intention of the term in the Bible is much more to treat them as 'native' or 'citizen'. The rise of Chinese heritage churches in Britain began primarily because of the language barriers. We see some shifting of this with the recent arrivals of BN(O)s, and their willingness to participate within local British churches.

But hospitality, welcoming, attendance and involvement are not the same as it *becoming* home. It's often suggested that multiculturalism and the multicultural church will help to create a home for migrants. Advocates for multiethnic and multicultural churches often point out that the gospel cuts across social, economic, racial and cultural barriers and that it's a theological imperative to work towards a church that does this. As Harvey Kwiyani puts it quite frankly:

> Monocultural churches, especially in contexts of cultural diversity, go against everything we read in the New Testament ... Monocultural churches in multicultural contexts paint an image of a God who pays attention to the needs of one racial or cultural group and not the others.[3]

Proponents of multicultural churches often believe that, by welcoming different ethnicities to the same service and venue, those groups will find the space to be at home.

Those who promote an intercultural church challenge those ideas as insufficient. Whereas a multicultural church *celebrates* racial, ethnic, theological and cultural differences, an intercultural church seeks to *be shaped* by the different cultures.[4] The premise is that an intercultural church allows those different cultures to be part of the conversation in creating a 'new' space in which all cultures are engaged. This creates a new home, you might say. The intercultural church invites different languages, different expressions and different cultures to be expressed in the same service, and engages leadership across those cultural bounds. It's this 'new' space that creates a 'new home' for all cultures. And amid these, the Chinese heritage church, with its multicultural sub-congregations, seeks to create a home by gathering those of a similar cultural heritage and giving them the space to worship within their own cultural expressions. But which one of these options creates a home for Chinese Christians? Are they better integrated into a multicultural church, adopted into a local British church and part of a new expression of an intercultural church, or within a Chinese heritage church that creates the closest thing to home for them?

In Chapter 9, Chow offers his own exploration of Chinese Christian place with his suggestion of an internetworked ecclesiology. This is a modular approach to different aspects of Christian life and faith, and finding which ones works best for each. The advantage of this is cross-cultural engagement in the areas of weakness, and similar cultural engagement for areas that require a deeper cultural understanding. Perhaps this is an alternative way of creating a home for Chinese Christians.

All of these are first steps into new directions. They are options and opportunities that open up as we begin to engage, appreciate, understand and release cultures. No one ethnicity or culture has a monopoly on God. It is through the mosaic of different people that we share and see a fuller picture of God. But if we remain blind to the beauty of cultures and ethnicities, we welcome nothing. For Christianity in Britain, it means appreciating the diversity, complexity, history and potential of the Chinese here, so that what is discovered can also be shared.

We often think of home as a singular place. We imagine the units that make up that home, the spaces, the styles and the forms. And so when we consider how the Chinese Christians might be at home in Britain, we consider their space, their style and even how they might 'fit in'. However, a broader way to think of it may be with home as a village. Home as a broader community or as part of a village is what makes people feel part of a place. Whereas in the West we are used to a single family or a single generation within a household, in China, historically, homes were much larger, with multiple generations and including multiple nuclear families in a single compound. So being at home in this village called Britain is more of the same – albeit across a more diverse family – where 'My Father's house has many, many rooms.' It's this context that may help to create an understanding of how a diversity of churches could fit in. There is space in a home for diversity. And even broader, there is space in a village for different types of church experiences. There is space in a village for a Chinese heritage, Mandarin-speaking church. There is space in a village for a Chinese-speaking home group as part of a large multicultural church. There is space in a village for an English-speaking congregation with those of a Chinese heritage background. There is space in a village for a new Hong Kong immigrant church. And as those churches give space for different groups to grow, their existence acknowledges that there isn't one singular way to do church but that each church makes part of the home together. It is a neighbourhood of churches, not a single expression of church.

The beauty of the church is in diversity, held together by the unified adoration, worship and obedience of God the Father, the Son and the Holy Spirit. The beauty is seen in the celebration of the variety of expressions of church. They all point towards the same God, are filled with people saved by the same redeeming and atoning work of Christ. But the village finds its beauty as we love our neighbour. If we choose to reject, ignore or disregard our neighbour, we lose the opportunity to be a blessing to them and to be blessed by them. The existence of the Chinese heritage church in the UK gives British Christianity an opportunity to love their neighbour. If they are blessed and released, then the joy is shared. If they are ignored or disregarded, the joy is missed out.

I grew up in Southern California, where the diversity in food is tremendous. Because of the large enclaves of ethnic populations, you were able to find some of the most authentic dishes. I know of one taco place where the owner would drive across the Mexican border to buy the flour to make their tortillas. I know of Chinese dumpling places that would use the same recipes that were passed down from generations. These distinct dishes and eateries were a valuable part of Southern California. It meant there was space for these things to exist, to flourish and to find connections to new generations. And because these deeply authentic places existed, it gave rise to new types of fusions. Whether it was a sushi burrito or a Korean fried-chicken waffle, these new mixes could find places to create new expressions. It was like an intercultural food experience. In the 'village' of Southern California there is room for all these culinary expressions. I think we desire too often a singular expression of church or we use theology to denigrate one form or to elevate another. In reality, we should see how individual expressions add to the broader mosaic of the Kingdom of God. Home isn't felt in the small unit but in the neighbourhood, the village, the city of God.

We started this Conclusion with a quote from Laozi, and the journey beginning with a single step. We recognize that the journey of the Chinese into faith and into Britain has been a long one but that the journey to deeper understanding of Chinese Christianity in Britain is just beginning. And it's this realization that makes the joy of the journey not the destination but the adventure itself. And for all Christians, the adventure is in the unified mission that Christ has set out for us:

> Go therefore and make disciples of all nations, baptizing them in the name of the Father and of the Son and of the Holy Spirit, teaching them to observe all that I have commanded you. And behold, I am with you always, to the end of the age. (Matthew 28.19–20, ESV)

For all of us are part of a shared journey with Christ, to be his witnesses, his disciples and his disciple-makers to this world around us. Every person, every culture, every ethnicity is an opportunity for us to see Christ in them and for Christ to be seen through them. But if we choose not to take a single step in the direction of another, then we will surely miss out on the journey we could have shared with Christ.

Notes

1 Sarah Shin, *Beyond Colorblind: Redeeming our Ethnic Journey* (Downers Grove, IL: IVP, 2017), p. 13.

2 In particular, Huang takes the 2021 census's broad categorization of Chinese as a singular ethnic group and examines it alongside place of birth, first language and national identity to better identify the types of Chinese across Great Britain.

3 Harvey Kwiyani, *Multicultural Kingdom: Ethnic Diversity, Mission and the Church* (London: SCM Press, 2020), p. 146.

4 Safwat Marzouk, *Intercultural Church: A Biblical Vision for an Age of Migration* (Minneapolis, MN: Fortress Press, 2019), pp. 14–15.

Index of Names and Subjects

Allen, Roland 177n15
Anglican xii, 21, 156, 166, 177n10
 and colonialism 30, 44–5, 82
 Anglican Minority Ethnic Network 66n5
 Church of England 3, 5, 24–5, 27n26, 50, 56, 57, 61, 66n3, 76, 92–3, 96, 103–8, 108–9, 165, 178n31, 178n33, 196
 see also The Teahouse
Anti-Extradition Law protests (2019–20) 16, 17, 63, 115

Bhabha, Homi K. 81, 87
Birmingham Chinese Evangelical Church (BCEC) xi, 24, 94–5
Black, Asian and Minority Ethnic (BAME) 7–8n10
Bonhoeffer, Dietrich 153–4, 156, 157
British and Foreign Bible Society 59, 66n3, 67n15, 146
British East and Southeast Asian (BESEA) 23, 25, 107

Catholic see Roman Catholic
catholicity 158, 171, 175, 178n29, 179n35
China Inland Mission (CIM) 43–5

Chinese catering 15–16, 17, 18, 22, 78, 96, 115, 184
 see also takeaway kid
Chinese Church in London (CCiL) 15–16, 17, 57, 157, 167–8
Chinese Overseas Christian Mission (COCM) xii, 15, 16, 17, 24, 66n5, 67n11, 78, 131, 132, 143n2, 143n7, 156–7, 167–8
Chinese Students' Christian Union of Great Britain and Ireland 14, 17
Chow, Alexander 94, 191n2
Choy, Renie Chow 4, 26n5, 96, 107–8
Christian and Missionary Alliance 16, 17, 21, 57
Church of England see Anglican
communist revolution 36, 138
 see also Cultural Revolution (1966–76)
covenant 93, 100, 102–3, 106, 117, 150, 152, 183–4, 184–6, 189
Covid-19 1, 2, 11, 16, 17, 23, 28n27, 48, 50, 74, 132, 135–6, 139, 148, 173
Cultural Revolution (1966–76) 14, 17, 116
 see also communist revolution

digital technology xi, 2, 3, 5, 46n6, 52, 67n13, 148, 173–5, 179n35, 179n36

East India Company (EIC) 30–1, 43–4
Elim Pentecostal Church 16, 17, 56, 57
eschatology 13, 75, 150, 169, 176, 183, 184, 189–90
exile 184–6, 187

Father 86, 152, 159, 183, 185–90, 194n36, 194n41, 198, 199, 200
forever foreigner *see* perpetual foreigner

Gospel Hall Christian Mission, Liverpool xii, 1, 13, 17, 48, 166–7

Holy Spirit 103, 114, 155, 159, 160, 183, 185, 188–90, 199, 200
Hong Kong British Nationality (Overseas) visa 1, 12, 16, 17, 20–1, 28n27, 53, 55, 78, 143n6, 146
Hong Kong Christian Church in the United Kingdom 63–4, 168
hospitality 119, 139–40, 141, 148, 149–50, 150–1, 152, 155, 157, 161, 169–70, 177n19, 197

identity
 adhesive 49, 116
 bicultural 12, 22–5, 90, 93–6, 96–100, 101, 102, 106, 171, 182, 183, 190–1
 multicultural 191, *see also* multicultural church
imago Dei (image of God) 119–21, 124, 138, 197
intercultural church 85, 197–8
see also multicultural church

Kandiah, Krish 18–19
Kirkham, George A. xii, 13, 26n7
Kwok, Pui-lan xii, 82–3

Lee, Daniel D. xii, 96–102, 106–8
Lee, Jung Young 94
Lee, Sang Hyun 95, 96
Li, Florence Tim-Oi xii
Lion Rock 112–13, 115–16, 121–4, 124n3
Liverpool Chinese Gospel Church 17
see also Gospel Hall Christian Mission, Liverpool
local ecumenical partnership 148, 173, 178n33

Mei, Yiqi 132
mental health 32, 42, 107, 113, 139
see also trauma
Methodist 3, 15, 16, 17, 21, 56, 57, 98, 148, 151, 153, 156–7, 158, 178n33, 179n39
missio Dei (mission of God) 87–9, 100, 188
Morrison, Robert 43–5
multicultural church 75, 83–4, 89, 197–8
see also intercultural church

INDEX OF NAMES AND SUBJECTS

Napoleonic Wars (1803–15) 12

one-child policy 140
Opium Wars (1839–42; 1856–60) 1, 4, 11, 12–14, 17, 30–6, 38, 46n3

pentecostal 6, 16, 17, 56, 57, 58, 65, 166
perpetual foreigner 6, 74, 107, 139–40
Phan, Peter C. xii, 113–14, 117, 120, 170, 178n24
pneumatology *see* Holy Spirit
Pohl, Christine 149, 150, 151
postcolonialism
  Orientalism 81–5
  strategic essentialism 5, 84, 88, 97
  hybridity 87, 93–6, 96–7, 100, 102–3, 106

racism 1, 2–3, 4, 12, 16, 17, 18, 19, 23–5, 27n19, 28n35, 74, 75, 100, 105, 139, 164, 171, 184, 193n19
Redeemed Christian Church of God 166, 168, 176n8
returnee 5, 15, 117, 122, 131–2, 134–6, 138, 141, 143n10
Roman Catholic 6, 17, 21, 27n26, 50, 52, 165, 171, 178n29, 178n33, 179n39

Said, Edward 81–3
St Paul's Cathedral 31–8, 41
salvation *see* soteriology
Schreiter, Robert 178n29, 179n35
Shen, Michael Fuzong 1
Sino-British Joint Declaration (1984) 11, 15–16, 17, 115

sonship 183, 185–90, 192n13
soteriology 6, 181–2, 186, 188–91, 192n4
Spivak, Gayatri 84
St Michael's Church, Liverpool 13–14

takeaway kid 23, 96, 184, 193n18
  see also Chinese catering
Taylor, Hudson 43–5
The Teahouse 24, 66n5, 108–9
Three-Self Patriotic Movement 134, 177n14
Tiananmen Square protests 15, 17, 115
trauma 99–101, 119, 145
  see also mental health
Treaty of Nanking (1842) 11, 33–4
Treaty of Tientsin (1858) 35–6, 38
Trinity 138, 155, 157, 159, 174, 159, 186–7

UKHK *see* Welcome Churches
Umbrella Movement (2014) 16, 17, 115, 146

Venn, Henry 167, 168

Wang, Stephen xii, 15, 156–7, 167
Welby, Justin 20, 25, 105
Welcome Churches 18–19, 57, 67n11, 67n14, 139
Wesley, John 157–8
Windrush 19, 28n35, 75, 78, 115
World Wars (1914–18; 1939–45) 12–13, 14, 17

www.ingramcontent.com/pod-product-compliance
Lightning Source LLC
Chambersburg PA
CBHW022054290426
44109CB00014B/1096